Imperfect Alte.......

Imperfect Alternatives

Choosing Institutions in Law, Economics, and Public Policy

Neil K. Komesar

The University of Chicago Press
Chicago & London

The University of Chicago Press, Chicago 60637
The University of Chicago Press, Ltd., London

© *1994 by The University of Chicago*
All rights reserved. Published 1994
Paperback edition 1996
Printed in the United States of America

03 02 01 00 99 98 97 96   2 3 4 5 6

ISBN: 0-226-45088-0 (cloth)
ISBN: 0-226-45089-9 (paperback)

Library of Congress Cataloging-in-Publication Data

Komesar, Neil K.
    Imperfect alternatives : choosing institutions in law, economics,
and public policy / Neil K. Komesar.
        p.   cm.
    Includes bibliographical references and index.
    ISBN 0-226-45088-0 (acid-free paper)
        1. Law—Economic aspects.   2. Public policy (Law)   3. Judicial
process.   I. Title.
    K487.E3K66   1994
    342′.041—dc20   93-49435
    [342.241]   CIP

To the memory of my parents,
and to the love and support
of my wife

Contents

Preface

My aim in this book is to recast the analysis of law and public policy, both economic and non-economic analysis. Such temerity requires qualification and explanation.

I am certainly not the first to emphasize the central need for the analysis of institutional choice—for comparative institutional analysis. As the body of the book indicates, Ronald Coase has long emphasized the importance of institutional choice and comparison. Twenty-five years ago, Harold Demsetz criticized Nirvana solutions and called for comparative institutional analysis.[1] Non-economists such as Richard Stewart, Kenneth Shepsle, and Barry Weingast have also called for comparative institutional analysis.[2]

As a general matter, the importance of institutional choice and the necessity of institutional comparison seem common sense. It is not odd, therefore, to find calls for institutional comparison or even instances of serious institutional comparison. What remains remarkable is the vast amount of law and public policy analysis that either ignores, trivializes, or poorly executes institutional comparison. In this book, I am attempting to answer the continuing calls for institutional comparison by extensively documenting the evils of failing to take it seriously and by offering an analytical framework with which to begin this difficult but necessary task.

I must also offer a qualification of ignorance. My own background and experience do not—indeed could not—match the sweep of my claims. I am an American law professor with training in economics. I have taught a relatively wide variety of American legal subjects, including property law,

1. Harold Demsetz, *Information and Efficiency: Another Viewpoint,* 12 J L & Econ 1 (1969). Indeed, an abiding concern with institutional comparison and institutional choice can be traced back to Adam Smith. James Buchanan makes such a connection in his summary of constitutional economics in *The New Palgrave: A Dictionary of Economics* (1987), 2:585.

2. Richard Stewart, *Crisis in Tort Law? The Institutional Perspective,* 54 U Chi L Rev 184 (1987); Kenneth Shepsle and Barry Weingast, *Political Solutions to Market Problems,* 78 Am Pol Sci Rev 417 (1984).

tort law, and constitutional law, and I have dabbled in contracts law. But the number of American law subjects that I have neither taught nor seriously thought about outnumbers those that I have. I also am largely ignorant about law and public policy outside the American context and have only touched upon disciplines other than economics and law. Notwithstanding these significant qualifications, however, I remain confident of the universal importance of institutional comparison and of the need to seriously advance comparative institutional analysis on all fronts. Only the consideration of more knowledgeable minds can test these convictions.

The breadth of this book also requires comment on my choice and treatment of those works I discuss and critique. I chose many of these works because they are among the most generally discussed and noticed. I often use them to show that the failure to carefully consider institutional choice infects and handicaps even the most prominent works. Each of these works has received considerable critical attention. Unless the criticism is pertinent to the points I am making, I have not made exhaustive reference to these critical literatures.

I have been writing about comparative institutional analysis for almost fifteen years, and I derive several parts of this book from my earlier articles. Despite attempts to update the various collateral references, I am sure that I have failed to be encyclopedic. My objective in this book is to improve the conceptualization and, therefore, the analysis of institutional choice. Given the large range of subject matter and the significant number of disciplines engaged by this book, I can only hope that the book will be judged primarily on its conceptualization rather than its erudition.

I am very grateful to the many colleagues and friends who contributed to this book. Many read and commented on various drafts of this book — Peter Carstensen, Larry Church, Bill Clune, Howard Erlanger, Marc Galanter, Dirk Hartog, Willard Hurst, Len Kaplan, Beverly Moran, Tom Palay, Richard Posner, Joel Rogers, Vicki Schultz, Leon Trakman, and Bill Whitford. Several were subjected to multiple drafts. Here I want to single out my old friend, David Goldberger, who diligently read, commented, and suffered through every draft and through drafts of virtually all the articles that foreshadowed this book. I owe special debts to Bob Wills and Richard Allen, who diligently and creatively edited this book, and to Theresa Dougherty, who by dint of extraordinary competence and effort turned chicken-scratchings and dictated mutterings into interminable typed drafts. I owe thanks to several anonymous readers and to one, Ronald Coase, who graciously waived his anonymity and whose supportive comments meant so much. I also owe a debt to the many friends and colleagues who have offered their support over the years. That support has spurred me on.

I owe a lifetime of debts to a wide variety of teachers. My first teachers were my parents. My mother, Jeanette, taught me a love for intellectual curiosity and creativity. My father, Hyman, taught me the importance of honesty and determination. His life was a lesson in quiet courage. These lessons were only a few of their many gifts to me.

My teachers at the College of the University of Chicago taught me to see ideas as a single fabric and my teachers in the economics department taught me a set of basic tools capable of examining that fabric. Through their skepticism (and even paranoia) about economics, my colleagues and students at the University of Wisconsin Law School have forced me to think hard about economic analysis, how to use it and how to explain it.

Last, my wife, Shelley Safer, has taught me lessons in joy, trust, and openness — and these may be the most important lessons of all.

}I{

Deciding Who Decides: The Comparative
Analysis of Institutional Performance

}1{

Taking Institutional Choice Seriously

Most of us live in massive and complex societies in which the quality of life is dependent on decision-making processes operating somewhere beyond the horizon. Amorphous markets determine what we get and what we pay. Decisions made by faceless bureaucracies, distant legislatures, and isolated courts mold our opportunities.

This book is about these decision-making processes. More particularly, it is about the way we choose to allocate authority to and among them. It is about deciding who decides.

This decision is the essence of such global tasks of social definition as the making of constitutions. Sweeping ideologies from laissez-faire capitalism to centralized socialism are defined by their positions on who decides. Moreover, choices between markets, courts, and political processes pervade law and public policy at all levels. These choices determine what one views as the correct response to air pollution and the correct pattern of tort reform. They underlie a full range of judicial decisions from, for example, the unconstitutionality of prayer in schools to the remedy for breach of contract. Scratch the surface of any important issue of law and public policy, and important and controversial questions concerning the choice between decision-makers will appear.

In this book, I refer to the decision of who decides as "institutional choice." The term "institutional" reflects the reality that the decision of who decides is really a decision of *what* decides. The alternative decision-makers are not individuals or even small numbers of individuals. They are complex processes, such as the political process, the market process, and the adjudicative process, in which the interaction of many participants shape performance. In turn, I refer to the analysis of institutional choice as "comparative institutional analysis" because the analysis of the choice among decision-making alternatives requires the sophisticated comparison of these alternatives. The argument in favor of comparative institutional analysis takes up part 1 of this book.

In addition to arguing that institutional choice is an essential part of

3

law and public policy choice, and, therefore, that comparative institutional analysis is an essential part of any analysis of law and public policy, I propose a framework or approach for *doing* comparative institutional analysis. I define this "participation-centered approach" below and develop it in parts 2 and 3 of this book.

My belief in the importance of institutional choice and comparative institutional analysis is not universally shared, however. There are, in fact, dramatic anomalies in the study of law and public policy when it comes to the subject of deciding who decides. For example, one would assume that the central issue of constitutional law is the choice of who decides — the choice between alternative social decision-makers such as the executive, the legislature, and the judiciary — and that, therefore, constitutional scholarship would be replete with sophisticated analyses of these alternatives. In turn, one would assume that, when economic analysts of law — usually non-constitutional law — consider the issue of who decides, these high priests of trade-offs and opportunity costs would know that one cannot decide who decides by examining only one alternative. Yet most constitutional scholars ignore the issue of who decides or at most treat it with superficial maxims. And when economic analysts of law address the subject of who decides, they often focus their attention on the attributes of only one alternative.

Constitutional law and the economic approach to law are important enough aspects of legal study that such anomalies standing alone would justify searching inquiry. But, in fact, these anomalies are only dramatic examples of a pervasive problem in the analysis of law and, more generally, of public policy. Although important and controversial decisions about who decides are buried in every law and public policy issue, they often go unexamined, are treated superficially, or, at best, are analyzed in terms of the characteristics of one alternative.

Most existing theories of law and public policy focus attention on social goals and values. The economic approach to legal analysis is cast in terms of a single social goal — resource allocation efficiency. Its critics attack that goal as insufficient both normatively and descriptively, while its proponents defend its validity. Constitutional law analysis is largely a debate about social goals and values such as resource allocation efficiency, Rawlsian justice, or Lockean protection of property.

Although the choice among social goals or values is an important ingredient in understanding and evaluating law and public policy outcomes, analysis of goal and value choices, standing alone, tells us virtually nothing about these outcomes — what they are or what they should be. Upon close inspection, each social goal bandied about in analyses of law and public policy is generally consistent with virtually any law or public policy outcome. In other words, a given goal can be seen as consistent with liability or no liability, regulation or no regulation, constitutional right or no constitutional right. Goal choice may be necessary to the determination of law and public policy, but it is far from sufficient.

A link is missing — an assumption overlooked — in analyses that suppose that a given law or public policy result follows from a given social goal. That missing link is institutional choice. Embedded in every law and public policy analysis that ostensibly depends solely on goal choice is the judgment, often unarticulated, that the goal in question is best carried out by a particular institution. Given the goal of protecting property, for example, the case for recognizing a constitutional right involves the implicit judgment that the adjudicative process protects property better than the political process. In turn, given the goal of promoting safety, the case for removing tort liability involves the implicit judgment that the market or government regulation promote safety better than the adjudicative process.

Goal choice and institutional choice are both essential for law and public policy. They are inextricably related. On the one hand, institutional performance and, therefore, institutional choice can not be assessed except against the bench mark of some social goal or set of goals. On the other, because in the abstract any goal can be consistent with a wide range of public policies, the decision as to who decides determines how a goal shapes public policy. It is institutional choice that connects goals with their legal or public policy results.

Institutional choice is difficult as well as essential. The choice is always a choice among highly imperfect alternatives. The strengths and weaknesses of one institution versus another vary from one set of circumstances to another. For example, whether the adjudicative process is the best protector of property rights or the worst determiner of safety is by no means obvious. Sometimes the courts will be the best protectors of private property, and sometimes that task will be better assigned to the political process. Sometimes the courts will be the best determiners of safety, and sometimes that task will be better assigned to the political process or the market.

Despite its importance, and perhaps because of its difficulty, most analysts omit any explicit consideration of institutional choice, treat it as intuitively obvious, or deal with it as an afterthought. Frequently, any institutional choice inconsistent with the analyst's preferred law and public policy position is summarily dismissed after reciting a long parade of horribles. In a world of institutional alternatives that are both complex and imperfect, institutional choice by implication, simple intuition, or even long lists of imperfections is deeply inadequate. These approaches do not take institutional choice or analysis seriously.

Even more serious institutional analyses, however, seldom shake the tendency toward "single institutionalism" — the focus on only one institution — that characterizes the less serious parade-of-horribles approach. Both the power of serious institutional analysis and the pervasiveness of single institutionalism are reflected in two of the most prominent theories now current in law — Richard Posner's economic analysis of the common law and John Ely's analysis of constitutional law. The strengths and weaknesses of these two well-known theories illustrate the need to go beyond current analysis to a more thorough comparative institutional analysis.

Both Posner and Ely employ serious institutional analysis to provide insights into a broad range of legal and public policy questions. Both are concerned with variation in the ability of a central institution. Both their theories provide valuable insights unavailable from existing non-institutional analyses. However, because both analysts attempt to make sense of judge-made law (common and constitutional law) by focusing on variation in the ability of a single, non-judicial institution, they fail to consistently compare institutions. Posner makes sense of the common law by seeing how well the market works in one common law setting relative to another. Ely makes sense of constitutional law by seeing how well the political process works in one constitutional law setting relative to another. The correct question, however, is not whether, following Posner, the market works better in one setting than the market works in another setting or, following Ely, the political process works better in one setting than in another.

The correct question is whether, in any given setting, the market is better or worse than its available alternatives or the political process is better or worse than its available alternatives. Whether, in the abstract, either the market or the political process is good or bad at something is irrelevant. Issues at which an institution, in the abstract, may be good may not need that institution because one of the alternative institutions may be even better. In turn, tasks that strain the abilities of an institution may wisely be assigned to it anyway if the alternatives are even worse.

As I will show, failure to employ a comparative institutional approach causes significant analytical problems in the work of Posner and Ely.[1] Moreover, that the theories of such respected and able analysts as Richard Posner and John Ely should contain such a basic flaw is indicative of a much larger problem. Comparative institutional analysis is very difficult. Institutions are large, complex, and hard to delimit. More importantly, comparing institutions requires identifying parallels across institutions in some acceptable, understandable, and useable fashion. Any adequate analysis must be able to pick up variations in institutional ability across the wide and varied landscape of law and public policy.

I recognize that my call for comparative institutional analysis must be accompanied by a strategy for identifying and comparing institutional capabilities. To that end, I provide an analytical framework—the "participation-centered approach"—that will permit analysts of law and public policy to organize studies of institutional choice in the various areas of law or public policy that interest them. Such a framework provides, minimally, a place to start—a way to organize data, intuitions, and arguments and to focus further inquiry. In this framework, I attempt to capture as much detail as possible given the desire that the framework be portable. I have tried to construct an analytical approach that generates insights into most law and public policy issues. I wish this framework to be accessible and comfortable to a broad audience of analysts.

In this framework, variation in the performance of an institution is tied to the participation of important institutional actors common to all the institutions. As such, I emphasize the activities of consumers, producers, voters, lobbyists, and litigants. At least initially, official actors in the political process and the judiciary—legislators and judges—play a secondary role.

The participation-centered approach identifies the actions of the mass of participants as the factor that in general best accounts for the variation in how institutions function. In this sense, the adjudicative and political processes are like the market, with its myriad of buyers and sellers. As is common with analyses of the market, the interaction of these many actors rather than the will of a few officials receives central attention in my analysis. The importance of officials vis-à-vis other actors varies across institutions and across issues, and this variation provides an important aspect of

1. I examine Posner's approach in chapters 2 and 6 and Ely's approach in chapter 7.

institutional comparison and choice. As a general matter, however, all these institutions are massive and all are strongly affected by the activity (or lack of activity) of the mass of actors.

The basic model of institutional participation is a simple economic one. The character of institutional participation is determined by the interaction between the benefits of that participation and the costs of that participation. The benefit side focuses on the characteristics of the distribution of benefits or stakes across the relevant populations. Here the central determinants I examine are the average per capita stakes and the extent to which per capita stakes vary within the population. The cost side focuses on the costs of participating in the institutions — transaction costs, litigation costs, political participation costs. These costs generally fall into one of two broad categories — the cost of information and the cost of organization. The cost of information is the more important category — in good measure, organization is itself dependent on information. Here the central determinants of cost I examine include the complexity or difficulty of understanding the issue in question, the numbers of people on one side or the other of the interest in question, and the formal barriers to access associated with institutional rules and procedures.

Nothing is new or startling about the participation-centered approach. Ronald Coase's transaction cost approach to the organization of production emphasized the cost of information in understanding institutional activity in general and transacting in particular.[2] The emphasis on the distribution of stakes can be traced to Mancur Olson's work on collective action.[3] That this analysis is simple and its components well known are major advantages — perhaps even necessary attributes — for my purposes. An analytical framework meant to serve so vast a range of possible investigations and investigators must be as simple, accessible, and intuitively sensible as possible. This framework provides the structure upon which more microanalytic examinations can be constructed.[4]

2. Ronald H. Coase, *The Nature of the Firm*, 4 Economica 386-405 (1937); Ronald H. Coase, *The Problem of Social Cost*, 3 J L & Econ 1 (1960).

3. Mancur Olson, *The Logic of Collective Action* (1965).

4. There are various approaches to individual institutions that stress greater microanalytic details such as "positive political theory," in the case of the political process, and "transaction cost economics" or "property rights theory" in the case of the market. These will be discussed in greater detail in chapters 3 and 4, respectively. I do not reject these more detailed inquiries. As I apply the framework at various points in the book, I add more microanalytic detail. But the simpler participation-centered framework provides a powerful strategy for initiating inquiry. That is the purpose of an analytical

This summary statement of the central propositions of the book leaves much to be explained. The next chapter examines more closely the relationship between goal choice and institutional choice. The third, fourth, and fifth chapters, comprising part 2 of the book, consider three major institutions — the political process, the market process, and the adjudicative process. These chapters develop and use the participation-centered approach and contrast it with other institutional analyses. Part 3 then takes the insights gleaned from examinations of these three institutions and applies the resulting comparative institutional framework to two major and seemingly quite different topics in law and public policy — safety, tort liability, and tort reform, on the one hand, and constitutional law and constitution making, on the other. From an institutional standpoint, these seemingly different topics are very much related. Constitution making and tort reform show remarkable similarity in the institutional issues that they raise and the tough institutional choices that they present. They even show a similar need for important, if necessarily limited, judicial activities.

Before moving on, I want to offer some general comments on my choice of institutions for study, on the relationship of my analysis to the standard law and economics approach, and on its relationship to three prominent works dealing with institutional choice. Although, for the purposes of this book, I lump institutions together into three general categories, market, political, and adjudicative, there is no magic about these categories. Institutions can be defined and aggregated in any number of ways depending on the focus for study. The categories are a compromise between conflicting analytical objectives — my desire to show the broad spectrum of institutional choice and my desire to examine law-related issues.

The first objective leads me to aggregate a wide variety of processes that others might wish to treat separately. Subheadings or sub-institutions are inherent in at least the market and political processes. For example, one can productively break out the administrative process from the political process, and I do that at several points in the book. Similarly, consistent with the view of many modern industrial organization economists, one can subdivide the market into firms, relational contracting, and atomistic spot markets. I explore these divisions in chapter 4. On the other hand, a special concern for law-related subjects leads me to separate the judiciary

---

framework. The extent to which additional material is added depends on the subject of investigation and the background of the investigator.

or adjudicative process from the political process. Analysts of public policy might not see the need to give separate attention to the courts. However, as the book shows, this relatively small institution, on occasion, has some important and interesting comparative advantages.

Some large-scale institutional decision-making processes, such as corporations and labor unions, are treated in this book as actors (producers in the market, members of interest groups in the political process, or litigants in the adjudicative process). However, for consideration of labor law or corporate law issues, for example, they might well be treated as institutional alternatives.[5] Although I do not discuss these institutional processes at length, the discussion of the institutions that are the focus of the book should be useful for analyzing corporations and unions as well. In particular, I believe that the discussion of the political process has important insights for corporations and unions, where majoritarian constitutions and the operation of concentrated interests can produce a range of responses similar to those in the general political process.

The analysis I present here is clearly related to what is called "law and economics." This book could be considered revisionist law and economics. I argue that good law and economics must be good comparative institutional analysis. Indeed, as I show, the most powerful insights to be gained from the economic analysis of law come from comparative institutional analysis. The proponents of law and economics believe its insights derive from the importance of the social goal of resource allocation efficiency. But resource allocation efficiency is connected to law and public policy through institutional choice, and its implications for law and public policy can only be realized through comparative institutional analysis.

But this book is not limited to law and economics. First, adequate economic analysis of public policy beyond the confines of the law depends on comparative institutional analysis as well. Second, and more important, any analysis of law and public policy—economic or not—depends on comparative institutional analysis. Institutional choice is the necessary connection between any social goal or goals and law and public policy. As such, this book can be considered revisionist law and sociology, revisionist law and political science, revisionist law and history, revisionist law and philosophy, revisionist law and critical thought, and so forth.

5. As I will show subsequently, however, the ultimate institutional choices for law and public policy even in areas like corporate or labor law will be among the larger institutional processes discussed in this book. See the discussion in chapter 4 of Oliver Williamson's work on vertical integration.

There are no shortcuts around the issues of institutional choice. Every law and public policy choice involves institutional choice. That is unavoidable. The question is whether these institutional choices are made implicitly or explicitly; whether they are made thoughtfully or haphazardly. In other words, the issue is the quality of law and public policy analysis. As I will show, any attempt to sidestep comparative institutional analysis leaves the resulting analysis (whatever its genre) profoundly vulnerable.

The participation-centered approach to comparative institutional analysis employed in this book is, however, not the only way possible to construct comparative institutional analysis. There are debatable aspects of the specification of institutions employed in this book. Throughout the book I will attempt to highlight these aspects and explain my choices. Showing the analysis at work allows a better understanding of its potential. In addition to those detailed applications found in part 3, each of the next four chapters is filled with applications of the analytical approach as well as examples of the problems created by such failures of institutional analysis as single institutional analysis. I discuss a large number and variety of law and public policy issues including the growth of the bureaucracy, the dynamics of market advertising and political propaganda, the determinants of deterrence, the choice between injunctions and damages in the enforcement of property rights, the interrelation between the First Amendment and the Political Question Doctrine, the framing of the Constitution, and the role of compensation for the taking of property. I revisit the work of Posner and Ely and address other social and legal commentators ranging from John Rawls to Richard Epstein. By the end, the reader will have the opportunity to see comparative institutional analysis in general and the participation-centered approach in particular in a variety of settings defined by various social issues, ideologies, and intellectual theories.

However, three major works on institutional choice, emanating from three different fields, require comparison to my approach at the outset. In *The Legal Process: Basic Problems in the Making and Application of Law*, a massive, unpublished, but influential work, legal scholars Henry Hart and Albert Sacks presented a theory of the legal process based on the interplay between the three branches of government, the executive, the legislature, and the judiciary.[6] This theory dealt with the full range of law—constitutional, common, administrative, and statutory. Despite the authors' interest

6. Henry Hart and Albert Sacks, *The Legal Process: Basic Problems in the Making and Application of Law* (tentative ed 1958).

in the role of the courts and their concerns with institutional competence, their approach is significantly different from mine. Hart and Sacks presented a largely idealized image of institutions. Each institution was assumed to be a contemplative, deliberative, rational decision-maker.[7] From my perspective, their conception of institutional behavior assumes away most of the difficulty and richness of institutional choice. It is quite different in conception and spirit from the participation-centered approach to institutional behavior and comparison championed in this book.

In *Politics, Economics and Welfare,* an equally celebrated work from political science, Robert Dahl and Charles Lindblom examined the relative merits of various combinations of "sociopolitical processes," including the price system, hierarchy, polyarchy, and bargaining.[8] This long, complex work is far more ambitious than mine. It is an attempt to determine the global issue of the organization of political and economic activity. In essence, it attempts to determine the optimal outcome from the capitalism-socialism spectrum. Although I hope that the framework I present can contribute to understanding these global questions, much more must be added to make it yield such solutions.

No doubt reflecting the strains of an ambitious agenda, Dahl and Lindblom, like Hart and Sacks, assume away important institutional issues with idealized institutional conceptions. More precisely, they assume a significant beneficial presence for pluralism, an important issue open to inquiry in my analysis.[9] More importantly, despite long lists of the advantages and disadvantages of each process, Dahl and Lindblom do not articulate or examine a finite set of factors that determine the comparative advantages of each institution and, most importantly, that determine how these advantages vary from policy setting to policy setting. My approach focuses on these factors. However one judges their relative merits, the two approaches differ significantly.

The work of public finance economists, and in particular the Musgraves'

---

7. For a more complete discussion of the problems associated with the idealized institutional conceptions of Hart and Sacks, see Nicholas Zeppos, *Justice Scalia's Textualism: The "New" New Legal Process,* 12 Cardozo L Rev 1597 (1991), and William Eskridge and Phillip Frickey, *Legislation, Scholarship, and Pedagogy in the Post-Legal Process Era,* 48 U Pitt L Rev 691 (1987).

8. Robert Dahl and Charles Lindblom, *Politics, Economics and Welfare* (1953).

9. The authors' subsequent discomfort with this assumption is reflected in the preface to their second edition. See Robert Dahl and Charles Lindblom, *Politics, Economics and Welfare* xxii (2d ed 1976). It is brought out even more strongly in Lindblom's subsequent book. See Charles Lindblom, *Politics and Markets* (1977).

classic *Public Finance in Theory and Practice,* is closer to home.[10] The Musgraves recognized that more than variation in the ability of the market is important in determining public policy. In an early chapter, entitled "Fiscal Politics," they provided a picture of the political process roughly analogous to the one I present in chapter 3. But, although the Musgraves recognized the importance of variations in the ability of both the market and the political process in the abstract, they focused almost exclusively on variation in the ability of the market in their specific applications. The ability of the political process was considered, if at all, only in a limited, technical way, focused primarily on the administrative costs of the government programs or the problems of coordinating the efforts of different political jurisdictions, ignoring the more robust analysis of political process behavior they had alluded to in the "Fiscal Politics" chapter. Thus, although the Musgraves recognized the need for sophisticated institutional comparison in the abstract, they ignored it in the particular. In that sense, their approach is analogous to Richard Posner's work, which discusses the relative merits of courts, legislatures, and the market in the abstract, but ignores their comparison in application.[11] I examine the problems with this single institutional focus in the next chapter.

10. Richard Musgrave and Peggy Musgrave, *Public Finance in Theory and Practice* (1976).

11. The recognition of institutional comparison appears in Richard Posner, *Economic Analysis of Law* ch 19 (4th ed 1992). The failures to apply it are detailed in chapters 2 and 6 of this book.

}2{

Social Goals and Public Policies:
Bridging the Gap between Them

In this chapter I offer an overview of the themes of this book by considering the issues raised by two quite different but important legal cases, the common law nuisance case, *Boomer v Atlantic Cement Company,* [1] and the constitutional law, freedom of the press case, *New York Times Co. v The United States* (the *Pentagon Papers* case). [2] These case studies examine two very different conceptions of social goals: resource allocation efficiency in connection with *Boomer,* and the constellation of non-efficiency goals, especially the protection of basic liberty captured in John Rawls's *Theory of Justice,* in connection with the *Pentagon Papers* case. This examination shows that the choice of social goals such as resource allocation efficiency or Rawlsian justice tells us very little about law and public policy — either from a descriptive or prescriptive standpoint. It also highlights the importance of institutional choice, the challenge of comparative institutional analysis, and the inadequacy of single institutional responses.

The comparison of the two cases also demonstrates that comparative institutional analysis, although essential to the effective economic analysis of law and public policy, is not limited to economic analysis. The discussion of the *Boomer* case shows that good law and economics must be good comparative institutional analysis. But, as the discussions of Rawls and of the *Pentagon Papers* case show, the need for comparative institutional analysis persists when the goal of resource allocation efficiency is dropped.

BOOMER, RESOURCE ALLOCATION EFFICIENCY, AND INSTITUTIONAL COMPARISON

The economic analysis of law is a powerful if controversial approach. This approach is cast in terms of a social goal — resource allocation efficiency. The central propositions of the economic analysis of law tie what the law is (and, to an appreciable degree, what it should be) to this social

1. 26 NY2d 219, 309 NYS2d 312, 257 NE2d 870 (1970).
2. 403 US 713 (1971).

goal. In particular, the proponents of the economic analysis of law argue that the outcomes of the common law (judge-made law) generally increase resource allocation efficiency and that common law outcomes can best be understood and anticipated in this way.[3]

As the subsequent discussion of the *Boomer* case shows, however, if economic analysis is to help us to understand the law, it must depend on important insights about the comparison of institutions to do so. That the common law is animated by a deep and abiding interest in efficiency, standing alone, yields no implications for law. Any such implications stem from crucial assumptions about the workings of the relevant institutions — the market, the courts, and the political process. The most powerful insights from existing law and economics have come from an analysis based heavily on institutional insights. This analysis, however, has been single institutional and, therefore, has failed to explicate and reveal the full range of legal outcomes consistent with efficiency. Analysis of the *Boomer* case shows the central role of comparative as opposed to single institutional analysis in understanding law.

The *Boomer* case is a good object of study for several reasons. First, it is short and its facts are relatively simple. Second, because it contains a dissenting opinion, it shows judges explicitly exploring both sides of the case. Both the position of the majority and that of the dissent seem plausible and sensible. Third, concerns about something approximating resource allocation efficiency are explicit in *Boomer*. It is a classic law and economics case. Fourth, it contains themes both traditional and contemporary. *Boomer* is about property rights in their most traditional forms and yet it is also about the important contemporary problem of air pollution.

The *Boomer* case arose from private litigation by seven neighbors against a large cement plant near Albany, New York. The seven neighbors brought an action in the state courts of New York arguing that the dirt, smoke, and vibration emanating from the plant constituted a common law nuisance and, therefore, violated their private property rights.[4] They sought the

---

3. Resource allocation efficiency focuses on the balance of social costs and benefits. As it is used in legal analysis, concern for resource allocation efficiency is often seen in judicial balancing of these aggregate impacts. More precisely, resources are most efficiently allocated when they go to the use for which they most are demanded. This demand is measured by the willingness of people to pay for these resources. A more complete definition of resource allocation efficiency and its deficiencies as a measure of social good are presented later in this chapter.

4. *Boomer*, 257 NE2d at 871.

traditional remedy for violation of these rights, an injunction against continuation of this injurious activity. The trial court found that the defendant was maintaining a nuisance, but, contrary to previous precedent, refused the plaintiffs' request for an injunction, offering them damages instead.[5] The 1970 opinion of the New York Court of Appeals, the highest state court, reviewed this unorthodox trial court response. With slight modification, the Court of Appeals sustained the approach taken by the trial court.[6] A strong dissent called for imposition of the injunction.[7]

The majority of the appellate judges voted to sustain the refusal of the injunction because they believed that the harm to the plaintiffs caused by the defendant's cement plant was less than the social value of the plant.[8] The trial court estimated the total loss to the seven plaintiffs at $185,000. The value of the defendant's plant was described as involving an investment of roughly $45 million as well as employing over 300 people.[9] The majority's logic for refusing an injunction in these circumstances was simple: it did not make sense to close down a valuable plant in order to avoid a much lower loss. Instead, the court chose to remedy this loss by awarding damages rather than enjoining the injurious activity.

It is easy enough to see the outcome in *Boomer* as the result of a central concern for resource allocation efficiency. The choice of remedy was determined by weighing the social costs and benefits of two alternative remedies — injunction and permanent damages. This rough balance of social benefits and costs is largely what efficiency means in the law and economics approach.[10] As with other legal outcomes, such as the famous Learned Hand formula in negligence law discussed in chapter 6, concern for the balance between social benefits and costs serves as a powerful indication of judicial concern with what economists term resource allocation efficiency.

Boomer can be taken as a classic example of law-making driven by re-

---

5. Id.

6. Id at 875.

7. Id (Jasen dissenting).

8. Id at 874–75.

9. Technically, the figures are not comparable. The loss to society of closing the defendant's plant might be less than $45 million, depending on the value of the plant (and the land on which it was located) for other purposes. Similarly, the loss to the employees from cessation of business would depend on their alternative employment opportunities. Nevertheless, the figures used by the court roughly relate to the losses that would be associated with a cessation of the defendant's operation. Id at 873.

10. The more technical definition of resource allocation efficiency is considered more extensively later in this chapter.

source allocation efficiency. Because it would cost society more to close the plant than society would gain from such a closing, an efficiency-oriented court would refuse to order the closing. Indeed, the apparent common sense of the decision both seems to transcend and to elevate the somewhat antiseptic notion of resource allocation efficiency. Upon closer inspection, however, it becomes less obvious that either efficiency or common sense is necessarily served by the majority's decision.

We can see the equivocal nature of the connection between efficiency and legal outcomes in general, and between efficiency and the refusal of the injunction in *Boomer*, by briefly examining traditional property law. In this connection, we are aided by a well-known and respected economic analysis of property rights. In an analysis that depends heavily on institutional factors, Richard Posner, one of the most prominent figures in law and economics, shows that the choice between injunction and damages (between property rights and liability rights) is more subtle than the simple logic of the choice made by the majority in *Boomer*. [11]

As a general rule, awarding injunctions for property rights violations is quite common. Unconditionally awarding an injunction to prevent a trespass is a basic tenet of Anglo-American property law. In common law trespass actions, courts award an injunction for the violation of a property right without ever hearing or being willing to hear arguments about the relative merits or values of the particular offending and protected uses. There is no place in these contexts for the sort of balance between competing uses found in the *Boomer* case.

The very existence of this simple, unconditional enforcement of property rights seems, at first blush, to conflict with the economic approach to law because it seems to resist the very comparison of social benefits and costs that is the core of economic efficiency. If a judicial balancing of social benefits and costs like that in *Boomer* proves that the logic of the common law is efficiency, then a refusal to carry out such a balance seems to disprove that thesis.

Posner responds to this apparent conflict between law and efficiency by arguing that the courts will not balance benefits and costs because this

---

11. See Richard Posner, *Economic Analysis of Law* at 56–61 (4th ed 1992). Posner's analysis reflects an earlier analysis by Guido Calabresi, a founder of law and economics. See Guido Calabresi and Douglas Melamed, *Property Rules, Liability Rules and Inalienability: One View of the Cathedral*, 85 Harv L Rev 1089 (1972). Although Calabresi's analysis is more qualified than Posner's, it contains much the same points and, therefore, shares both the credit and criticism given Posner here.

balance can be accomplished better elsewhere. In particular, in the simple case of injunctions for trespass, the merits of the relative uses are worked out by market transactions. If the offending use is more valuable, then the offending user, precluded by injunction from simply imposing his or her use, will purchase that right to use from its owner. The market transaction manifests in a straightforward manner that the benefits of the use are greater than its costs. Courts do not have to directly resolve this issue.[12]

Posner illustrates this situation by a hypothetical controversy over the use of a garage. A, the owner of the land and garage, brings an action against neighbor B who has been using A's garage without A's permission. Suppose now B, like the cement company in *Boomer*, attempts to defend his use by arguing that B's use of A's garage is more valuable than A's use of the garage. Without knowing much property law, anyone would sense that such a defense would be rejected. And it is. Unlike *Boomer*, courts are unwilling to hear such a defense. There would be no hesitation; an injunction would be issued against B. Posner sees this simple property rule as efficiency-enhancing because, if B's use of A's garage is more valuable, then B will purchase the use of A's garage. Courts do not balance the uses because they do not have to.[13]

Posner's analysis is powerful and simple. It shows that an important area of law — traditional protection of property rights — can be explained as promoting efficiency. From this standpoint, however, the majority position in *Boomer* no longer seems so obvious. The implication that *Boomer* demonstrates a connection between property law and efficiency seems precarious on that account. Based on Posner's hypothetical case, it would seem that enjoining the use need not force the cement company to cease socially efficient production. If the benefits to the cement company of continuing the offending use exceed the detriments to the plaintiffs, the cement company, once it has been enjoined, can acquire the right to continue its use by purchasing that right from its owners, the plaintiffs. Contrary to the fears of the *Boomer* majority, the traditional injunction asked for by the plaintiffs would not be inefficient. Thus, we are left to wonder why we ever see courts in the business of comparing benefits and costs as they did in the majority opinion in *Boomer* and as they do in many areas of law.

Posner, however, is not at a loss to explain this outcome. Where the

12. Id at 56.
13. Id.

difficulty of transacting increases and, therefore, the likelihood of a beneficial transaction decreases, it is less likely that the market will correctly
balance costs and benefits in the context of an injunction. To Posner, the
simple injunctive response of trespass law makes less sense and the greater
role of courts in balancing benefits and costs makes more sense as the cost
of transacting increases. As Posner puts it, where the market works, the
courts allocate the efficiency decision (the balancing of costs and benefits)
to the market; where the market does not work, the courts make the efficiency determination themselves.[14]

From this perspective, one can see an important difference between Posner's simple garage example with its two participants and the actual setting
in *Boomer,* where the company would have to deal with seven parties.
A larger number of parties results in higher costs of transaction simply
because more transactions (six more) must be accomplished. More importantly, the presence of seven parties each of whose rights must be pur-
chased means that the defendant faces seven parties each of whom holds
veto power over the project. If each person tries to push the defendant
to its limit, the defendant could be faced with a cost significantly (approximately seven times) in excess of the value of its use. Under these
conditions, it is entirely possible that no transaction would take place and,
therefore, the dire (and inefficient) social result envisioned by the majority — the closing of a far more valuable plant — would occur.

Having momentarily resurrected the majority position in *Boomer,* however, it is wise to carefully examine the law and economics analysis that
allowed the resurrection. The analysis employed by Posner is institutional
as that term is used in this book. The difference between property rules,
liability rules, and complex property rules,[15] according to Posner, lies in
variation in the efficacy of market participation — of market transactions.
If market transactions are easy and likely, then the outcome is (and should

14. Id at 62–63.
15. Although the choice in *Boomer* is between injunctive relief and damages, the
issues raised by the choice between market balancing of relative uses and court balancing of relative uses can include a wide choice of remedies. If courts choose to balance
relative uses, they can still opt to issue an injunction. That is the logic of the dissent's
position. As we shall see, such a position really subsumes another level of choice between injunctions and damages — whether precluding the offending use is more effectively carried out by injunction or by permanent damages. This choice, as we shall also
see, is also comparative institutional. All this will become clear soon. For present purposes, it explains why I include "more complex property rules" along with liability
(damages) rules.

be) the straightforward application of simple property rules. If market transactions are difficult and unlikely, a different legal regime or result based on judicial balancing of costs and benefits occurs (and should occur).

An important aspect of law and economics is, therefore, driven by institutional concerns. The goal, resource allocation efficiency, standing on its own does not determine these results. Only by adding important institutional insights can Posner provide his creative explanation for the difference between property and liability rules.

If my sole point was to exhibit that law and economics and its concerns about efficiency were centrally tied to institutional concerns, this example would suffice. On the other hand, not much is accomplished by simply calling upon economic analysts of law to relabel their considerations as institutional. Far more important, for the analysis of cases like *Boomer*, for the understanding of law and economics, and for the understanding of the analysis presented in this book, however, is the realization that the institutional analysis upon which the Posnerian insights about law are based is inherently incomplete. Much more than mislabeling is involved here.

The problem with Posner's analysis is that it is single institutional rather than comparative institutional. Posner asks how the market works in two different settings and bases his vision of law on variations between these two settings. Thus, he associates injunctions with instances in which transaction costs are low or the market works well and other solutions such as liability rules (the awarding of damages) with higher transaction costs or instances in which the market does not work well. Something is missing.

The legal issue that Posner and the judges in the *Boomer* case confront is not single institutional but comparative institutional. The question, as posed by Posner himself, is under what conditions will the market balance the costs and benefits and under what conditions will the courts balance the costs and benefits. Where the market is the preferred balancer, we have simple property rules; where the courts are the preferred balancers, we have liability rules (or more complex property rules). If the issue involves two institutions — the market and the courts — then why does Posner only ask about variations in the ability of the market? Something needs to be said or at least assumed about the other institution — the courts.

Posner implicitly assumes that, where transaction costs are "low" or the market "works," it makes the allocation decision better than the courts. A hidden comparative institutional judgment lies buried in this single institutional formulation — that where transaction costs are low, the market

is always superior to the courts as the balancer of costs and benefits.[16]
Under this assumption, it seems plausible that the market is the superior
balancer.

Follow what happens to the Posnerian analysis, however, as one moves
from the simple setting of low transaction costs and market dominance to
the world of high transaction costs. According to Posner, we change legal
outcomes. We move from simple property rules to more complex property
rules or liability rules; the judiciary becomes the balancer of benefits and
costs. Again we have the peculiar outcome that a greater role for the judiciary is based solely on variation in the characteristics of the market with
no explicit consideration of variation in the ability of the judiciary. More
importantly, the implicit assumption of judicial superiority is subject to
serious doubt or at least qualification.

One can envision Posner's argument applied in the *Boomer* setting.
Boomer represents a more complex transaction setting than the two-party
setting imagined for the garage example. The larger number of parties in
Boomer makes the transaction more difficult. Bargains involving more actors generate higher transaction costs. But our question is not whether
market performance improves or deteriorates with larger numbers of parties, but rather whether the market works better or worse than the courts.
The correct legal response involves a choice between the market and the
courts in each setting.

Even assuming that the ability of the courts does not worsen as we increase the number of relevant parties, we cannot say with certainty that we
have reached the point where a greater judicial role is called for—only that
the case is better. Still, if the issue were merely one of finding the appropriate switching point, then my point would seem only picky. In the difficult world of legal analysis, Posner's analysis should not be expected to
give the exact point at which a worsening market becomes worse than the
courts. As long as the judiciary's ability to resolve the dispute does not vary
as one moves from one setting to another, variation in the ability of the
market is the major factor and Posner's articulation is a good first approximation of the more accurate comparative institutional articulation.

However, Posner's analysis is not even a good first approximation because the implicit assumption of unvarying judicial ability is faulty. As

16. I examine whether it is ever either correct or necessary to talk about "low transaction costs" in the real world in chapter 4.

with the market, the courts' ability decreases as the number of parties increases, for example, as we move from two to eight parties in the *Boomer*
case. The problems of collective action that plague market transactions as
numbers increase also plague adjudication. As the number of potential
plaintiffs or defendants increases, the costs of bringing actions increase
and the dynamics of litigation become more complex. Larger numbers of
parties means higher basic litigation costs such as service of process, notice
of motions, depositions, and other forms of trial preparation. Larger numbers also mean that negotiations over settlement are more complicated
and less likely to reach a value-enhancing result. The analysis here is the
same as for market transactions: larger numbers mean more hold-outs and
greater likelihood of a failed transaction.

In addition, the task of comparing benefits and costs and of setting
damages becomes more difficult for the courts as the number of parties
and the complexity of the interaction of their land uses increases. The
courts must now listen to and balance a larger number of views on the
situation. Thus, as the number of parties affected increases, the ability of
courts to make accurate assessments decreases, as does the likelihood that
the issue will be brought to court and sufficiently contested. Like the market process, the adjudicative process becomes less effective as numbers
increase.

The comparative ability of institutions viewed in a consistent and parallel fashion is the essence of valid comparative institutional analysis. It is
not sufficient to note the existence of the other institution and the possibility that it too may be imperfect or expensive. The crucial question
concerns the *relative merits* of the two institutions, when compared to
each other.[17]

---

17. Posner has sections of his book in which he speaks of the limits of the adjudicative process. See, for example, chapters 20, 21, and 22. He even has sections in which he
speaks generally about the relative merits of the market, the political process and the
courts. See chapter 19. The problem is that this general concern for institutional comparison does not show up in his legal analysis, such as his analysis of property rules. In
chapter 6, I return to this same problem in his analysis of tort law.

The same problem exists in a more subtle fashion in the analysis of property rules by
Guido Calabresi and Douglas Melamed, *Property Rules, Liability Rules and Inalienability:
One View of the Cathedral*, 85 Harv L Rev 1089 (1972). Although the authors are careful
to refer in general to the relative abilities of the "collective" solution to which they
compare transacting, sources of variation in institutional ability, such as greater numbers, come to play in their analysis only in considering variations in the ability of the
market not in the ability of the unspecified collective solution mechanism — presumably, the courts, administrative agencies, or legislatures. Although mention of the exis-

I do not mean to suggest that the same problems confront the adjudicative process as confront the market process. Indeed, the very essence of comparative institutional analysis is that relative merits often do not remain the same over differing situations. My only point — and it is central — is that the same factors that change the ability of one institution across two situations very often change the ability of its alternative (or alternatives) in the same direction. Quite commonly, albeit not always, institutions move together. When one institution is at its best or worst, the alternative institutions are often at their best or worst. As we have seen, increased numbers cause the performance of the market to become a less trustworthy indicator of efficiency, but they can also cause the performance of the courts to be less trustworthy as well. Because institutions commonly move together, Posner's single institutional analysis of the market (market works well, market works badly) has no claim even as a good first approximation of the relevant issue of comparative institutional performance. Comparative institutional issues like the choice of legal response cannot be determined or even roughly approximated by single institutional analysis.

To better understand the implication of greater numbers on the adjudicative process as well as to understand the range of remedies discussed in the *Boomer* case, we return to the damage remedy actually granted in the *Boomer* case and the criticism of that remedy by the dissent. The majority refused to give the traditional injunction and instead awarded damages of $185,000. The dissent criticized the remedy as inadequate to handle the larger problems inherent in particle pollution in the Hudson River Valley. Instead, the dissent argued that an injunction should have been issued after an 18 month period if no avoidance mechanism were found.[18]

Despite its quite different solution, however, the dissent's position showed as much concern with efficiency as the majority's position. The dissent disagreed with the majority's position because the dissent disagreed with the majority's definition of relevant social benefits and costs. The dissent emphasized that these seven homeowners were not the only people harmed by the defendant's activity. The dissent pointed out that the defendant is only one of many polluters in the Hudson River Valley and that its activities as well as the activities of the other polluters affect

---

tence of parallel alternatives may be an improvement over ignoring their existence, it is the parallel consideration of these alternatives that is necessary to make institutional comparison work.

18. *Boomer*, 257 NE2d at 877 (Jasen dissenting).

most of the citizens of the Hudson River Valley.[19] The dissent concluded that an injunction would produce the necessary incentives to induce the defendant and others similarly situated to discover technology
sufficient to eliminate or at least reduce the dirt, smoke, and vibration
caused by their plants.[20] Thus, the dissent too was interested in efficiency
and yet came to quite a different conclusion about the law than did the
majority.

Here, as with the majority position, the concern for efficiency — in this
instance measured on a more global scale — relates to the dissent's legal
position only through comparative institutional analysis. Once again that
analysis is hardly trivial. The dissent's position, just like the majority's, is
dependent on one's assumptions about the functioning of institutions.

The majority's concern about the inadequacies of injunction would
have been unfounded if the market worked frictionlessly. Similarly, the
dissent's concern about the inadequacies of permanent damages to take
account of the full social effect of the pollution would be unfounded if the
adjudicative process worked frictionlessly. The damage remedy is available, in theory, to anybody harmed by the pollution of the Atlantic Cement Plant or any of the other plants in the Hudson River Valley. These
plants would then be subject to actions for damages from all the citizens
injured by the pollution, including presumably all injuries to property and
to health. Faced with this prospect, these companies would have the incentive to consider these court awarded damages as costs, "internalize" these
costs, and reach the correct allocative solutions. If the potential damage
awards the company would have to pay were greater than the costs of
avoidance, it would be efficient to avoid the damage and the companies
would do so. In other words, they would have the correct incentives to
search for modes of avoidance including relocation without any need for
injunctions.

From this perspective, it would appear that the majority's damage
remedy would achieve efficiency not only in terms of the eight parties to
the case but also in terms of the larger portion of society of concern to the
dissent. If all the victims foreseen by the dissent brought actions (or there
was a serious threat that they would bring actions), the more global pollution problem that worries the dissent would be solved by the damage remedy suggested by the majority. Like the transaction-costless world where

19. Id at 876 (Jasen dissenting).
20. Id at 877 (Jasen dissenting).

market transactions would internalize everything, the frictionless adjudicative world would also send the correct signals. In this frictionless adjudicative world, we could trust that what we saw in terms of polluter behavior was the efficient solution.

Alas, like the transaction-costless market, the frictionless adjudicative process is a fiction. The adjudicative process is neither frictionless nor costless. More importantly, its frictions and costs increase as numbers of litigants, size of individual damages, and disparity of interests increase.

Quite likely, the sizable social problem of pollution in an area like the Hudson River Valley is characterized by small impacts on a great many victims. Thus, we have a large social loss dispersed over many victims each of whom suffers relatively low loss and, therefore, has relatively low stakes in any subsequent litigation. These impacts, as well as the sources of pollution, are complex, subtle, and difficult to recognize. Even if victims recognize these losses and their causes, the low stakes may not justify the significant threshold costs of litigation. Litigation has significant economies of scale — one does not buy any serious lawyering for the expenditure of $100 or even $1,000. Because of these limitations on adjudication, the *Boomer* judges could not reasonably expect all the people in the Hudson River Valley to bring or credibly threaten to bring permanent damage actions against Atlantic Cement or other local polluters.[21]

The *Boomer* example shows that the increased numbers of parties that plague the market also plague the courts. Increased numbers of effected parties reduce the effectiveness of damage remedies to achieve efficient solutions. Where there is a highly dispersed victim group, the damage remedy becomes a highly questionable means to control the behavior of prospective injurers.

In short, the *Boomer* case, a classic instance of judicial concern about resource allocation efficiency, shows that Posner's approach omits the most important aspect of the interaction between efficiency and law. Posner recognizes that the essence of the connection between law and efficiency lies in institutional concerns. But, because he does not employ

21. The courts have fashioned responses to this problem of litigation by dispersed interest. Predominant among these is the class action, which allows the joining together of dispersed interests and the sharing of the expenses of the collective legal action. Class actions and the other responses, however, only somewhat reduce the immense problem. The prospects of litigation still go down if the stakes are dispersed and the effect is particularly pronounced when there are widely dispersed interests. The subject of class actions and the other judicial responses to dispersion are discussed in chapter 5.

comparative institutional analysis, he envisions a deterioration in the ability of the market as numbers increase but fails to note a parallel deterioration in the ability of the adjudicative process. As numbers increase, substantive issues become more complex and difficult to deal with, and the dynamics of litigation can inhibit the ability of the court to send adequate signals.

I have not, however, squeezed all I can from the *Boomer* case; there is yet another important institutional comparison in the debate between the majority and dissent. The majority and the dissent agreed that neither the permanent damage remedy nor market transactions were feasible solutions to the general problems of regional air pollution. As we have seen, the dissent favored the issuance of an injunction based on an adjudicative determination that the costs of the offending use were sufficiently severe to justify forcing plant closure. The majority, also aware of the general problems of pollution, justified its more modest adjudicative role by placing greater reliance on yet another institution — the political process.

At least at first blush, the majority's position on this issue seems straightforward and sensible. Pollution in the Hudson River Valley is a far flung, complex phenomenon. The political process with its wide range of investigative, implementive, regulatory, and taxing alternatives seems the preferable choice when compared with an adjudicative process strained, as we have seen, by determinations that involve a vast number of victims. Allocating such global and complex issues to the political process is a response commonly found in judicial opinions from all areas of the law. To the majority, this ended the issue. Should it have?

To answer that question, we must employ the same kind of analysis we used to understand the relative roles of the adjudicative and market processes. Clearly, like the frictionless market and the frictionless adjudicative process, a frictionless political process is an obvious solution. In fact, of course, the political process is never frictionless. On the simplest level, time and other resources are needed to investigate, legislate, and implement. The more complex the issue and the larger the number of people involved, the higher these costs.

More importantly, the widely dispersed stakes associated with regional air pollution cause problems for the political process by affecting the political participation of various constituent interests in such activities as lobbying and voting. These effects on the dynamics of the political process are dramatic enough to be captured in two traditional and paradoxically opposite perceptions of political malfunction — the overrepresentation of concentrated interests (special interest legislation) and the overrepresentation of dispersed larger interests (the tyranny of the majority). In subsequent discussion, I refer to these two traditional perceptions of malfunctions as minoritarian bias and majoritarian bias. In the pollution setting, the familiar scenario involves a large but mostly dormant majority who are basically unaware of the problem or unwilling to bear the expense of fighting against more aggressive special interests with their larger per capita stakes. The result in that scenario is special interest legislation or minoritarian bias. This is a subject we will return to in the next chapter.

Without validating this particular image of the political process, we can see, even at this juncture, that the political process, like the market and adjudicative processes, may function more poorly as numbers increase and the distribution of stakes becomes more complex and more dispersed. Thus, although it is quite sensible for the majority in the *Boomer* case to see the political process as a viable alternative to adjudication for the general environmental issue, it is also quite sensible for the dissent to have been far less sanguine about this alternative. Just as the choice between an injunction and damages involved an implicit choice between the adjudicative and market processes as balancers of benefits and costs, it also involved the choice between the adjudicative and legislative responses to pollution. The decision required evaluation of the relative merits and limitations of all three institutions. The majority and dissent reached different conclusions based on different perceptions of the relative capacities of the alternative institutions.

Certain generalizations or lessons can now be drawn from this brief discussion of the *Boomer* case. First, identifying a goal—in this case efficiency—tells us virtually nothing about law and public policy. Insights about law and public policy require the comparative analysis of institutional performance. Second, this analysis cannot be carried out through single institutional analysis no matter how careful or creative. The same factors that cause one alternative institution to vary often affect all the alternative institutions. Changes in numbers, per capita stakes, and the cost of participation—the factors to which the participation-centered approach pays particular attention—cause the ability of all the major institutions to vary, often in the same direction.

For an analyst interested in understanding and describing the position of the judges in the *Boomer* case, perhaps with the hope of predicting their reaction to a new case with some different facts (a common concern for lawyers), the mere realization that they are interested in efficiency is not helpful. The analyst must understand the views of the judges on the work-ings of institutions like the market, the adjudicative process, and the po-litical process in order to understand the position each took in *Boomer* or is likely to take in some variant of *Boomer*. Positive or descriptive analysis requires comparative institutional analysis.

The same is true for normative or prescriptive analysis. Judges (or any-one else) interested in the goal of efficiency would have to involve them-selves in serious comparative institutional analysis. The judges' positions in *Boomer* suggest a rough and intuitive comparative institutional analysis. But judges can do better, and it is the job of legal analysts to help them do so.

LESSONS FOR LAW AND ECONOMICS: AVOIDING THE TEMPTATIONS OF A FRICTIONLESS WORLD

For the discipline of law and economics, the lesson of the foregoing discussion is simple and essential: good law and economics means good comparative institutional analysis. Law and economics gets its analytical richness from identifying variations in institutional characteristics, not simply from recognizing the central role of efficiency. By emphasizing comparative institutional analysis, economic analysis of law can become richer and avoid single institutional fallacies.[22]

The realization that comparative institutional analysis lies at the core of good economic analysis of law also calls into question strong assertions that have been made about the efficiency effects of Anglo-American com-mon law.[23] As the analysis of the *Boomer* case indicates, for any complex setting, there are a number of plausibly efficient scenarios. In *Boomer,* under a plausible range of circumstances, the injunction would have been

---

22. The need to explicate and emphasize the comparative institutional core of law and economics is dramatically revealed by law and economics analyses of the choice of contract remedies. The choice between specific performance and damages has received sophisticated comparative institutional analysis. See, e.g., Anthony Kronman, *Specific Performance,* 45 U Chi L Rev 351 (1978); Alan Schwartz, *The Case for Specific Performance,* 89 Yale LJ 271 (1979); and Thomas Ulen, *The Efficiency of Specific Performance: Toward a Unified Theory of Contract Remedies,* 89 Mich L Rev 341 (1984). Yet the choice between specific performance and expectation damages addressed in these analyses is only a spe-cial example of the choice between property and liability rules addressed single institu-tionally by Posner and Calabresi.

23. Posner succinctly states this central maxim as follows: "Although the correlation is far from perfect, judge-made rules tend to be efficiency-promoting while those made by legislatures tend to be efficiency-reducing." Posner, *Economic Analysis* at 523 (cited in n. 11).

efficient. In turn, under a plausible range of circumstances, the permanent damage remedy actually awarded would have been efficient. It is difficult, without significantly more evidence, to claim that the position of the majority was more likely to move society toward efficiency than would the position of the dissent.[24]

Members of the law and economics community justifiably celebrate the awarding of a recent Nobel Prize in Economics to Ronald Coase. Coase's famous 1960 article, *The Problem of Social Cost,* forms a significant part of the foundation for the modern economic analysis of law.[25] The famous Coase theorem, that, given zero transaction costs, the awarding of property rights (and therefore, law) does not affect resource allocation efficiency, stems from that article. Paradoxically, the Coase theorem that has led so many to spend so much time analyzing the implications of the world of zero transaction costs was part of an argument showing the irrelevance of zero transaction costs (or any parallel assumption of frictionless institutions).

Coase proposed the analysis subsequently labeled the Coase theorem to show the inherently incomplete nature of a prominent form of economic analysis, Pigouvian welfare economics. Pigou argued that the existence of market imperfections formed a sufficient condition for government intervention.[26] Implicit in the Pigouvian position was a virtually frictionless institution — the government response. Coase's analysis showed that, if one were to make similar assumptions about frictionless transacting, the market process would achieve efficiency without the aid of government. Assuming that a frictionless (perfect) institutional process (either adjudicating, regulating, or transacting) exists truncates any analysis of law or public policy to trivial proportions. Neither the frictionless government nor the frictionless market is a useful construct for public policy analysis except to show the absurd nature of assuming the existence of the other.

The call for comparative institutional analysis inherent in Coase's work seems not to have been heeded. Some see many real world markets as close

---

24. I considered this issue more extensively in an early work on comparative institutional analysis. See Neil Komesar, *In Search of a General Approach to Legal Analysis: A Comparative Institutional Alternative,* 79 Mich L Rev 1350, 1356–62 (1981). In chapter 6, I return to this same theme in the broader context of tort law and again show the wide range of results consistent with resource allocation efficiency that can be generated by varying institutional assumptions.

25. Ronald Coase, *The Problem of Social Cost,* 3 J L & Econ 1 (1960).

26. Government intervention for Pigou included injunctions or damage awards under nuisance law or taxation imposed by the legislature.

approximations of the transaction-costless world and, using this perception, truncate comparative institutional analysis and institutional choice.
As we shall see in the chapter on the market, real world markets are often
good institutional choices, not because they are costless or even nearly so,
but rather because, although they are always costly, markets are less imperfect and costly than their alternatives.

The lessons to be drawn from the *Boomer* discussion in particular and
from this book in general are, however, as relevant for those who do not
espouse law and economics methods and even for those who despise
them. The points made here about economic analysis of law, with its focus
on the social goal of efficiency, are true for any analysis and any social
goal. What can be said about efficiency can be said about any goal or end
value, whether it is the difference principle of John Rawls, the Marxist
principle of to each according to their needs and from each according to
their ability, or the principles of liberty, autonomy, or equality. Each social
goal requires difficult social determinations — often balancing or integrating aggregate social impacts. Defining, realizing, and implementing these
goals requires the operation of complex and imperfect social decision-
making processes or systems like the market, the courts, and the political
process. How these processes are constituted and how responsibilities are
allocated among them determines the content of these broad goals. Therefore, comparative institutional analysis would seem to be essential for understanding and reforming law and public policy no matter what the social
goal or end value contemplated.

Because I fear that this important point is likely to be misunderstood,
I next consider the relationship between institutional choice and non-
efficiency goals in greater depth. First, I discuss the very real limitations
and problems with resource allocation efficiency as a single goal or measure of social good. Second, I consider the range of goals that substitute for
or augment efficiency. Third, I consider one such constellation of goals,
the *Theory of Justice* of John Rawls. Fourth, I show that, as with efficiency
in the *Boomer* case, these other goals cannot yield meaningful law and public policy without serious consideration of institutional analysis and institutional choice. In that connection, I will analyze the *Pentagon Papers* case.

BEYOND EFFICIENCY

Resource allocation efficiency is a simple and attractive goal. Society's
scarce resources are optimally allocated (or efficiently allocated) when no
one could be better off without making someone else worse off. This situation is termed "Pareto optimal" or "Pareto efficient." In turn, a change

that made someone better off without making anyone worse off is termed "Pareto superior." If we assumed that the only social effects of closing the Atlantic Cement Plant in *Boomer* were a benefit of $185,000 for the seven neighbors and a loss of $45 million for the cement plant, we can imagine a better solution in which the neighbors are paid some amount between $185,000 and $45 million and the plant remains open. Everyone would be better off or at least no one would be worse off.

To see this example is to understand the heuristic power of the world of zero transaction costs associated with the Coase theorem. Where transactions can take place frictionlessly, we have an ideal process or institution to test efficiency. In this frictionless world, a transaction makes at least one party better off and the other at least as well off; therefore, a more efficient state of the world prevails. In other words, we know that the transaction constitutes a move toward Pareto efficiency — it is a Pareto superior move.

If one can imagine but not arrange such a transaction, that is, if one believed that in the transaction-costless world such a transaction would take place, then it would seem possible that, by forcing such a transaction (imposing it by government fiat or court order), one could increase resource allocation efficiency. Such a reallocation of resources would not be efficient in the Pareto sense because there would or could be net losers. The forced transaction is efficient only in the sense that if a transaction could have taken place it would have been Pareto efficient. The result may be positive in the aggregate, but there can be individual losers. This form of efficiency has taken on the name of "Kaldor-Hicks efficiency." When economists speak about a law or a program as advancing efficiency they usually are speaking of Kaldor-Hicks efficiency rather than Pareto efficiency because, in the real world, compensating the losers is usually too expensive or otherwise impracticable.

Thus, to return to the *Boomer* setting, if the cement plants in the Hudson River Valley were forced to reduce or stop pollution by employing filtering devices or even relocating, society might benefit in an amount that could make both the residents and the cement plants better off. In other words, the benefits to all the residents of the Hudson River Valley of having pollution reduced would be sufficient to cover the costs to the cement plants. But if, as is likely, the cement plants were not compensated, imposing the pollution abatement requirements would be efficient only in the Kaldor-Hicks sense.[27]

---

27. In chapter 8, I discuss the mechanics and implications of such a compensation system in the consideration of the Takings Clause.

In its Kaldor-Hicks manifestation, resource allocation efficiency is a form of cost-benefit analysis in which one concludes that the benefits of a given legal or public policy decision are sufficient to justify the costs even though the compensation necessary to assure that there are no losers is never in fact paid. That this is not the actual distribution of the net benefits is not relevant to Kaldor-Hicks efficiency.[28]

As an ethical norm, resource allocation efficiency is incomplete. Pareto superior transactions are intuitively attractive; they suggest the possibility of making some people better off without harming others. However, Pareto efficient transactions are determined by willingness to pay or willingness to be paid. Such willingness is related to ability to pay and to need, and hence to wealth. As a result, what would count as efficient could vary with differing distributions of wealth. Because Pareto efficiency takes the distribution of wealth as given, it ignores the fundamental question of equity or distributive justice: whether in fact society's current distribution of wealth and opportunity is itself conducive to social well-being. Thus Pareto efficiency, by its nature, is an incomplete description of the good.

In addition to sharing the incompleteness of Pareto efficiency, Kaldor-Hicks efficiency with its possibility of forced transactions involves additional tensions with equity or distributive justice. Under a Kaldor-Hicks approach, the result is efficient even if no voluntary transaction or associated compensation takes place so long as such a transaction would have taken place at zero transaction costs. Here there are losers and winners — not everyone is better off. Under these circumstances, the characteristics of the winners and losers — their moral attractiveness — can come into play. Thus, although Kaldor-Hicks efficiency might be fulfilled by a forced transaction without compensation, our sense of justice might not be. In the context of the *Boomer* case, we might feel that simply refusing any relief to the plaintiffs — an outcome that under the numbers used by the majority would have been Kaldor-Hicks efficient — would not be fair because they were at the location first or because they were poor or poorer than the owners of the cement plant. On the other hand, that the cement plants should be forced to employ filtering equipment or to relocate with-

28. Interestingly, in *Boomer* the remedy constitutes at least a rough approximation of Pareto, rather than Kaldor-Hicks, efficiency because it reflects the view that, given compensation, no one would be worse off, by requiring compensation of $185,000 in the form of permanent damages paid to the injured neighbors. As the term resource allocation efficiency is used in the law and economics literature, however, this compensation would be irrelevant for efficiency and often not present. See Posner, *Economic Analysis* ch 1 (cited in n. 11).

out compensation might seem fair because they are considered wrong-doers or because they are wealthier.[29]

A range of possible efficient outcomes raises even deeper doubts that efficiency is always good. We can imagine Pareto efficient transactions that are deeply unjust. One example is slavery. It is at least arguable that it is unjust for society to tolerate someone selling himself or herself into slavery. The right to control one's life, at least in the sense of being free of slavery, would then be an inalienable right. Society would not want to enforce or allow such a transaction even if the prospective slave chose that status knowledgeably and voluntarily.

A large range of social goals or interests can make legitimate claims on any theory of what is good or just. One can see a world divided between efficiency and equity, as most economists do, or one more particularly divided among a range of goals such as autonomy, equal liberty, distributive justice, and equality of opportunity, to which one might add efficiency. It is very difficult to believe that anyone has a sense of the good that does not involve a number of these concerns.

To the extent that multiple goals exist, however, one obvious challenge is melding them into a workable sense of the good. Whenever these notions (including efficiency) are in conflict, there must be some way of resolving how much of one and how much of another society considers to be just. Some theories of justice seek a single metric, such as utility; others make the tradeoffs or decisions via weights raised from intuitive senses of justice and applied in particular situations. Whatever the method of integrating these various goals, the decision rules remain complex and the basic constructs remain broad and vague enough to require definition at future points given future factors and, most importantly, by future institutions.

29. Each of these propositions is debatable. They are also based on debatable facts. For example, the distributive effects of placing the costs on the companies might end up placing those costs on people poorer than the beneficiaries of the compensation payments or of the pollution control, such as poorer workers or consumers. The important point is that some distributive results might be more attractive than others. As a general matter, a just society might want to reallocate wealth — the basis for ability to pay and therefore willingness to pay — in a more equitable and, in some rough sense, more equal fashion, and it might want to consider the worthiness of winners and losers in determining legal and public policy outcomes. Redistributing income or wealth or changing opportunities can have efficiency effects in that changing the distribution of wealth can involve administrative costs and additional costs as targets of the redistribution react by making their wealth less accessible. Changing the status quo always requires resources. The same of course may be said for any public policy or legal program whose purpose is to improve efficiency.

This need to define, implement, and meld social goals returns us to the central purpose of this discussion of goals. It is the choice of institutions not the choice of goals that concerns us here. As we saw in the discussion of efficiency, the choice of goals standing on its own dictates virtually nothing about law and public policy. Depending on a range of plausible institutional assumptions and institutional behaviors, either a given legal solution or its opposite may be the more efficient choice. Institutional choice plays a similar role where the definition of goals is broader.

Since efficiency, in one form or another, is usually one of the goals to be integrated into the constellation of goals, the same institutional choice issues and insights concerning efficiency are applicable when we consider a more complex constellation of goals. Comparative institutional analysis becomes at once more difficult and more necessary than it was in the context of resource allocation efficiency alone. As goals become more numerous and complex, dictating specific results in advance, as through a detailed constitution, becomes prohibitively difficult. More of the task for defining and implementing these complex goals must be allocated to future decision-makers, such as legislatures, administrative agencies, and courts. As more responsibility and power are assigned to these decision-making processes, their behavior and the allocation of decisions among them becomes increasingly important. If turning resource allocation efficiency into law and public policy requires extensive and difficult institutional choice and analysis, then, a fortiori, turning more complex configurations of social goals into law and public policy requires extensive and difficult institutional choice and analysis.

RAWLS AND THE *PENTAGON PAPERS* CASE

In order to convey a deeper appreciation of the range of non-efficiency goals and the difficulty of integrating them, I will make use of John Rawls's theory of justice.[30] Rawls's theory is useful because it captures all the non-efficiency concerns discussed in the previous section. Few if any works in philosophy have been so widely read not only in that field but, more importantly for my purposes, in the fields of law and public policy.[31] So far as I can tell, it is the most well-known discussion of social goals.

30. John Rawls, *A Theory of Justice* (1971).
31. There are an almost uncountable number of articles and books about *A Theory of Justice.* These various commentaries and critiques offer a wide variety of interpretations and extrapolations of the book. Rawls in turn has responded to many of these. So volu-

I employ Rawls's theory in two related ways. In the second part of this section, I examine a famous First Amendment case, *New York Times Co. v United States*[32] (the *Pentagon Papers* case), in terms of one of Rawls's non-efficiency goals, the protection of basic liberties. As with the goal of resource allocation efficiency, acceptance of the validity of a social goal tells us virtually nothing about what law is or should be. As we shall see, whether protection of basic liberties is consistent with strong constitutional protections or no constitutional protections at all depends on difficult questions of institutional choice. There is, however, reason to briefly examine the institutional components or underpinnings of Rawls's theory itself. Rawls's theory of justice is as close to a pure theory of goals and goal choice as is possible. He explicitly eschews institutional issues and, in turn, carefully avoids any law and public policy announcements. But even this strenuous attempt to avoid institutional choice by moving to a high level of abstraction and by refraining from law and public policy is problematic. The failure to confront issues of institutional choice troubles even Rawls's theory of justice.

Rawls's *Theory of Justice*

In his book, Rawls sets out two major principles, some subprinciples, and a system for ordering or ranking these principles. Rawls's first principle secures basic liberties for each person; the second provides for distributive justice or social and economic equality. In turn, social and economic equality is divided into equality of opportunity to hold offices and positions and equal access to society's primary goods. Rawls's ordering of goals places liberty first, equality of opportunity second, distribution of wealth third, and efficiency fourth. Liberty is traded only against liberty; individual liberty is curtailed only to the extent necessary to provide and protect the liberty of others. The most unusual and controversial component of Rawls's theory is his "difference principle": an increase in the inequality of opportunity or of other primary goods is acceptable only if it enhances the condition of those with lesser opportunity or other primary

---

minous is this exchange that there is at least one book (in excess of 600 pages) devoted to simply cataloging the various works about Rawls and the various issues raised and positions presented; see J. H. Wellbank, Denis Snook, and David T. Mason, *John Rawls and His Critics* (1982). The progression of commentary, response, and additional commentary has not to this time abated.

32. 403 US 713 (1970).

goods. That is, some people can be made *relatively* worse off only if they are, at the same time, also made *absolutely* better off.[33]

Rawls claims that his theory of justice is the only viable alternative to utilitarianism as a systemic approach to social justice. Unlike utilitarianism, he offers a special priority to liberty and distributive equality. Other non-utilitarian theories, which Rawls refers to as "intuitionist," designate only a constellation of goals, but not a method for integrating them, and are, therefore, not concrete alternatives to utilitarianism. In contrast, Rawls offers ordering and difference principles as means of defining just outcomes. These are, at any rate, Rawls's claims. In the vast literature about Rawls's theory, these propositions are debated. Rawls's critics have attacked the validity of these assertions, the substance of his goals, and, in particular, his willingness to redistribute wealth and opportunity.[34]

I am not in position nor do I want to assess the validity of any of these claims. I am interested instead in what even such an extensive and much discussed articulation of social goals as Rawls's theory of justice tells us about law or public policy. For that purpose, I accept Rawls's choice and ordering of social goals. Rawls's list provides a valuable and respected set

33. Rawls's exact articulation in *A Theory of Justice* (at 302–3) is as follows:

First Principle. Each person is to have an equal right to the most extensive total system of equal basic liberties compatible with a similar system of liberty for all.

Second Principle. Social and economic inequalities are to be arranged so that they are both: (a) to the greatest benefit of the least advantaged, consistent with the just savings principle, and (b) attached to offices and positions open to all under conditions of fair equality of opportunity.

First Priority Rule (The Priority of Liberty). The principles of justice are to be ranked in lexical order and therefore liberty can be restricted only for the sake of liberty. There are two cases: (a) a less extensive liberty must strengthen the total system of liberty shared by all; (b) a less than equal liberty must be acceptable to those with the lesser liberty.

Second Priority Rule (The Priority of Justice Over Efficiency and Welfare). The second principle of justice is lexically prior to the principle of efficiency and to that of maximizing the sum of advantages; and fair opportunity is prior to the difference principle. There are two cases: (a) an inequality of opportunity must enhance the opportunities of those with the lesser opportunity; (b) an excessive rate of saving must on balance mitigate the burden of those bearing this hardship.

General Conception. All social primary goods—liberty and opportunity, income and wealth, and the bases of self-respect—are to be distributed equally unless an unequal distribution of any or all of these goods is to the advantage of the least favored.

34. This debate is catalogued in Wellbank, Snook, and Mason, *John Rawls and his Critics* (1982).

of non-efficiency goals. In the next part of this chapter, I will borrow one of these goals, liberty, and show that institutional choice is once again an essential link between goals and law and public policy. Before I do so, however, I offer some comments about the place of institutional choice in Rawls's theory in general.

From an institutional perspective, two general aspects of Rawls's theory of justice stand out. First, a great deal of attention is spent on the "original position," a perfectly functioning institution analogous to the transaction-costless world, which Rawls employs to derive his theory of justice. Second, serious attention to real world institutions and institutional choice is virtually absent. The first is interesting; the second is troubling.

Rawls derives his results from an ideal institutional setting in a manner analogous to the way that economists derive efficient results from the transaction-costless world or the perfectly competitive market. This setting, called the original position, is complex, and Rawls is sometimes ambiguous about some of its basic conditions. But its most important attribute is the suppression of information. The decision-makers in the original position have "no information about particular individuals: they do not know their own social position, their place in the distribution of natural abilities, and/or their conception of the good."[35] Much as the idealized world of zero transaction costs produces efficient results by frictionlessly taking into account everyone's willingness to pay, the original position produces justice as fairness. It forces the representative person to become the "every person" and, therefore, to internalize and take into account the interests of everyone.

The original position, like the transaction-costless world, is a powerful expository and analytic device. It has received considerable attention both by Rawls and his critics.[36] In stark contrast, however, Rawls focuses virtually no attention on real world institutions and institutional choice.

Much of this absence of attention is advertent. Rawls declares disinterest in attempting to set out what he calls "non-ideal" conditions for carrying out his theory of justice. His stated objective is to establish a theory of justice, not a theory of law and public policy. His theory is purposely

35. Rawls, *Theory of Justice* at 197.
36. In particular, his critics have argued that Rawls's difference principle implies a virtually infinite risk averseness. The person in the original position is seen not only seeking insurance against some downside risks but against *all* downside risks. In other words, there would be an unwillingness to take any risk of ending up being disadvantaged no matter how large the expected benefits of that transaction. See Dennis Mueller, *Public Choice* 235–46 (1979).

articulated at a high level of abstraction. When he refers to institutions, he means idealized rules, not real world decision-making processes. Rawls simply alludes to a vague multi-sectored governmental process that will protect liberty (including property rights), dispense distributive justice, and police the market. For each function, the correct agency will arise. He does not describe the decision-making process that characterizes this government or even whether he is speaking of separate branches for each function or separate functions carried out by one branch. Although he flirts with basic institutional issues, he does not confront them. For example, he speaks in favor of majority rule but does not see it as essential. He alludes to a wide range of constraints on majority rule but eschews any discussion of their form.

Given Rawls's interest in a global definition of justice rather than a set of specific programs, this disinterest in institutions might be acceptable — albeit disappointing to someone interested in institutional choice. Rawls could be seen as interested in goal choice while I am interested in institutional choice. Since Rawls does not attempt to dictate specific law and public policy, the absence of consideration of institutional choice could be acceptable.

This division of responsibility, neat as it sounds, is more troubling than it initially appears. Any attempt to articulate a theory of justice, even in the abstract, must ultimately be based on assumptions about the workings of social institutions. Leaving these assumptions unexplored creates problems even for Rawls. His detailed theory of justice reflects unarticulated but basic senses of the workings of society's institutions that are inconsistent with his necessary conditions for a just society. This tension reveals that difficult institutional choice and analysis is necessary even to make sense of Rawls's theory.

At least one careful reader of Rawls argues that his theory of justice requires that all (or most) citizens of a nation must largely share (and be willing to act on) the same conception of justice. If such a perception means that these citizens must universally be prepared to abide by the Rawlsian principles even after a fall from the original position — even after they realize their actual position and advantages — then the conditions are either unlikely to be fulfilled or, if fulfilled, would remove much of the need for Rawls's theory. As Brian Barry puts it:

> Given his premises, the problem of constitutional design poses itself for Rawls as either very simple or insoluble: if people pursue justice single-mindedly it scarcely matters how the rules for decision-making are drawn up, since the results can hardly fail to be good; if they don't do

this then all is lost. . . . Indeed, it is difficult to see why, on Rawls's premises, there is any reason for the constitutional entrenchment of the personal liberties dealt with by the first principle of justice, since, if men
behave justly, they will vote to preserve them anyway. Perhaps this explains why his remarks on the subject are so vague and tentative.[37]

If Barry's interpretation of Rawls is correct, then one must divorce Rawls's
principles from his conception of institutions — or his non-conception of
institutions — in order to turn his principles into any meaningful discussion of law and public policy or, on a more general level, into even the
broadest outlines of a real-world just society. Barry is quite correct when
he suggests that under this interpretation there would be no reason for the
first principle and, indeed, it is doubtful that any principle would need
articulation.

The resulting Rawlsian constitution might need be only a preamble that
sets out Rawls's principles. This preamble would serve at most as a rough
reminder to society's citizens of what they would want to do anyway.
All decisions about the structure of government and the allocation of
decision-making could be left to the future, and institutions would not
be difficult to design or redesign as society went along. Liberties, as protections against government, would be unnecessary. Rights would be
unnecessary. Judicial review and other structural mechanisms would be
unnecessary. Just as the zero-transaction-cost market achieves efficiency
whatever the status of the law, a truly justice-seeking, consensus-achieving,
altruistic populace makes concern about constitutions, constitutional
rights, and constitution making superfluous. Such a worldview is both
etherial and arid.

Simplistic, frictionless institutional specifications always make institutional choice trivial and empty. The Rawlsian constitution would not even
need Rawls's principles. It would require no more than an intuitionist notion of justice with component parts — liberty, equality of opportunity,
and so forth — that would be later assembled and implemented by the just
citizenry.

Rawls's detailed theory of justice with its carefully articulated separate
principles, its rules of priority, and its focus on a difference principle
presupposes a non-idealized conception of institutions. The existence of
Rawls's first principle with its concern for the protection of liberty bespeaks a notion of the behavior of citizens and, therefore, of social institutions different than the simplistic idealized conditions. So does the

37. Brian Barry, *The Liberal Theory of Justice* 143 (1973).

special concern for the least advantaged. Only by explicating and analyzing these institutional implications can we begin to see why we need a
specification like Rawls's.

Paradoxically, just as the detail in Rawls's theory of justice bespeaks the
importance of institutional features and institutional choice, so does the
inevitable ambiguity. Rawls's articulation of his principles and priorities
contains a wide range of open-ended constructs like equal basic liberties,
the least advantaged, social and economic inequalities, and equal opportunity. The justness of society will be determined by how these constructs
are defined and applied. Consequently, justice is tied to the character of
the real world decision-making processes, or institutions, that will define
and apply these constructs.

Take, for example, Rawls's difference principle. Important and difficult
substantive issues surround the operation of this principle, not the least of
which is the definition of "the least advantaged." According to Frank
Michelman, a careful and sympathetic reader of Rawls, the needs implied
in Rawls's articulation of the difference principle are unclear. This ambiguity is a source of significant variation both in who is considered the least
advantaged and in what is considered a just outcome:

> If we really thought that the only need people had was the undifferen-
> tiated need for more income, then under Rawls's 'general conception' of
> justice as fairness the 'worst-off' would simply be the class of those
> whose incomes were below the highest guaranteed minimum income of
> which the economy was capable. Conversely, if individualized needs on
> the order of basic health are considered discrete components of expec-
> tations, it is hard to see how any simple notion of worst-off representa-
> tive persons can satisfy the precept of maximum which characterizes the
> general conception.[38]

Michelman goes on to show that Rawls's conception of fairness must
include a significant dose of those discrete individualized needs and that
this requirement makes it difficult to establish any "simple notion of
worst-off representative person." Michelman's reading of Rawls and, in
particular, his reading of the intuitive outcomes of Rawls's original position make this interpretation persuasive. However, even if we assume that
the difference principle could be fulfilled by the simpler definition of
those "below the highest guaranteed minimum income of which the

38. Frank Michelman, *Constitutional Welfare Rights and "A Theory of Justice,"* in Nor-
man Daniel, ed, *Reading Rawls* 329–30 (1975).

economy were capable," the resulting test is hardly simple and straightforward. The need for guesswork and discretion in applying even a simplified
standard requires careful concern about the character of the institution
applying the test.[39]

Ambiguity and discretion move institutional choice to center stage.
Suppose, for example, that the legislature (or any other branch of government) assigned the task of implementing this standard is dominated by
the rich or even the non-poor. One might expect a relatively stingy guaranteed minimum. This stinginess might stem from an intentional distor-
tion of justice or it might reflect the honest but still biased view of officials
and constituents that, if the guaranteed income were any higher, the pie
would shrink so much that the poor would be worse off in the long-run.
Recognizing the possibility of a biased legislature, a constitution-maker
might consider a wide range of design choices including a legislature structured to better represent the poor, another branch of government to review the determination of the first (presumably that reviewer branch
would be structured differently than the reviewed branch), or a detailed
schedule of guaranteed income specified in the constitution itself. The important point here is that even the most straightforward version of Rawls's
difference principle depends for its real substance on the decisions of the
institutions that Rawls neglects to examine.

Even the constitutions of totalitarian states have contained high-
sounding announcements of rights. The welfare of the populace depends
on the presence of institutions capable of translating high-sounding principles into substance. Issues of institutional representation and participation seem especially important for the least advantaged, who almost by
definition have had difficulties with representation and participation in
existing institutional processes. If representation and participation are important for resolving the simpler version of the difference principle, they
would seem even more important in confronting the more complicated
standard that Michelman derives from Rawls. They would seem more important yet when society faces the immense task of fulfilling a measure of

39. Consider Richard Posner's comparison of Rawls and Bentham: "Rawls's principle
of social justice resembles Bentham's principle of maximizing income equality subject
to the constraint of preserving the individual's incentive to engage in productive activity. In both cases, the optimal degree of equality depends on empirical hunches re-
garding the size and shape of individuals' marginal-utility schedules and the disincentive
effects of egalitarian policies. The necessity of making such hunches imparts to Rawls's
theory the same indefiniteness that plagues Bentham's." Richard Posner, *The Economics
of Justice* 59 (1981).

justice that seeks to integrate this difference principle with the concepts of equal opportunity and liberty. Determining the character of the legislature or agency given the task of this integration seems central here. The real content of Rawlsian justice depends on such a determination.

Any theory of justice capable of even minimally capturing our basic sensibilities has many loosely defined components. Because such loosely defined elements and complicated standards are inherent in goal choice and articulation, the character of the institutions that will define and apply these goals becomes an essential — perhaps *the* essential — component in the realization of the just society. The more complex and vaguely defined the conception of the good, the more central becomes the issue of who decides — the issue of institutional choice. The discussion of *Boomer* showed that these questions of institutional choice dominate issues of resource allocation efficiency — a definition of the social good more confined and better defined than broader conceptions of the good such as Rawls's theory of justice. The lessons about the importance and complexity of institutional choice derived from *Boomer* are even more appropriate with more complex definitions of the good.

Rawls purposely and expressly abstracts from concerns about institutions and institutional choice. Under such circumstances, perhaps it was unfair for me to raise the subject in criticism of his theory — however limited that criticism. I did so for two reasons. First, I wanted to show that implicit assumptions about institutional choice exist within even the most carefully constructed abstractions and that, if left unexamined, these hidden assumptions can have adverse effects on the internal structure of the theory. Second, I wanted to show that such abstraction from institutional choice severely constrains the robustness of the resulting theory. Any attempt to employ Rawls to explore the character of the just society, as opposed to justice in the abstract, requires abandonment of the vow of non-institutionalism.

Rawls and the First Amendment

To better understand how institutional choice links any conception of social goals to meaningful law and public policy, I close this chapter by examining the implications of Rawls's first principle for constitutional law and constitution making. In particular, I consider the First Amendment of the U.S. Constitution and an important Supreme Court case interpreting it — the *Pentagon Papers* case.[40] Rawls first principle calls for "an equal right

40. *New York Times Co. v United States,* 403 US 713 (1971).

to the most extensive total system of equal basic liberties compatible with a similar system of liberty for all." Not surprisingly, Rawls considers the freedoms of speech and of the press as primary examples of "basic liberty." This emphasis on basic liberties is probably the least controversial and most straightforward component of Rawls's theory of justice. Including freedoms of speech and press among these liberties is traditional. Yet even an affection for basic liberties tells us little about the character of constitutions.

By his use of the term "right," Rawls indicates that a constitution consistent with his view of liberty should constrain the political process on the subject of speech and press. Calling something a "right" is an institutional statement. As Michelman noted in his consideration of the application of Rawls's second principle, a right means that there are "demands that are to be met despite a currently opposed legislative will."[41] On the other hand, the political process — the state — is important to the achievement of liberty. A society intent on achieving the highest liberty for all runs smack into a basic institutional quandary: liberty requires both protection *by* the government and protection *from* the government.

Faced with this institutional quandary, the vague, idealized institutions contemplated by Rawls easily support polar opposite constitutional responses. As noted earlier, the idealized conditions seemingly required by Rawls for achievement of justice would not demand any constraint on the legislature or the public will in general. The decision when and how the goal of equal liberty is to be achieved could be decided by *any* political process without fear. Speech and press rights could be treated like the awarding of patent rights in Article II, section 8 of the U.S. Constitution. They would be among those many subjects left within the discretion of the legislature. Seen from a different perspective, however, the same idealized conditions of human behavior support a perfect market in ideas (constitutional scholars commonly refer to the "marketplace of ideas"). As such, we would not need government action in regulating speech and press. The Constitution could simply deny the government any role in this area.

I am not belittling Rawls's declaration of principles. Like many others, I favor a strong concern for liberties in general and speech and press freedoms in particular. But these concerns remain largely meaningless without an accompanying concern for institutions more serious that Rawls's idealized conditions. To make Rawls's first principle relevant to any issues

41. Michelman, *Constitutional Welfare* at 326 (cited in n. 38).

of constitution making and constitutional law, we must recognize and make difficult institutional choices. The importance and difficulty of these choices can be seen in constitutional law cases like the *Pentagon Papers* case.

The *Pentagon Papers* Case

In June 1971, the *New York Times* and *Washington Post* published parts of a top secret defense department study of the Vietnam War. This long and detailed study, known popularly as the Pentagon Papers, contained information about the formulation of United States policy in Southeast Asia including information about secret diplomacy and military operations. The federal government brought action in federal district courts in New York and Washington to enjoin any further publication of the Pentagon Papers, claiming that such publication would interfere with the national security, lead to the death of soldiers, undermine our foreign alliances, and prolong the war. In an abbreviated legal process, the cases were heard at the district court level, appealed and heard by the Supreme Court, and the Supreme Court issued decisions in a period of approximately fifteen days. By a vote of 6 to 3, the justices of the Supreme Court refused the government's request to enjoin publication.[42]

The *Pentagon Papers* case raises basic constitutional and social issues. Whether it is framed as a determination of whether less extensive liberty in this case will strengthen the total system of liberty shared by all — a Rawlsian statement — or more generally as the issue of the confrontation between liberty and order, the constitutional issue posed in the case is among the most fundamental imaginable. Even a superficial glance at the *Pentagon Papers* case reveals the importance and difficulty of this issue. Nine separate opinions (one for each justice) reflected six votes to deny any injunction and three votes in dissent. None of the opinions of the six majority justices constituted an opinion of the Court. Instead, the decision of the majority was simply and briefly announced in a per curiam opinion.

As all the judges in *Boomer* could be seen as concerned with efficiency, so all the justices in the *Pentagon Papers* case can be seen as concerned with establishing "the most extensive total system of equal basic liberties compatible with a similar system of liberty for all." As with the *Boomer* case, the same configuration of goals or balance of liberties can be seen in the positions of all the justices and, therefore, can be seen as consistent with

42. *New York Times,* 403 US at 714.

any of the radically different positions. This configuration of goals is as consistent with the dissent as it is with the majority.

Institutional assumptions dictate radically different positions from the same goal. On one extreme, if the political process were ideal, there would be no need for a First Amendment or for judicial review. No justice holds such a view. On the other extreme, if the behavior of individuals in exercising their individual liberties posed no threat to order or "the total system of liberty shared by all," there would be no reason to allow governmental action regulating speech at all. It could be argued that three of the Pentagon Papers justices held such a view. Justices Douglas, Black, and Brennan took an "absolutist" position that prior restraint of publication of political information is simply prohibited under any circumstances.[43] All three justices were impatient that the determination took so long and that injunctions — no matter how temporary — had been issued at all.

The absolutist position of these justices can be seen as the liberties counterpart to the efficiency view of the absolute property right against trespass. There the zero- or low-transaction-costs market could be trusted to make the correct efficiency balance. Here a perfect "marketplace of ideas" allows an absolute right. It is difficult, as well as unnecessary, to believe, however, that any of these three justices believed that the marketplace of ideas is perfect or nearly so.[44] Imperfections in the marketplace of ideas do not make the absolutist position untenable. Because the issue is institutional choice, even a highly imperfect market would be the choice over more imperfect alternatives. The institutional logic of the absolutist position lies as much, if not more, in the distrust of both the political and adjudicative processes than in trust of the market. For the absolutists, words may, like sticks and stones, sometimes break your bones, but a few fractures are better than censorship.

The three dissenting justices, Burger, Harlan, and Blackmun, recognize the long history of distrust of the political process inherent in the First Amendment in general and the distrust of prior restraint of publication in particular. They have a different perception of the institutional balance than the absolutists. Their dissenting opinions reveal that they signifi-

43. "Both the history and language of the First Amendment support the view that the press must be left to publish news, whatever the source, without censorship, injunctions, or prior restraints." Id at 717 (Douglas concurring).
44. Justice Brennan, at least, seemed to hold the view that there was a narrow set of instances in which the courts might determine that an injunction would issue. See id at 726 (Brennan concurring).

cantly distrust the marketplace of ideas and, in particular, they distrust the decisions of the press.[45] We cannot tell how distrustful they are of the government, but they must have reservations about it as well because they bring in a third institutional alternative — the courts. The major complaint of the three dissenters is that the adjudication was so abbreviated and that the federal courts were not allowed to fully consider the substance.[46]

Thus, both the three absolutist justices and the three dissenting justices seem to be balancing liberties consistent with Rawls's first principle. Their different conclusions can be traced to very different perceptions of the institutional alternatives — the market, the political process, and the adjudicative process.

Most interesting are the positions and opinions of the other three justices, the swing justices whose votes disallow the injunctions. These three, Justices Stewart, White, and Marshall, are more equivocal than the absolutist justices who they join in the majority. Like the dissenters, the swing justices are not comfortable simply leaving the marketplace of ideas to determine the balance of liberty and order. They cannot dismiss the possibility that, in some settings, newspapers might publish material that created real dangers to national security. All three justices recognize the need of the government for confidentiality in the area of international relations and national defense.

Although the swing justices vote with the absolutists in refusing to enjoin publication, they offer a much different view of the liberty right involved. All three swing justices suggest a quite different outcome in the case would have occurred if the substantive issues had been decided by a different configuration of institutions within the political process. All three justices suggest that they would have decided differently if the president's attempt to seek an injunction had been made pursuant to congressional action. Justices Stewart and White even suggest that the result would have been different if the president had based his request for an injunction

45. See, for example, critical appraisals of the behavior of the *New York Times* by Chief Justice Burger and Justice Blackman at 403 US at 749–50 and 403 US at 759–60, respectively.

46. Here the comments of Justice Harlan are typical of the views expressed by all three judges: "With all respect, I consider that the Court has been almost irresponsibly feverish in dealing with these cases. . . . [T]his frenzied train of events took place in the name of the presumption against prior restraints created by the First Amendment. Due regard for the extraordinarily important and difficult questions involved in these litigations should have led the Court to shun such a precipitate timetable." Id at 755 (Harlan dissenting).

on a pre-existing executive regulation.[47] Thus, it appears that protection of the liberty of political speech against prior restraint of publication can be importantly qualified by seemingly marginal variations in the institutional configuration of the political process.

This peculiarly compromised right seems to fly in the face of the tradition of strong judicial response to governmental attempts at prior restraint and to the significant distrust of the government it suggests. Few, if any, prior restraints have survived judicial scrutiny. Faced with prior restraint of publication of political speech, courts have examined with great care and skepticism any governmental determination that such restraints serve the public good. There are many reasons to suspect the political process in its determination of whether or not to constrain political speech, including the traditional fears that the political process may suppress speech that is embarrassing to political leaders. This is a subject which I will examine in greater detail in chapters 3 and 7. It seems odd then to allocate this decision back to the political process, as the swing justices suggest.

The peculiar position of the swing justices becomes easier to understand, however, in the context of the institutional choices revealed in a quite different category of constitutional law decisions. When litigants have attempted to enlist the courts to review governmental determinations about international relations and national defense, the courts have often declared such issues "political questions"—a rare explicit judicial announcement that there will be *no* judicial examination for such issues. At least ostensibly, the announcement that an issue is a political question means that the political process will have the only and last say about the question. This complete deference to the legislature reflects the view that the adjudicative process with its generalist judges, formalistic adversarial process, and limited case-by-case determination has serious deficiencies in dealing with issues of national defense and security that are complex and global and whose sensitivity often requires some level of secrecy.[48]

Because the *Pentagon Papers* case involves a government attempt to obtain a prior restraint based on serious claims of injury to national defense and security, it forces a clash between two very different institutional choices and, therefore, two quite different constitutional outcomes—high skepticism of governmental claims accompanied by a very active judicial

47. See id at 729 (Stewart concurring); id at 731 n 1 (White concurring).
48. For a more extensive discussion of the political question doctrine, see Neil Komesar, *Taking Institutions Seriously: Introduction to a Strategy for Constitutional Analysis*, 51 U Chi L Rev 366, 380–84 (1984).

role in the case of prior restraints of the press versus judicial abdication and acceptance of the balance imposed by the government in the case of political questions. Not surprisingly, this tension is most directly reflected in the positions and opinions of the three swing justices—the justices most likely to feel the pull of both strains. But, as we have seen, it is also reflected in the opinions of all the justices.

Like Rawls, all the justices who decided the *Pentagon Papers* case were concerned with balancing individual liberty and liberty for all. Yet a wide variety of outcomes are represented by their positions in this case. To understand and assess these different positions one needs a great deal more than an idea of what social goal or interest is involved. Underlying these differences are differences in perception about who should resolve the uncertainties inherent in carrying out the social goals.[49] Rights—constitutional or otherwise—are institutional choices in service of social goals. They involve the choice of one institutional decision-maker over another. The value or validity of rights in serving these goals depends on the validity of the underlying institutional choices.

As with the *Boomer* case, *Pentagon Papers* illustrates a general concern with a perfectly plausible set of social goals. *Boomer* appears to reflect concerns about efficiency; *Pentagon Papers* appears to reflect concerns about ordered liberty. In both cases, a large range of legal outcomes can be seen as consistent with the proposed social goal. To understand or evaluate any of these legal outcomes, one needs to ask about more than social goals. One must ask who will define, implement, and weigh the social goal or goals in question. The issue of institutional choice, not goal choice, seems to dominate the debate and decide the issues in these cases.

Rawls and his followers could accurately suggest that his theory of justice is not aimed at understanding or dictating individual legal decisions. But, unless they are willing to give up virtually any connection between their theory of justice and a theory of the just society, Rawls and his followers cannot walk away from the kinds of issues raised in this discussion of the *Pentagon Papers* case. If Rawls's theory is not meant to directly inform individual cases, it is at least meant to inform larger questions of the character of constitutions and the character of constitution making. Just societies are based not on the announcement of broad principles but on the design of real world institutional decision-making processes and the

49. The mere fact that the Supreme Court was the ultimate arbiter in this situation is a function of institutional arrangements suggested by the United States Constitution and solidified in subsequent cases, as shall be seen in chapter 7.

designation of which process will decide which issues. Justice is forged in the crucible of institutional choice.

SUMMARY

In this chapter, I have dealt with two themes — first, the necessary connection between institutional choice and law and public policy choice and, second, the need to study institutional choice from a comparative institutional rather than a single institutional perspective. An analysis based solely on goal choice can never reach conclusions about law and public policy. Any institutionally sophisticated reader confronted with a goals-based analysis — even one accompanied by a single institutional analysis — can always offer a valid two-word response: "So what?"

For the purposes of this book, I accept the need to study both goal choice and institutional choice. On a more sophisticated level, however, many goal choices are deep-seated institutional choices. Rights to basic liberties are impossible to understand without recognizing that they imply a distrust of government. That people feel so strongly about protecting these liberties reflects primal senses about malfunctions in government. Natural rights are derived, not from a sense of nature, but from a sense about the nature of society and its limitations.

As the discussion of Rawls's analysis showed, the debate over goals and goal choice might profit from a more thorough explication and examination of these implicit institutional choices. In this connection, Rawls, in work subsequent to his *Theory of Justice,* grounds his understanding of "political conceptions of justice" in the workings and structures of actual social and political institutions.[50] Unfortunately, this work still does not involve a careful consideration of the character of these institutions and of the complex and rich patterns they reveal. If the conception of justice is to be derived from the workings of actual social and political institutions, then Rawls and his followers must more thoroughly shoulder the task of comparative institutional analysis.

I will, however, leave to the moral philosophers the debate over broad definitions of justice and good. I take on what I consider the more important if less glamorous task of examining the institutional choices necessary to transform these grand goals into law and public policy.

I frequently discuss these institutional choices against a background of

---

50. John Rawls, *The Idea of an Overlapping Consensus,* 7 Oxford J Leg Stud 1 (1987). This work was subsequently incorporated into John Rawls, *Political Liberalism* (1993).

something roughly akin to resource allocation efficiency. This tendency reflects both my economics background and the expositional simplicity gained by using this relatively well-defined goal. It does not reflect a view of the ethical supremacy of efficiency. My focus on efficiency is not exclusive. I also regularly consider the kinds of concerns reflected in more complete and complex constellations of goals like that embodied in Rawls's theory of justice. In chapter 8, for example, I extensively and critically examine the complex institutional choices presented by another important example of non-efficiency goals — Lockean libertarianism.

Whatever the social goal in question, however, the institutional analysis that follows should provide important information about the characteristics of available alternative institutional decision-makers and should allow any analyst to get at least a rough picture of the issues of institutional choice involved. The same institutional alternatives are available whatever the goal, and the same institutional behavior confronts the implementation of all goals. Although institutional choices and, therefore, law and public policy choices can vary depending on the goal, these same insights about institutional character and behavior will be relevant no matter what the goal.

Economic analysts, wedded to the sort of single institutionalism displayed by Posner, may be tempted to retain their single institutional approach by labeling institutional comparison as a secondary adjustment — a sort of "second best" consideration — to be addressed later, if at all. Besides denying the evidence in this book, such treatment would violate a basic tenet of economics: opportunity costs. No economist can study any social choice except in terms of its alternatives. Economic analysts of law are studying institutional choices, usually one between the market and the courts. They cannot simply rely on single institutional notions, like market failure. Here the need to consider and compare institutional alternatives is primary, not secondary, to competent economic analysis.

The rest of this book examines in greater detail the major institutional alternatives at play in cases like *Boomer* and *Pentagon Papers*. I begin where the *Boomer* discussion left off and *Pentagon Papers* began — with the political process.

}II{

Who Plays, Who Doesn't: The Participation-
Centered Approach to the Political Process,
The Market, and the Courts

}3{

The Political Process: The Power of the Few and the

Power of the Many

I begin examination of the three major decision-making institutions with the political process because politics allows for the easiest introduction of several themes important to all the institutions. First, others have employed the participation-centered approach championed in this book in its most straightforward form in analyses of politics. As such, a discussion of the political process provides a comfortable place to introduce the approach in detail. Second, the use of the participation-centered approach to analyze politics raises issues, such as the role of the motivations of official actors, that are important, albeit not so clearly raised, in other institutional settings.

This chapter, however, does much more than introduce general themes. Its major purpose is the introduction and exploration of a different approach to understanding politics—the two-force model of politics. The two-force model is an alternative approach to understanding the political process that builds upon, but significantly alters, the so-called interest group theory of politics (IGTP).

Despite its impressive credentials,[1] the IGTP has been criticized by a wide variety of commentators.[2] These critics point to many instances of legislation that are inconsistent with narrowly defined interest group politics. Too much legislation at least appears to have a broad public interest. These critics argue that the IGTP is flawed because it assumes that public officials are motivated by narrow self-interest—that public officials behave like the proverbial economic person.

Contrary to the assertions of both proponents and opponents of the

---

1. George Stigler and James Buchanan received Nobel Prizes in economics based in good part on their significant contribution to this economic-based theory of politics.

2. See, e.g., Richard Posner, *Theories of Economic Regulation,* 5 Bell J Econ & Mgmt Sci 335 (1974); Abner Mikva, *Foreword,* 74 Va L Rev 167 (1988); Mark Kelman, *On Democracy-Bashing: A Skeptical Look at the Theoretical and "Empirical" Practice of the Public Choice Movement,* 74 Va L Rev 199 (1988).

IGTP, however, self-interest is neither a sufficient nor a necessary condition for the working of the IGTP. The debate about motivation is largely irrelevant. The narrow and incomplete coverage of the IGTP stems not from its misconception of motivations but from its narrow and incomplete institutional conception of the political process.

The IGTP places almost exclusive emphasis on overrepresentation of concentrated interests, usually at the expense of larger, less organized groups. Although this conception of the political process clearly has validity, it is incomplete. A polar opposite conception also deserves consideration — the power of the many over the few.

In order to fill this gap, I propose a theory based on the pull or tradeoff between these two forces — minoritarian versus majoritarian influence. I use the factors of the participation-centered approach to determine the relative strength of each of these influences. In some identifiable instances or contexts, minoritarian or special interests prevail. In others, majoritarian influences can counteract minoritarian influence, producing public policy that is less narrowly based and that often seems more public interested. In turn, just as minoritarian influence can become severe minoritarian bias, the overrepresentation of the concentrated few, so too at some stage the power of majoritarian influence can severely skew political results and produce what might be termed majoritarian bias, the overrepresentation of the many. The two-force model of politics proposed here integrates the many features of the political process left out of the one-force model that characterizes the IGTP.

The first section of this chapter sets out the IGTP and its limits. The second section takes up the issue of the relevance of motivation that has occupied so much attention. The third section details the two-force model of politics, compares it to the one-force model used by the IGTP, indicates those factors that determine the relative strength of majoritarian and minoritarian influences, and considers the role of countervailance between the two forces in understanding the political process. The fourth section uses the two-force model to examine the growth of the bureaucracy.

THE INTEREST GROUP THEORY OF POLITICS AND THE ONE-FORCE MODEL

Much of what economists have contributed to the analysis of politics, especially the recent work that has found its way into law, is based on a simple but powerful image — the dominance of small, concentrated interest groups. These groups are small in number and concentrated in the sense that each member has a high stake in the political outcomes in question. In this scenario, the small, concentrated interest groups have substantially greater political influence than groups larger in number but with smaller per capita stakes even though the total stakes for the larger group may significantly exceed that for the smaller.[3]

3. Here the prominent works are George Stigler's analysis of economic regulation and the body of work which studies "rent-seeking." George J. Stigler, *The Theory of Economic Regulation,* 2 Bell J Econ & Mgmt Sci 3 (1971). The "rent-seeking" theory is captured well in James M. Buchanan, Robert D. Tollison, and Gordon Tullock, eds, *Toward a Theory of the Rent-Seeking Society* (1980).
  These two major branches of the economic theories of politics differ primarily in the focus of their inquiry. Stigler generated a model of government behavior that emphasizes the degree to which concentrated interests prevail in a process in which self-interested political officials provide legislation to the highest bidder — the interest group that will provide the most (dollars, votes, prestige, etc.) to the political official. Because concentrated interests prevail even where their gains are less than the losses imposed on the dormant majority, there are losses to societal resource allocation efficiency. Accepting this notion, rent-seeking analysts point out an additional and, in their view, dominating source of resource allocation efficiency loss: the waste of resources employed to gain government favors or advantages. This emphasis on the losses associated with rent-*seeking* rather than those associated with rent-*acquiring* distinguishes the rent-seeking branch of the economic theories of politics.
  The basic assumptions about interest group representation embodied in both these branches are summarized well in Sam Peltzman's restatement of George Stigler's economic theory of regulation:

> To summarize the argument briefly, the size of the dominant group is limited in the first instance by the absence of something like ordinary-market-dollar voting in politics. Voting is infrequent and concerned with a package of issues. In the case of a particular issue, the voter must spend resources to inform himself about its implication for his wealth and which politician is likely to stand on which side of the issue. That information cost will have to offset prospective gains, and a voter with a small per capita stake will not, therefore, incur it. In consequence the numerically large, diffused interest group is unlikely to be an effective bidder, and a policy inimical to the interest of a numerical majority will not be automatically rejected. A second major limit on effective group size arises from costs of organization. It is not enough for the successful group to recognize its interests; it must organize to translate this interest into support for the politician who will implement it. This means not only mobilizing its own votes, but contributing resources to the support of the appropriate political party or policy: to finance campaigns, to persuade other voters to support or at least not oppose the policy or candidate, perhaps occasionally to bribe those in office. While there may be some economies of scale in this organization of support in neutralization of opposition, these must be limited. The larger the group that seeks the transfer, the narrower the base of the opposition and the greater the per capita stakes that determine the strength of opposition, so lobbying and campaigning costs will rise faster than group size. The cost of overcoming "free riders" will also rise faster than group size. This

The overrepresentation of concentrated interests is a notion that under-lies a significant range of analyses of the political process in both the eco-nomics and political science literature. Variously called the capture theory, special interest theory, or interest group theory, all of these notions de-pend substantially on the concept of disproportionate influence of the concentrated few over the dispersed many.[4] For simplicity sake, I lump this entire body of work into the IGTP and refer to the disproportionate influ-ence of the concentrated few as "minoritarian bias."[5]

The classic example of legislation thought to be subject to minoritarian bias is the tariff that effectively reduces competition from foreign sources for the benefit of local producers and to the detriment of local consumers. The power of the few lies in their control of information and ability to organize effective political influence.[6] The process often takes place away from the public view, although the public action it produces later may be cloaked in public interest garb. Consumers, each of whom bears only a relatively minor cost, do not even have the incentive to understand these negative effects let alone to organize activity to combat them.

Despite the power of this basic and traditional conception of political bias, there are two sources of doubt about its adequacy as a general theory of politics. Many doubters, including economists, have observed that too much legislation seems to be broad-based, ideological, and even public interested to justify complete reliance on the IGTP.[7] For critics of an eco-

---

    diseconomy of scale in providing resources then acts as another limit to the size of the group that will ultimately dominate the political process.

    In sum, Stigler is asserting a law of diminishing returns to group size in politics: beyond some point it becomes counterproductive to dilute the per capita transfer.

Sam Peltzman, *Toward a More General Theory of Regulation,* 19 J L & Econ 211, 213 (1976).

    4. See, for example, Theodore J. Lowi, *American Business, Political Policy, Case Studies, and Political Theory,* 16 World Pol 677 (1964); James M. Buchanan & Gordon Tullock, *The Calculus of Consent* (1962); Morris P. Fiorina, *Group Concentration and the Delegation of Legislative Authority,* in Roger G. Noll, ed, *Regulatory Policy and the Social Sciences* 175 (1985); Paul H. Rubin, *On the Form of Special Interest Legislation,* 21 Pub Choice 79 (1975).

    5. Whether the influence of either the few or the many is disproportionate depends on the social goal in question. For the IGTP, resource allocation efficiency (or some-thing roughly like it) has been the social goal. Although, for most purposes in this chapter, I discuss "overrepresentation" in these terms, I consider the implications for non-efficiency goals at several points.

    6. See note 3.

    7. See, for example, Posner, 5 Bell J Econ & Mgmt at 335 (cited in n. 2); Susan Rose-Ackerman, *Progressive Law and Economics — And the New Administrative Law,* 98 Yale LJ 341 (1988); Douglas North, *Structure and Change in Economic History* 47–48 (1981); Joseph P.

nomic approach to politics, the existence of this wide range of outcomes provides sufficient reason to abandon it altogether, although they usually offer no analytical framework to replace it. Those more friendly to the economic approach tend to accept its validity for some purposes but to explain nonconforming results as "slippage" — instances in which interest group theory does not apply and legislators can act without the control of interest groups.[8]

The second source of doubt about the IGTP's fixation with minoritarian bias is even more dramatic. Tradition, history, and contemporary observation all point to important instances of the overrepresentation of concentrated minorities.[9] The IGTP has added analytical sophistication to these basic insights. Like most useful theories, its consistency with basic observation, both contemporary and historical, strengthens its appeal.

The IGTP fails this same criterion, however, when it ignores another bias in the political process with as much tradition and historical pedigree, that is, the overrepresentation of the many over the few (majoritarian bias). Especially for proponents of the IGTP who are concerned with constitutional political economy, the failure to notice and integrate traditional concerns about the "tyranny of the majority" leaves a significant gap.[10] Our own constitution is as much, most likely more, a product of fear of the dominance of many over the few as it is a product of the opposite fear. The *Federalist Papers* reflect greater fear of majoritarian bias than of minoritarian bias, and the Constitution produced in significant part by the authors of those papers reflects this concern.[11]

Kalt and Mark A. Zupan, *Capture and Ideology in the Economic Theory of Politics,* 74 Am Econ Rev 279 (1984); Daniel A. Farber and Philip P. Frickey, *The Jurisprudence of Public Choice,* 65 Tex L Rev 873, 893–900 (1987).

8. See Posner, 5 Bell J Econ & Mgmt at 340–41 (cited in n. 2); Kalt and Zupan, 74 Am Econ Rev at 282–84 (cited in n. 7).

9. The notion of government providing favors to the well-placed few at the expense of the general populace (usually as consumers) has been with us for a long time. In England, concern over preference for the privileged few in the form of the grant of monopolies by the Crown was a substantial source of complaint in the seventeenth century and had its role in leading to the constitutional reforms of that century. See Charles Hill, *The Century of Revolution, 1603–1714,* 31–33 (1961), suggesting that the mass of the populace as consumers bore the brunt of these special privileges while the few close to the Crown gained, even if the monopolies often were granted ostensibly to promote laudable ends.

This same view is reflected in the views of Adam Smith. See George J. Stigler, *The Citizen and the State* 41 (1975).

10. James Buchanan is the most prominent contributor to the political economy part of the economic theories of politics. See James Buchanan, *Liberty, Market and the State* (1985); Geoffrey Brennan and James Buchanan, *The Reason of Rules* (1985).

11. I return to this point in chapter 7.

The IGTP's failure to integrate both majoritarian and minoritarian influences and their interaction into a single analytical framework misses a straightforward way to account for the larger range of political outcomes, including both broad-based legislation and legislation in which the interests of the majority are overrepresented. The two-force model I introduce below attempts to increase the coverage and efficacy of the IGTP without dropping the basic logic of interest group politics. First, however, I want to clarify the existing debate by exorcising (or at least diminishing) an issue that has received entirely too much attention — the motivation of political actors.

THE LIMITED RELEVANCE OF MOTIVATION

Many critics of the IGTP assume that its major characteristic is the assumption that political actors — in particular, public officials like legislators — are motivated by "narrow self-interest" as opposed to public interest or ideology.[12] Some have vigorously attacked this assumption, presuming

12. The following comments are indicative of the content and tone of the debate about self-interest. Judge Abner J. Mikva, in his foreword to a recent symposium on public choice theory, opens with the following: "After studying the articles in this symposium, I realize why I have found it hard to read or to profit from the 'public choice' literature. The politicians and other people I have known in public life just do not fit the 'rent-seeking' egoist model that the public choice theorists offer. Perhaps I am still one of those naive citizens who believe that politics is on the square, that majorities in effect make policy in this country, and that out of the clash of partisan debate and frequent elections 'good' public policy decisions emerge." Mikva, 74 Va L Rev at 167 (cited in n. 2).

Similarly, Mark Kelman, an outspoken critic of public choice, centers a great deal of his analysis on what he sees as its central assumption: "The standard public choice models posit that politics can best be understood as a market in which officials, seeking to maximize their own fortunes, 'sell' what is seen as the government's unique service, the capacity to steal from less politically potent citizens, to voters motivated by the desire to steal. Obviously, at base, such a claim is grounded in the idea that wealth-maximizing motives best account for both voter and official behavior." Kelman, 74 Va L Rev at 205 (cited in n. 2). Kelman spends much of the rest of his article attempting to show that politics is better understood as motivated by ideological concerns rather than narrow self-interest.

Susan Rose-Ackerman, a law and economics scholar more sympathetic to the IGTP, also notes their self-interest core and the dismal picture they paint of the political process: "Most of this positive work is skeptical about the normative claims for democratic government. Self-interested, vote-maximizing behavior does not seem broadly compatible with the production of efficient public policies." Rose-Ackerman, 98 Yale LJ at 346 (cited in n. 7).

Daniel Farber and Philip Frickey, in their review of the jurisprudence of public choice, present a similar view of the basic motivational assumptions of the economic models versus other approaches:

The core of the economic models is a revised view of legislative behavior. In place of their prior assumption that legislators voted to promote their view of

that their attack if successful robs the theory of its power.[13] Even those sympathetic to the theory believe that the unrealistic assumption of narrow self-interest limits the set of political activity to which the theory is applicable.[14]

One can easily see how these commentators got the impression that narrow self-interest, as contrasted with public interest motivation, constitutes the major building block of the IGTP. Those who have contributed to this theory have emphasized self-interest. The following quote from one of the founders of the rent-seeking branch of the IGTP, James Buchanan, underscores this assumption:

> Although we do not believe that narrow self-interest is the *sole* motive of political agents, or that it is necessarily as relevant a motive in political as in market settings, we certainly believe it to be a significant motive. This differentiates our approach from the alternative model, implicit in conventional welfare economics and widespread in conventional political science, that political agents can be satisfactorily modeled as motivated solely to promote the "public interest," somehow conceived. *That* model we, along with all other public choice colleagues, categorically reject.[15]

In this passage, Buchanan equates the approach of welfare economists, who saw the government as the automatic responder to imperfections in the market, with the perception that political agents are public spirited and the IGTP with the perception that political agents are narrowly

---

the public interest, economists now postulate that legislators are motivated solely by self-interest. In particular, legislators must maximize their likelihood of re-election. A legislator who is not re-elected loses all the other benefits flowing from office.

The two kinds of economic models of legislation have in common the rejection of ideology as a significant factor in the political process. They assume that ideology, defined simply as individual beliefs about the public interest, influences neither voters nor legislators. Thus, the heart of the economic approach is the assumption that self-interest is the exclusive causal agent in politics.

Farber and Frickey, 65 Tex L Rev at 891–93 (cited in n. 7).

13. See Kelman, 74 Va L Rev at 205 (cited in n. 2).

14. See Farber and Frickey, 65 Tex L Rev at 891–93 (cited in n. 7); Rose-Ackerman, 98 Yale LJ at 346 (cited in n. 7).

15. Geoffrey Brennan and James M. Buchanan, *Is Public Choice Immoral? The Case for the "Nobel" Lie,* 74 Va L Rev 179, 181 (1988). Brennan and Buchanan are defining "narrow self-interest" as wealth maximizing: they envision the economic man as a "wealth-maximizing egoist." Id at 180. See also Geoffrey Brennan and James Buchanan, *Predictive Power and the Choice among Regimes,* 93 Econ J 89, 89 (1983).

self-interested. These perceptions associate perfect governmental outcomes with public-interested public officials and distorted governmental outcomes with self-interested public officials. Motivation seems central.

Yet, despite the focus by both proponents and opponents of the IGTP on motive, this assumption is unimportant if not irrelevant to the IGTP, especially as it is employed in legal and public policy analysis. Put succinctly, narrow self-interest is neither a sufficient nor a necessary condition for the outcomes associated with this theory. The same sorts of distortions and biases occur in the presence of public-regarding, public-interested, or ideological motives. Moreover, unbiased and undistorted results can coexist with narrow self-interest. The degree and direction of the biases or distortions in the political process are determined by the character of that process, by institutional factors, not by the character of individual motives.

The mistaken focus on motive is unfortunate in several respects. First, it continues a traditional stereotype of economics as a discipline concerned with the materialistic and based on a cynical and simplistic perception of individual character. This prejudice unnecessarily taints the use of economic analysis for many who might otherwise gain from and contribute to the genre. Second, the mistaken focus on motive by those who debate the IGTP parallels a similar mistaken focus by legal analysts interested in politics in general. This focus on motive has infected judicial decisions, especially those involving racial and gender discrimination.[16] Third, and most important for this book, the debate about motivation reveals a failure to understand the significant difference between individual and institutional decision-making. The behavior of massive and complex social institutions is only tenuously related to the motives of the individual participants.

It is odd that economists place so much emphasis on individual motivation in their analysis of the behavior of the political process. In economic theories of the market, most economists recognize that individual motivation is unimportant in determining either the quality or the character of market outcomes. In the perfect market, for instance, the self-interest of market actors when funneled through the complex interactions of competition translates into a public interest not intended by any individual actors, namely resource allocation efficiency. Economists do not assume that producers are interested in serving the interest of consumers

16. See *Washington v Davis*, 426 US 229 (1976), and its progeny. I explore this issue in Neil K. Komesar, *A Job for the Judges: The Judiciary and the Constitution in a Massive and Complex Society*, 86 Mich L Rev 657, 708–11 (1988).

let alone some global interest in the efficient allocation of resources. Producers are seen as *self*-interested, as attempting to maximize their own income or wealth or utility. Any publicly valuable result, such as resource allocation efficiency, is a by-product of this self-interest funneled through the aggregative mechanisms of the perfect market. The well-worn maxim that private vice can be public virtue reflects this idealized process.

Bad outcomes and systemic distortions do not correspond to narrow self-interest. That private vice is not always public virtue — that the market is not always perfect — does not stem from any variation in the assumed motive of market actors. Instead, according to standard economic theory, inefficient outcomes result from institutional imperfections in the market, sometimes called market failures. The conventional list of these market failures includes ignorance (lack of perfect information), unincluded third-party effects (externalities), and monopoly.[17] The presence of these factors and their effects on market outcomes do not depend on the presence or absence of such motivations as narrow self-interest or wealth maximization.

One can see the importance of institutional factors and the limited relevance of motives in economic analysis by returning to the Coase theorem introduced in chapter 2. If transaction costs are zero, parties, whatever their motivation or tastes, understand their situation and work out an economically efficient arrangement. The same result would seem to hold for the political process. If it is costless to recognize one's position and to organize effective political activity, the same sort of efficient results arise from the political process whatever the motives of the actors.

Consider here the classic example from the IGTP — the protective tariff favoring producers usually at the expense of consumers. This economically inefficient tariff results from the greater ability of producers to understand the political situation and to organize effective political action. Without such institutional elements, the inefficient result would not occur no matter how self-interested the motives of the public officials involved. Thus, for the sake of simplicity, assume the most narrowly self-interested perception of legislator behavior: a model of government based on graft or bribery. Given such a perception, an inefficient tariff would result if producers are in a better position to bribe these self-interested legislators. But if consumers were also in a position to represent their interests in the political process, for example, by amassing a fund to bribe public officials, the inefficient tariff would not be imposed. By definition, the cost of the

17. I discuss these concepts in chapter 4.

tariff would exceed its benefits and the consumers' bribe would be greater than the producers'. This efficient result (no tariff) would not require that we change our assumptions about self-interest. It requires only that we change assumptions about the actors' relative abilities to organize effective political activity (in this case, a bribe).[18]

This discussion establishes only that narrow self-interest is not a sufficient condition; it establishes that institutional factors such as the costs of organization and information are necessary to produce the distortions or biases that are the core of the IGTP. The more difficult question is whether narrow self-interest is even a necessary condition for such outcomes: If legislators or constituents were motivated by public interest or ideology as opposed to narrow self-interest, would we eliminate the biases, distortions, or other attributes of politics established by the IGTP? The answer is no. The same problems manifested in the classic examples of the IGTP remain in the presence of these broader motives. Whether the final results are resource allocation efficient, just, or equal, or meet any other social criterion depends on the characteristics of the representation of interest groups in the political process, not the motivations of their members.[19] Thus, the sort of overrepresentation of concentrated interests associated with the IGTP can occur with public-interested public officials.

If, for example, we adopt the criterion of resource allocation efficiency that often underlies the IGTP, serious distortions and biases can easily occur even if we assume public-interest motivations. The results depend on institutional characteristics such as the availability of information. An omniscient public official motivated by the public interest of promoting efficiency can glean the concerns and interests of his or her constituents and choose policies subject to efficiency criteria. But, if we drop the assumption of perfect knowledge, we find distortions and biases analogous to those in the situation where self-interest prevailed. The now partially ignorant, but still public-interested, official must depend on others to provide

18. Similarly, inefficient rent-seeking would also cease in a world of transaction costless politics even if we retain the assumption of narrow self-interest. Rent-seeking occurs when profit-seeking individuals attempt to obtain the rents (wealth redistributions) associated with subsidies or tariffs. The social loss from the attempt to gain subsidies or tariffs is both the loss associated with the inefficient subsidy or tariff itself and the resources expended by parties who compete for that government action. By definition, rent-seeking, a form of political transaction, would be costless in a transaction costless world. More important analytically, an effective consumer group would make such rent-seeking activity fruitless and, therefore, would deter it.

19. For a non-efficiency example, see the discussion in chapter 2 of the role of representation in the implementation of Rawls's difference principle.

information on the desires of his or her constituents and the relationships between those desires and policy alternatives. Assuming, as does the IGTP, that concentrated groups have significant advantages in understanding and effectively representing their viewpoints, the public-interested official will garner a distorted picture of constituency desires and public policy implications. The interests of concentrated groups would be given too much weight in final results.[20]

In addition to being able to present a distorted picture of the public interest to the public-interested but ignorant public official, overrepresented interest groups can alter outcomes through the election process. Legislators with ideological or public-interest perceptions consistent with those of the overrepresented constituent interests are more likely to be elected.[21] So long as candidates exist who represent a range of views on the public interest, the same biased results can occur by an evolutionary process of replacing public officials whose views of the public interest are inconsistent with the views of the overrepresented group with public officials who have consistent views.

In effect, an interest group can obtain a favorable result in three ways —

20. The central importance of information and the difficulties confronting far less than fully informed legislators is reflected in the following observations by two political scientists who have recently studied the activities of organized groups in the congressional setting: "Legislators' greatest need is for information. Members of Congress are confronted with a staggering number of complex issues about which they are expected to make informed judgments. In the fact of these complexities, members of Congress need all the help they can get in trying to determine the consequences of their assorted legislative decisions — who will be affected, in what ways, to what extent, and with what reaction. The kind of detailed, up-to-the-minute information that legislators need is often difficult to obtain and expensive to collect. Nevertheless, organized interests find it useful to try to produce such information when congressional policy issues touch their area of concern." Kay Lehman Schlozman and John T. Tierney, *Organized Interests and American Democracy* 297 (1986).

21. The reality of such a tactic is reflected in this comment by Schlozman and Tierney: "That organized interest devotes so much energy to activities associated with the electoral process implies, of course, a recognition of how much elections affect them. . . . One objective in electoral activity is to influence the outcome of electoral contests and, by affecting who wins or loses, thereby to elect more sympathetic public officials. The implicit assumption is that candidates who are like-minded on the broad or narrow set of issues with which the organization is concerned would, if left to their own devices once in office, promote the causes dear to the organization; therefore, what is needed is quite simply to make sure that such candidates are victorious. The goal of electing ideologically congenial candidates and defeating hostile ones dictates that the organization locate races in which there is a genuine choice on salient issues and support the ideologically compatible candidate with endorsements and campaign assistance." Id at 206–7.

propaganda, replacement (by election), and inducement (bribes, contributions, and so forth). Only the last is eliminated by assuming that public officials are public interested.[22] Since both propaganda and replacement can carry the distortions in organization and representation that are the core of the IGTP, public-interest motivation is not a necessary condition for these distortions.

The situation does not change if we assume that constituents are also motivated by public interest or ideology rather than narrow self-interest. Even if constituents' desires or motivations are public interested or ideological, problems arise from a skewed representation of conflicting interests. Contests between conflicting ideologies or perceptions of the public interest can involve strong pressure groups and cause substantial redistributions (albeit not necessarily pecuniary redistributions) by the operation of the same sorts of biases and distortions as those associated with more narrowly self-interested contests.

As a general matter, environmentalists, anti-Communists, welfare rights advocates, law and order proponents, and others who might be seen as public interested or ideological are participants in the same political process as producers who seek tariffs or farmers who seek price supports. When one interest group or another is overrepresented because they are better organized or better informed or otherwise more influential, we have reason to worry about serious political malfunction regardless of whether the overrepresented group has ideological or pecuniary interests. Both sides in the abortion issue are dominated by ideology or public interest rather than narrow pecuniary issues. Does the presence of ideology rather than narrow self-interest remove concerns about political determinations about this issue? Is there any doubt that there is the potential for serious redistributions inherent in these determinations?

Thus, self-interest is neither a sufficient nor a necessary condition for the kinds of distortions in political outcomes and the political process rep-

22. Inducement may also be relevant to the case of the public-interested public official depending on how singularly public interested the motivation must be and how we treat re-election. The analysis in the text assumes fanatic public interest — legislators will never trade off the public interest at any margin. If something less than fanatic public interest would still be considered public interest, then even inducement is possible. A likely tradeoff, consistent with a plausible definition of public interest, might be the tradeoff with re-election. Under the maxim that you cannot do good if you are not in office, one might imagine a "public interest" legislator trading a little public interest for a large campaign contribution (or bloc of votes).

resented in the IGTP. To be clear, I am not arguing that the results of a political process are the same when one varies the motivations of political actors. If politically influential groups or actors change their desires or motivations, the output of the political process, such as the content of legislation, would presumably change. But such changes in the content of legislation are as likely to occur when there are changes *within* the set of what might be called narrow self-interests or *within* the set of what might be called public interests or ideologies as they are when there is a shift from self-interest to public-interest. More importantly, given any of these shifts in interest, the problems in the political process emphasized by the IGTP remain as long as institutional distortions in representation remain because of such systemic features as the distribution of impacts, acquisition of information, and the abilities to organize. There is no a priori reason to suppose that these systemic distortions are highly correlated with any categories of interests.[23]

THE TWO-FORCE MODEL

Recognizing the limited relevance of motivation clears the debate about the IGTP of a nagging element. We can turn now to the valid concerns about the narrow scope of the IGTP—the failure to comfortably incorporate legislation that distributes its benefits more broadly than the narrow special interest contemplated by the IGTP, let alone those historically important instances in which dispersed majorities have benefited disproportionately at the expense of concentrated minorities. The IGTP can be augmented or broadened to include these political outcomes without abandoning its basic analytical logic by recognizing the role of majoritarian as well as minoritarian influence.

Majoritarian influence can represent a countervailing force to minoritarian influence, given the possibility that a majority, even though it has lower per capita stakes, may be able to use its greater numbers to influence and even dominate political outcomes. The power of this second force will vary from the virtually nonexistent or dormant force imagined by the IGTP to a dominant, even oppressive force captured in phrases like "tyranny of

---

23. This analysis is analogous to the economic analysis of market behavior when tastes change. Market outcomes would change, but distortions or problems in market behavior and the associated economic analysis of market behavior are unlikely to vary. Similarly, as one varies motivations, results in the political process vary; but the underlying problems and the analytical approach remain the same.

the majority." This variation in majoritarian influence and the tradeoffs or tension between the majoritarian and minoritarian forces is the core of the two-force model.

The existence of this majoritarian effect and its tension with the more commonly recognized minoritarian effect is actually reflected, but undeveloped, in the basic literature on the IGTP. George Stigler, whose emphasis on minoritarian bias we discussed earlier, explains why those industries capable of obtaining a state-supported cartel are not also able to avoid selective excise taxation, as "a special case of the obvious characteristic of democratic political life: special minorities (including industries) can exploit uninterested majorities but will be exploited by interested majorities."[24] Unfortunately, this short comment remains cryptic and undeveloped: so far as I can tell, Stigler at no point explains either when majorities will be interested or uninterested or the extent to which any majoritarian influences can or will overcome his basic reliance on minoritarian bias.[25] His comment remains, however, a provocative suggestion for a larger theory of politics.

Along the same lines, Anthony Downs, whose book, *An Economic Theory of Democracy*,[26] remains one of the most influential economic analyses of politics, closes that work with two "testable propositions" that seem in tension with one another: "Proposition 6: Democratic governments tend to redistribute income from the rich to the poor. . . . Proposition 7: Democratic governments tend to favor producers more than consumers in their actions."[27] Downs presents an example in which a dispersed majority (the poor — or the poorer) is able to redistribute income from the rich (a smaller, higher per capita group) alongside an example that represents the classic minoritarian bias of producers over consumers. Like Stigler, Downs offers a fleeting recognition of this tension but goes no further in resolving it: "Thus the vote market evolves towards an unstable balance of power between two sets of groups: (1) high-income groups, whose funds give them

24. George Stigler, *The Citizen and the State* at 162 (cited in n. 9).
25. At another point, Stigler suggests that the failure to develop such issues remains a basic problem for the economic theory of regulation: "A central problem with the economic theory of regulation . . . is to determine the nature and arguments of the function defining the political power of a group. The theory of coalitions is not well developed, and we do not know the specific affects of the various constellations of numbers and gains (including homogeneity of interests, duration of interest, etc.) upon the political activity and the effective political power of a group." Id at 139.
26. Anthony Downs, *An Economic Theory of Democracy* (1957).
27. Id at 297.

initial dominance, and (2) emergent low-income collective-bargaining centers, which may eventually gain a numerical edge."[28]

Even when not explicitly recognized, majoritarian influences play a central if unseen role in the basic propositions of the IGTP. Thus, in explaining why concentrated interests attempt to extract redistribution indirectly through regulation or the granting of a monopoly rather than directly as a cash subsidy, Gordon Tullock, a major contributor to the rent-seeking branch of the IGTP, explains that "the pushing through of such a benefit for a special class requires that the cost of the benefit not be obvious to the very much larger collection of voters who will be injured by it. This, in turn, requires a certain degree of complexity in the subsidy, and direct cash payment raised out of direct taxes would normally not meet that requirement."[29] Tullock's analysis implicitly assumes that the power of the concentrated minority depends on keeping the majority uninformed and, therefore, uninterested and dormant.

Thus, buried in the theories of three of the major architects of the economic analysis of politics are the seeds of a notion of majoritarian influence that, although undeveloped, suggests a force different from and indeed countervailing to the strong minoritarian force that animates the IGTP. We need now to know when and to what extent this majoritarian force affects political outcomes. We need to know the determinants of the tradeoff between minoritarian and majoritarian influence. When will majorities become "interested" in Stigler's terms or make use of their "numerical edge" in Downs' terms?

The Tradeoff between Minoritarian and Majoritarian Influence: The Benefits and Costs of Political Action

On one level, that so many theories of politics focus on minoritarian forces is remarkable. In the simple world of grade school civics, democracy is dominated by majority rule. Numbers are central. The many dominate the few.

Modeling modern political behavior according to such simplistic majoritarian notions would, of course, be appallingly naive. Complex political structures and a massive heterogeneous population are only two among many factors that remove actual politics from the simple world of civics. These complexities of political action have been with us so much and so

28. Id at 190.
29. Gordon Tullock, *The Transitional Gains Trap,* in Geoffrey Buchanan, Robert Tollison, and Gordon Tullock, eds, *Toward a Theory of the Rent-Seeking Society* 219 (1980).

long that it has become second nature to assume strength in concentration and weakness in numbers. But sophistication and an awareness of complexity should also lead us to recognize that variation in the factors that separate political reality from simple majoritarianism can cause variation in the degree of dominance of concentration over numbers. In this section, I examine the reasoning behind the minoritarian or concentrated interest model with a particular eye to those factors that determine the strength of minoritarian influence and the sources of variation in that strength.

The IGTP focuses on the distribution of the benefits of political action. In describing political behavior, the most important factors are the per capita stakes and their distribution across various interest groups.[30] Interest groups with small numbers but high per capita stakes have significant advantages in political action over interest groups with larger numbers and smaller per capita stakes.

Higher per capita stakes make it more likely that the members of the interest group will know and understand the issues. In the extreme but not uncommon case, the members of the losing majority (often consumers or taxpayers) do not even have the incentive to recognize that they are being harmed. In some instances, they may even be convinced that they are being aided. Legislation that effectively excludes competition is often cast in terms of consumer health and safety.[31] The majority is not stupid or

---

30. For a succinct summary of this view and its role in prominent theories of politics, see Fiorina, *Group Concentration* at 181–82 (cited in n. 4).

31. A classic example is the legislation involved in the *Carolene Products* case, *United States v Carolene Products Company*, 304 US 144 (1938), whose famous footnote is discussed extensively in chapter 7. The legislation at issue banned the interstate sale of "filled milk," or skim milk supplemented with nonmilk fats such as coconut oil. See Filled Milk Act of 1923, Pub L No 67–513, 42 Stat 1486, codified at 21 USC § 61–63 (1982). Congress and many state legislatures had banned this product, ostensibly because it was "adulterated" by the nonmilk additions, which provided less vitamin A than did butterfat. Although the Pure Food and Drug Act (see Pure Food and Drug Act of 1906, Pub L No 59–384, 34 Stat 768 [repealed 1938]) already required that imitations or blends be labeled as such and given a unique brand name to avoid confusion with the generic product, Congress prohibited sales of filled milk ostensibly because retail dealers were still successfully promoting the product either as identical to pure milk or as the equivalent of pure milk, and because the product also was being sold in bulk to boarding houses and ice cream manufacturers, who in turn supplied it to a public that believed it was receiving pure milk or pure milk ice cream. See *Carolene Products,* 304 US at 148–51 nn 2–3.

It does not take much scrutiny to see the dairy lobby at work behind the passage and

innately passive. In these instances, the per capita impact on each member of the majority is so low that it does not even justify the expenditure of resources necessary to recognize the issue involved.

But, even if a member of an affected group recognizes the impact of the legislation and his or her per capita benefit exceeds the allocate share of costs of political participation (or even if the per capita benefit exceeds the *total* costs), one may observe no willingness to contribute from this member and, more importantly, no collective action from this group. Whatever benefits an individual might gain by producing the collective action through his or her contribution, the net benefits to that individual would be even greater if he or she did not have to contribute. There is, therefore, an incentive to refuse to contribute and allow others to bear the costs of political participation; in other words, there is an incentive to free ride.

The severity of the shortfall in the representation of a group depends on the degree or extent to which members of the group free ride. At one extreme, if only a few free ride and the efforts of others take up the slack, there is no underrepresentation. At the other extreme, if all free ride, they will have no political representation and everyone in the group will lose.

The extent or probability of free riding can be related to group size and the characteristics of the distribution of impacts. Small groups have an advantage in collective action because the costs of overcoming free riding and inactivity are lower for them. Small groups can more easily make and police an agreement among the members. Because groups with small numbers and higher per capita stakes are less likely to face free riding problems,

---

enforcement of the "filled milk" act. See, e.g., 67 Cong Rec 4981–82 (1923) (statement of Sen. Stanley that bill was a "plain attempt to utilize the dread powers of legislation to destroy one business in order to foster another"). The bill's sponsor felt obliged to note that the measure had the support of more than 30 dairy and farming groups. Id at 3949–50 (statement of Sen. Ladd). Indeed, the dairy industry's efforts to employ legislation to keep "adulterated" products from grocery shelves and vending booths have a long history, extending from before *Lochner v New York,* 198 US 45 (1905), to the present. See Morton Keller, *Affairs of State* 413 (1977); Alton Lee, *A History of Regulatory Taxation* 12–27 (1973); Johannes van Stuijvenberg, *Aspects of Government Intervention,* in Johannes van Stuijvenberg, ed, *Margarine: An Economic, Social and Scientific History, 1869–1969,* 281 (1969). This activity suggests that concern for the dairies' pocketbooks rather than for the consumer's health best explains the dairy lobby's efforts. In turn, the filled milk legislation ostensibly aimed at helping consumers may have harmed them. Consumers were "saved" from "adulterated" products at the cost of higher prices, while the dairy industry benefited from reduced competition. See Keller, *Affairs of State,* at 413–14. For an extensive discussion of the politics behind the legislation in *Carolene Products,* see Geoffrey Miller, *The True Story of* Carolene Products, 1987 Sup Ct Rev 397.

they are more likely to produce collective political action and be better represented in the political process.

The same analysis of free riding also suggests that results might differ among large groups depending on the unevenness of the distribution of per capita stakes in the large group. In this connection, George Stigler suggests that a large group with a very uneven distribution of stakes can be analyzed in much the same fashion as the small number group:

> The small number solution has a wider scope than a literal count of numbers would suggest. The size distribution of individuals is highly skewed when these individuals have a size dimension (sales of firm, property of family). The large individuals in a group may therefore properly view themselves as members of a small number industry if their aggregate share of the group resources is large.[32]

The analysis points to two aspects of the distribution of per capita stakes that can affect the likelihood of political action by larger groups. First, the higher the average per capita interest of the larger group (albeit still low relative to the average per capita interest of the smaller group), the more likely that members of the larger group will incur such basic expenses as acquiring an understanding of their position. Second, the greater the heterogeneity of the distribution, the greater the likelihood of collective action on behalf of the larger group because of the existence of small, high per capita stakes subgroups.[33]

32. George Stigler, *Free-Riders and Collective Action: An Appendix to Theories of Economic Regulation*, 5 Bell J Econ & Mgmt 359, 362 (1974). Similar observations surface in treatments outside the field of economics, such as Russell Hardin's *Collective Action* (1982), an often discussed work of political science, and the recent consideration by sociologists Pamela Oliver, Gerald Marwell, and Ruy Teixeira, *A Theory of the Critical Mass: I. Interdependence, Group Heterogeneity, and the Production of Collective Action*, 91 Am J Soc 522 (1985).

I have introduced a similar notion of heterogeneity and an associated concept called "the catalytic subgroup." See Komesar, 86 Mich L Rev at 674–75 (cited in n. 16). As I show subsequently, the activities of the subgroup differ from other small group activities to the extent that the smaller group, because it is a subgroup of a majority, has available to it a greater possibility of awakening the dormant larger group and, therefore, of offering the threat or contribution of votes as well as funds.

33. The availability of alternative institutions can also be a factor in determining the potential benefits of political activity. The market or the courts may provide an even better route to achieve the group's desires.

For an analysis of the tradeoffs between political action and cartelization in the market, see Posner, 5 Bell J Econ & Mgmt Sci at 345–46 (cited in n. 2). I return to the general subject of the substitution of market or adjudicative activity for political activity in chapters 5, 6, and 7.

Thus, the degree and form of political action for both large and small groups depends in good part on certain characteristics of the benefits of political action — in particular, the distribution of the per capita benefits of political action, including the mean, variance, and skewness of that distribution. The greater the mean per capita stakes the more likely a particular group member will benefit from political activity. Greater skewness and variance indicate pockets of high-benefit group members.[34]

In addition to the level and distribution of benefits, the degree and form of political action also depend on the costs of political participation and, in particular, the costs of overcoming the free-rider problem. Foremost is the cost of information.[35] It shows up in several forms. As we have already seen, one important form of information is the basic recognition of the existence of an interest. The most dormant groups are those whose members do not even recognize a need for political action. The more complex the social issue the more difficult or expensive it is to recognize one's position.

Information costs are also associated with organizing collective action. Included here are the costs of identifying others who are in a similar position and determining when would-be members are failing to contribute. In addition, information costs include expenditures to acquire knowledge and sophistication about the political process and its various channels of

34. The benefits of political action, like most benefits, also have a time dimension; certain political actions have longer term effects than others. Increased durability of benefits may be associated with patterns of legislative action or administrative implementation. Constitution making is probably the most durable of political activities. Thus, Robert McCormick and Robert Tollison, major contributors to the economic theories of politics, recognize the possibility that even usually dormant majorities may exhibit greater activity in connection with constitution making: "A second general point about analyzing constitutional choice is that we would expect the citizen-consumer-taxpayer to play a larger role in constitutional processes than in normal political processes. The reason for this resides in the net expected benefits facing the individual in the two cases. Constitutions are more durable than any one politician or group of politicians, and the individual voters stake is thus larger when considering constitutional issues." Robert E. McCormick and Robert D. Tollison, *Politicians, Legislation, and the Economy: An Inquiry into the Interest-Group Theory of Government* 127 (1981).

35. Most of the major contributors to the IGTP have emphasized the importance of information and its costs. The earliest work along these lines is by Anthony Downs. His *Economic Theory of Democracy* (1957) contains a substantial section describing the implications of information costs. See Part III, 207–78. Gordon Tullock makes this theme central in his book *Toward a Mathematics of Politics* (1967); see chapters 6, 7, 8, and 9. See also Posner's review of Stigler's theory of economic regulation, Posner, 5 Bell J Econ & Mgmt at 353–55 (cited in n. 2) and McCormick and Tollison, *Political Legislation* at 17 (cited in n. 34).

influence. The more complex and extensive the political process, the more difficult it is to understand its rules and discover its channels of influence—both formal and informal. These various costs of information and the associated costs of organizing political action often have a threshold or fixed quality.[36]

When one combines this analysis of costs with the analysis of benefits presented earlier, it is relatively easy to see why the dominant image of the political process and its biases is minoritarian. The concentrated few with their substantial per capita stakes have the incentive to understand their interests, organize for political activity, and determine the correct channels of influence in a complex political process. Their small numbers make organization and collective action easier. Once they have overcome threshold or start-up costs, subsequent activity becomes less expensive. From this vantage, it is easy to see why the few are active and the many are dormant.

There is, however, a significant range of variation for each of the factors we have discussed; consequently, there are significant sources of variation or gradation in the dominance of the few and the dormancy of the many. These factors and, therefore, the degree of majority dormancy vary across political issues and political jurisdictions. As the *absolute* per capita stakes for the majority increase (even holding constant the ratio between majoritarian and minoritarian per capita stakes), members of the majority will more likely spend the resources and effort necessary to understand an issue and recognize their interests. In turn, variation within the distribution of the per capita benefits of political action—the degree of heterogeneity—affects the probability of collective action on behalf of the majority by subgroups of higher stakes individuals. This collective action can take the form of informing and organizing lower per capita stakes members of the majority, thereby increasing the chance that an otherwise dormant majority will act. In these instances those with higher stakes operate as a catalytic subgroup, activating the more dormant members.

36. McCormick and Tollison make this point in connection with organization costs: "A second general point about organization costs is that these costs are like start-up costs. Once they are born, they do not effect marginal costs (though if the 'firm' is to survive, they must be born over time). Groups that have already borne the start-up costs, for reasons unrelated to lobbying, will have a comparative advantage in seeking transfers and will therefore be more successful in procuring transfers as a result. This is simply a point about jointness in production. Some groups will be able to produce political lobbying as a by-product of performing some other function, thereby avoiding start-up costs for lobbying. There are many examples of such groups in the economy, among which are labor unions, trade associations, corporations, and the like."
McCormick and Tollison, *Political Legislation* at 17 (cited in n. 34).

On the cost side, the probability of majoritarian response varies as the costs of political action vary. These costs depend on the rules and structural characteristics of the political process such as size and population of the jurisdiction, size of the legislature (number of legislators), frequency of election, size and scope of the legislative agenda, and the rules of the legislature (and agencies). Smaller jurisdictions or polities and, therefore, smaller numbers of voters and fewer issues for majoritarian response may decrease the associated connection between majority positions and free riding and increase the probability of majoritarian response.[37]

Complexity and, therefore, the cost of information also vary with the subject matter of the issue in question. The degree to which someone understands any issue also depends on that person's stock or endowment of general information. This stock is in significant degree determined by cultural symbols, formal education, and the coverage of the press and media. Each culture has certain subjects such as religion or ethnicity that are part of the common experience of the members of that culture. This stock of "simple symbols" provides some social issues with easy recognition. Because the press and the media provide cheap and accessible information, press and media response is a central element in determining the degree of majoritarian influence.

Therefore, the political influence of concentrated minorities varies depending on the complexity of the issue involved, the absolute level of the average per capita stakes of the larger group, the unevenness of the distribution of the larger group and the chance that this heterogeneity will produce catalytic subgroups, and the availability of free or low cost information to the larger group. In other words, the prospect of majoritarian activity and majoritarian influence and, therefore, the majority's ability to offset minoritarian influence, is determined by variation in much the same factors employed by the IGTP to generate its conclusions of minoritarian dominance. I have simply broadened the scope of the factors to cover majoritarian as well as minoritarian participation.

Taken to its logical conclusion, this analysis suggests not just that the relative advantage of the concentrated group will vary, but that there may even be instances in which the larger group can dominate and be

---

37. Not surprisingly, in the context of suburban and exurban local land use regulations one finds lower per capita majorities in the form of present homeowners dominating high per capita minorities in the form of housing developers. See, e.g., Neil Komesar, *Housing, Zoning, and the Public Interest*, in Burton Weisbrod, Joel Handler, and Neil Komesar, eds, *Public Interest Law* 218 (1978). I will return to this subject in the discussion of the Takings Clause in chapter 7.

overrepresented. This potential for domination stems from the simplest dimension of the difference between larger and smaller groups — the number of members in the two groups. This is the simple civics model with which we began. In the most straightforward sense, larger numbers of members translates to political power via voting.[38] Voting provides large groups with a form of political action that, in the right circumstances, can be a powerful substitute for the organizational advantages of special interest groups. Catalytic subgroups within a majority who can threaten to turn out the vote hold a special bargaining chip unavailable to other concentrated interests in negotiating with political actors.

The vote-based source of majoritarian influence, however, forces consideration of the "paradox of voting" — the difficulty of understanding voting from an economics perspective. The paradox of voting is simple. The costs of voting may be low, but the benefits are minuscule: the possibility that any one vote could affect an outcome is virtually zero in any but the smallest jurisdictions. Given this view, no one should be expected to vote and, therefore, any strategies based on numbers of votes must be empty. The paradox here is that people do vote in significant numbers. This voting, explicable or not, provides a means for translating larger numbers into majoritarian influence.[39]

However haltingly and awkwardly, the power of the majority and their threat at the ballot box are felt. The fear of majority influence has a long history, and its imprint can be found in present day politics in many

---

38. Voting is not necessarily the only way in which numbers translate into political influence. Even in political systems without effective elections, large numbers may be important. Revolts, mobs, demonstrations, passive resistance, and sabotage allow political costs to be imposed by large numbers on a government otherwise ruled by the few.

39. Social scientists have advanced two general theories to explain the paradox of voting. The first, the "consumption value" theory, simply sees voting as a form of directly pleasurable activity — a sense of civic participation and so forth. See William Riker and Peter Ordeshook, *A Theory of the Calculus of Voting,* 62 Am Pol Sci Rev 25, 28 (1968). George Stigler has advanced an alternative explanation for voting based on more familiar "investment motives." Stigler argues that, as it is for most phenomena, it is wrong to believe that election outcomes are simply all-or-nothing and, in turn, that vote margins are unimportant: "If election outcomes are *not* all-or-nothing (49% is defeat) and instead influence a monotonically increasing function of vote share, then the probability that one's vote will make a difference is *unity,* not some infinitesimal fraction. This restatement does not in turn magically dispose of the paradox, because the additional influence achieved by one more vote for one's party is usually 'small.' The cost of voting is also tolerably 'small,' however, and no conclusion can be drawn at this level of generality with respect to the rationality of voting." George Stigler, *Economic Competition and Political Competition,* 13 Pub Choice 91, 104 (1972).

ways—most obviously in the tremendous effort public figures expend on public and press relations. Although the power of the vote and the influence of the majority is not so straightforward as it appeared in grade school civics, it is hardly illusory.

The Advantages of the Two-Force Model: Countervailance and the Possibility of Majoritarian Bias

As we have seen, even those sympathetic to the use of economics in understanding nonmarket phenomena have noted a great many examples of legislation that does not seem narrowly self-interested or designed to simply redistribute wealth to concentrated special interests. The two-force model presented here offers a straightforward way to understand this broader range of political behavior and political outcomes through the interaction between minoritarian and majoritarian influence. Results can be traced to variation in the strength of the two influences and, in turn, to the factors of the participation-centered model—the distribution of stakes and the costs of information and organization. Where the majority is dormant and the majoritarian influence is negligible, we get the results of the IGTP—the same results as we would get from a one-force, minoritarian bias model. But as the majoritarian influence grows, we can get a countervailance of sorts between the two forces and, with it, political outcomes that are more "balanced" than predicted by a model that focused on only one force.

Given countervailance, broad-based legislation can occur even in the context of strong, narrowly selfish motivation on the part of either elected officials or interest groups. Moreover, even in the presence of very strong forces, the resulting legislation or political action may show few overt signs of either force. Countervailance in the presence of strong forces of both varieties could even be sufficiently offsetting to result in unbiased results. The two forces and their countervailance present the possibility of attractive outcomes dictated by the interaction of individuals and groups none of whom act from attractive motives. In short, public virtue can result from private vice in the political process as well as in the market process.

The interaction between the two forces, however, is not necessarily salutary. Where minoritarian influence predominates, the model generates the unattractive results of the IGTP. Even where countervailance is strong, the resulting broad-based legislation may be illusory. As we shall see, what majorities may win at one level of government may be undone by minorities at another level.[40] As we shall also see, active majorities can be manipulated and misled.

Most importantly, the two-force model recognizes a political evil beyond the purview of the one-force model and even its critics — overwhelming majoritarian influence leading to majoritarian bias. Some of the most dramatic evils done by government are represented here. Although these evils have often been observed, there has been little effort to understand them. When de Tocqueville used the phrase "tyranny of the majority" or Madison spoke of the deleterious effects of majoritarian factions, they did not explain the characteristics of these evils. Many contemporary scholars have used similar phrases with no attempt to define them.[41] The two-force model provides a way to understand when and why majoritarian bias (or minoritarian bias) is likely to occur.

Both majoritarian and minoritarian bias share a common context — an uneven or skewed distribution of impacts. That is, one side or interest is more concentrated (higher per capita impacts or stakes, fewer people) than the other. The skewed distribution, however, relates differently to minoritarian and majoritarian bias. The distinction between *influence* and *bias* is important here. In a democracy, majorities gain their influence relative to minorities simply from numbers. This source of influence does not depend on the skewed distribution. By contrast, at least in terms of the IGTP, minorities gain their influence relative to majorities primarily through the existence of the skewed distribution. Although there may be some advantages to organizing smaller numbers whatever the distribution of stakes, the most substantial benefits are realized because the greater individual incentives inherent in higher per capita stakes raise the chances of recognition, organization, and other forms of political participation. The relative strength or influence of minorities depends on the determinants of the two-force model.

Influence is a positive or descriptive issue. By contrast, bias is a normative or prescriptive issue. As always, it depends on the social goal in question. From the standpoint of resource allocation efficiency, minoritarian bias occurs when a concentrated high per capita minority prevails over the dormant low per capita majority even though the total social costs imposed on the losing majority are greater than the total social benefits gained by the successful minority.

40. See the discussion of the growth of bureaucracy in the section "The Two-Force Model Applied: The Growth of the Bureaucracy" in this chapter.
41. During the period 1980–88, over fifty law review articles employed some variant of the phrase "tyranny of the majority." None defined it.

In turn, from the standpoint of resource allocation efficiency, majoritarian bias occurs when the majority wins even though the total social impact on the majority is less than that on the minority. In the context of resource allocation efficiency, majoritarian bias depends on the existence of the skewed distribution. With a uniform (non-skewed) distribution, greater numbers would mean greater social net benefit and, therefore, increased efficiency—at least in the commonly employed Kaldor-Hicks sense of efficiency. In the simplest sense, majority rule means that *numbers* not *intensity of preference* or *need* will prevail. With a sufficiently skewed distribution, counting noses produces problematic results.

We can see the dynamics of majoritarian bias and its interaction with minoritarian bias by returning to the *Boomer* case discussed in the previous chapter. The location of the cement plant and its neighbors is represented roughly in the following diagram:

A	B	C
D	E	F
G	H	I

Using the figures employed by the *Boomer* majority, the stakes of the cement company, located on plot E on our diagram, would be $45 million while the stakes of the neighbors (A, B, C, D, F, G, H and I in the diagram) would total $185,000 or $23,125 each.[42] We can see the implications of majoritarian bias by imagining that the nine boxes constitute a jurisdiction—a small local government. Under the simplest rule of democratic government—one person, one vote—the more numerous neighbors would pass an ordinance prohibiting the activities of the cement company. Since the social costs of such a prohibition ($45 million) far exceed the social benefits ($185,000), this would be an inefficient result. It would occur because numbers not impacts are counted. This is the simple civics model gone astray.

Several reasons suggest that such a result might not occur. Given the vast gulf between the impacts on the company and the neighbors, the company might buy the votes of at least four neighbors. The chance of

42. I have taken the artistic liberty of including eight rather than seven plaintiffs in order to make the diagram symmetrical. The changes in numbers and per capita impact are not significant to the example.

such an arrangement is reduced, however, if we increase the number of neighbors from eight to eighty and reduce the associated per capita impact to $2,312.50. Now the company would have to purchase the votes of forty neighbors and all the transactional problems we discussed in the *Boomer* case would come into play.

We could further complicate matters by supposing, as seems likely, that this larger citizenry is associated with a more complex government in which decisions were made by representatives rather than by all citizens. Here the company would only have to pay off a majority of representatives. The willingness of these representatives to accept a bribe would, however, depend on their honesty as well as their fear of losing office or of prosecution for bribery. The last two possibilities would, in turn, depend on the likelihood that the majority or at least enough of its members have sufficient incentive to actively participate in the political process to the extent of voting the offending officials out or at least placing sufficient pressure to see them prosecuted for bribery. These prospects are not at all impossible, since we still have a relatively small jurisdiction (81 voters) and per capita stakes for the majority that are relatively high.

If we now expand the number of neighbors to eight thousand (and the per capita stakes drop to $23.12), the prospect of such majoritarian reaction is reduced. Successful political action would take more people. The stakes might no longer justify political participation by enough of the neighbors to pass an ordinance (or to prevent bribery), especially because problems of free riding and of the technical complexity of pollution effects are likely to increase as numbers increase. There is no way to know at what point the chances of majority dominance become less than minority dominance. But we can easily trace out the continuum of possibilities in terms of the determinants of institutional participation.

In contrast, we can also envision those instances in which minority dominance is inefficient by turning to the issue of pollution in the Hudson River Valley. Suppose that the social impacts of the removal of the cement plant pitted the $45 million loss to the cement company against $50 million going to the occupants of the Valley, who number, let us say, 5 million. Per capita impact now averages $10 per person. As we saw from the previous example, as the numbers rose and per capita impacts fell, the chance of effective majoritarian participation fell. Such a setting would likely also be characterized by a more complex governmental structure (a state government, for example) with more legislators to watch and more complex records to police. Greater complexity would also likely exist in tracing the relationship between the activities of the Atlantic Cement Company and the loss to the populace. All these factors make it more likely that the majority will be dormant and that, therefore, efficiency-increasing regulations would not be imposed. One can fiddle with these hypothetical fact patterns by, for example, altering the governmental process or introducing low-cost information in the form of a journalistic exposé on pollution. These variations underscore my point that a skewed distribution of impacts can itself be consistent with a variety of outcomes and even with diametrically opposed outcomes; which outcome comes about depends on those factors considered by the participation-centered approach.

Land use decisions by small jurisdictions are classic examples of instances in which large numbers with lower per capita impacts (residents of developed parcels) can dominate small numbers with higher per capita stakes (residential developers or owners of undeveloped land). Yet if we increase the size of the majority, decrease the per capita impact, and throw in greater complexity as to impact and as to political participation, we can quickly come to a setting for public land use decisions in which the concentrated minority prevails.[43]

Having traced out the mechanics of majoritarian and minoritarian bias for the goal of resource allocation efficiency, some comment on other goals is needed. Whether either majoritarian or minoritarian dominance is a social evil and, therefore, associated with terms like majoritarian or minoritarian bias depends on the goal in question. For example, those who value a more equal distribution of wealth may have a different conception of majoritarian bias than those who value only resource allocation efficiency. Where votes are more equally distributed than wealth, a political process characterized by one person, one vote may be more attractive to

43. I discussed the dynamics of an early version of the two-force model in the zoning setting in Komesar, *Housing, Zoning and the Public Interest* (cited in n. 37). One can get a glimpse of the various forces in conflict in a real world setting in *Construction Industry Assoc. v City of Petaluma*, 522 F2d 897 (9th Cir 1975), where developers and local residents were eventually joined respectively by civil rights and environmental groups. The increase in the chances of minoritarian bias as the size of the jurisdiction increases helps to explain why those outside the local jurisdiction — potential purchasers of housing — do not use their greater numbers to influence the larger jurisdiction of which they are a part. Thus, for example, those within a state who are excluded by local zoning could, in theory, seek to have the zoning decision taken from the locale and allocated to a state or regional zoning authority. That they do not do so is a sign of the increasing propensity for minoritarian bias as the size of the jurisdiction increases. At the state level, the battle is more likely to be between two concentrated groups — the representatives of the local jurisdictions and the developers.

those devoted to greater equality than to those devoted to resource allocation efficiency. Majoritarian influence would be seen less often as majoritarian bias. On the other hand, those with a strong concern about the
preservation and protection of private property rights against the government might see the prospects of minoritarian influence as less threatening
or evil in some settings than would the devotees of resource allocation
efficiency (let alone the devotees of greater equality of wealth or income).
They may even sometimes favor a rule of unanimity for political decision-
making.

I qualify each of these assertions because the complexity of institutional
choice makes the connection between a law like majority rule and any goal
considerably less than straightforward. In some settings, majority rule
might even be most preferred by libertarians and least preferred by egali-
tarians.[44] My point is that the normative implications of the two-force
model and, therefore, characterizations like majoritarian or minoritarian
bias can (but do not necessarily) vary with the choice of goal.

None of this detracts from the importance of comparative institutional
choice in general or of the two-force model in particular. As the discussion
in chapter 2 showed, converting any social goal or set of goals into law and
public policy requires institutional choice. Adequate institutional choice requires understanding the working of institutions like the political process
which, in turn, requires understanding the two-force model. The conditions that produce majoritarian and minoritarian dominance are important even if the normative judgments associated with these outcomes may
vary with the goal choice. As goals vary, the normative perception of institutional behavior varies but the institutional behavior does not. Understanding institutional behavior remains essential for normative analysis
no matter what the goal.

As a general matter, the intuitions that underlie the concepts of minoritarian and majoritarian bias relate to a broad (if amorphous) sense of social goals — much broader than just resource allocation efficiency. The
excesses of majoritarianism captured in phrases like "tyranny of the majority" are not the product of economists or other devotees of resource
allocation efficiency. Similarly, antipathy to the overrepresentation of concentrated interests does not require any special allegiance to resource allocation efficiency. The common vocabulary and the popular press reflect

44. See, for example, the discussion of the complex and surprising institutional implications of libertarianism in the section on takings in chapter 8.

concern about the excessive power of special interests. This concern predates any formal articulation of the IGTP. The concepts of majoritarian and minoritarian bias capture the pervasive, though amorphous, intuition that both simply counting noses without considering the degree or extent of impacts and simply ministering to the desires of the active few can sometimes lead to severe injustice.[45]

The Extent of Majoritarian Bias

Establishing the theoretical existence of majoritarian bias, however, does not establish that it has any real importance. Even traditional concerns about the protection of concentrated minorities reflected in the Equal Protection and Takings Clauses of the U.S. Constitution may be either outmoded or overblown.[46] The two-force model would still be valuable even if the spectrum of political outcomes had only one polar evil — minoritarian bias. Recognizing that minoritarian and majoritarian influences vary enhances our understanding of broad-based, non-minoritarian outcomes. But the existence of majoritarian bias both demonstrates that the two-force model is needed and shows that normative judgments cannot be made simply on the existence of a broad distribution of legislative benefits. Broad-based legislation is not necessarily good legislation.

The extent — quantity and severity — of majoritarian bias, however, is not easy to gauge. Quite likely, the quantity of government activity characterized by minoritarian bias significantly exceeds that characterized by majoritarian bias. But the severity of majoritarian bias — its total impact on society — may rival that of minoritarian bias. The mistreatment of minority races in this country has wrought great hardship and social cost. Jim Crow laws and Japanese relocation are only the most obvious examples. The treatment of racial, religious, and ethnic minorities across the world and through time has generated and promises to generate atrocities.

In addition to the mistreatment of traditional minorities, there are less seen but nevertheless quite pervasive forms of majoritarian bias. As the reexamination of *Boomer* suggested, one can find majoritarian bias in local zoning. The majority of voters in small jurisdictions are able to impede high-density residential development. Majoritarian bias in local zoning is

---

45. For an example of majoritarian bias in a non-efficiency setting, see my discussion of the role of majoritarian bias in understanding the characteristics of the constitutional protection of racial, ethnic, and religious minorities under modern American equal protection law in Komesar, 86 Mich L Rev at 675–77 (cited in n. 16), and in chapter 7.

46. I address such an assertion by Bruce Ackerman in chapter 7.

not a trivial problem. The impact on the cost of housing and on the integration (social and racial) of the population arguably constitutes one of the more pervasive social impacts in our society. Overregulation by local zoning authorities impacts everything from school segregation to the plight of the homeless. The developers represent many potential buyers who are excluded from the jurisdiction by severe restrictions. Sizable court battles have been fought in which developers, joined by housing and civil rights groups, have faced local homeowners, joined by environmentalists.[47]

One can also see flashes of majoritarian bias in other settings. Richard Pierce suggests that there have been cycles of minoritarian and majoritarian bias in public utility rate-making.[48] In general, as simple, more dramatic issues arise or the intermittent gaze of the media falls on an issue, majorities can be activated and, in some of these instances, majoritarian bias can occur.

Majoritarian bias in its various forms has been and continues to be a serious social evil. Whether majoritarian bias is, in general, a greater social evil than minoritarian bias is not central for law and public policy. Comparative institutional examinations in the later chapters show that the important question is not the frequency or severity of a bias, but rather the extent to which a bias in a given context can be corrected by substituting other institutions such as the courts or the market or by reforming the political process. Even if majoritarian bias occurs less frequently than minoritarian bias (which it probably does) and, in total, is less severe (which is not so obvious), majoritarian bias may sometimes be the more relevant bias if it is in general more amenable to institutional substitution or reform. For example, majoritarian bias may often be a better match for judicial correction than minoritarian bias.[49]

Catalytic Subgroups and the Line between Majoritarian and Minoritarian Activity

As we have seen, sometimes concentrated subgroups within the more dispersed majority operate on behalf of the larger group. If concentrated

47. See, for example, *Construction Industry Assoc. v City of Petaluma*, 522 F2d 897 (9th Cir 1975) and *So. Burlington NAACP v Township of Mt. Laurel*, 67 NJ 151, 336 A2d 713 (1975). This is not to suggest, of course, that all zoning and environmental decisions are cases of majoritarian bias. The difficulty of finding an institution that can discern the biased from the unbiased is the key to reform. I return to this comparative institutional issue in chapter 7.

48. Richard J. Pierce, Jr., *Public Utility Regulatory Takings: Should the Judiciary Attempt to Police the Political Institutions?* 77 Georgetown LJ 2031 (1989).

49. See chapters 5 and 7.

interests are operating on behalf of both the majority and the minority, it becomes more difficult to distinguish majoritarian from minoritarian activity. Upon closer inspection, however, the activities of these catalytic subgroups of the majority differ from the activities of classic concentrated interests because they have available as a tactic the threat of awakening the larger group to political action. Demagogues, throughout history, have drawn on the power of the majority and have often exploited the vulnerability of some concentrated minority. The exclusion of racial or religious minorities from jobs, education, and the other benefits of society may in some instances serve concentrated special interests who compete with them.[50] But in most of these instances of majoritarian bias, unlike most instances of classic minoritarian bias, subterfuge is unnecessary. All too often, the majority enthusiastically supports such activity.

The extent to which subgroups within the majority can activate the rest of the majority or at least credibly threaten to do so again depends on the factors that are the focus of the participation-centered approach. The higher the per capita stakes of the remaining majority, the simpler the issue, and the more endowed information possessed by the majority, the lower the cost to the subgroup of activating the majority. If the prospect of majority activation is high enough, then the subgroup can use the credible threat of that activation to influence legislators.

Variations in these same characteristics can lead to problems in defining majoritarian activity and influence. Majorities faced with complex issues and limited incentives to independently investigate may be manipulated or misled into supporting positions that are detrimental to them. One could distinguish majoritarian subgroups from other concentrated groups based on their ability to call upon or credibly threaten to call upon the rest of the majority. Under such a definition, concentrated interests capable of misleading the majority would be majoritarian even though the end effect

50. Thus, for example, the forced detention of Japanese-Americans during World War II may have been promoted by such special interests: "Special interest groups were extremely active in applying pressure for mass evacuation. See House Report No. 2124 (77 Cong., 2nd Sess.) 154–56; McWilliams, *Prejudice*, 126–28 (1944). Mr. Austin E. Anson, managing secretary of the Salinas Vegetable Grower-Shipper Association, has frankly admitted that 'we are charged with wanting to get rid of the Japs for selfish reasons. We do. It's a question of whether the white man lives on the Pacific Coast or the brown man. They came into this valley to work, and they stayed to take over. . . . They undersell the white man in the markets. . . . They work their women and children while the white farmer has to pay wages for his help. If all the Japs were removed tomorrow, we'd never miss them in two weeks, because the white farmers can take over and produce anything the Jap grows. And we don't want them back when the war ends, either.' " *Korematsu v United States*, 323 US 214, 239 n 12 (1944) (Murphy dissenting).

of their activity would be to harm the majority. The emphasis would be on the capacity to activate the majority. Alternatively, one could distinguish majoritarian subgroups from minoritarian influence according to whether the subgroup had the same interests as the majority without regard to whether they could activate the majority. One could also combine the two and define majoritarian subgroups as those parts of the majority whose interests coincide with the majority and who have some ability to activate the majority. Each of these definitions has relevance in the consideration of political behavior. To avoid confusion, unless otherwise indicated, I will use the term "catalytic subgroup" in only the third sense.

Augmenting the Two-Force Model

Both the two-force model and the IGTP are participation-centered analyses of the political process. The two-force model retains the central role of constituency control, but sees that constituency control from a broader vantage point by adding a majoritarian force that interacts with the minoritarian force of the IGTP. Public interest results, as well as the extremes of minority or majority tyranny, are the product of these countervailing forces. These results are generated by variation in a small set of factors — the distribution of stakes and the costs of information and organization.

Such an approach is sparse by design. In order to produce a comparative institutional framework useful across a broad range of law and public policy, I have kept its political process component relatively simple. In individual applications, the framework will often require augmentation. There is a growing body of work on the political process that examines the implications of the various forms or structures of politics such as the congressional committee system. Such insights enter the two-force model as sources of variation in the costs of political participation and, therefore, as sources of variation in the extent and pattern of that participation. The two-force model will require such information for many applications.[51]

---

51. In chapter 7, I examine the implications of various structural alternatives involved in the construction of the United States Constitution.

There is a growing literature on the implications of various structural elements. This literature has been termed "positive political theory." For an example, see *Symposium: Positive Political Theory and Public Law*, 80 Georgetown LJ 457 (1992). The terminology, the background, and the future of this work is ably discussed in Daniel A. Farber and Philip P. Frickey, *Foreword: Positive Political Theory in the Nineties*, id.

Even here, however, confusions about the role of motivation cast their shadow. Farber and Frickey see the absence of unflattering assumptions about legislator motivation as a major advantage for positive political theory over the IGTP. Farber and Frickey, id at

Similarly, some applications may require greater emphasis on the behavior of public officials than that provided by the participation-centered approach of the two-force model.

That this framework is ecumenical should not diminish the central importance of its simple participation-centered analytical core. Many analyses critical of the narrowness of the IGTP offer useful detail about the political process but lack the analytical structure necessary to explain or prescribe basic political process outcomes. Thus, for example, although there have been a number of detailed multi-interest group alternatives to the IGTP, these multi-force theories do not specify the conditions under which any interest will be weaker or stronger.[52] Similarly, another set of

----

468–71. As the earlier discussion in this chapter showed, the IGTP can operate without these assumptions and, therefore, positive political theory holds no real advantage on this account.

52. Thomas Gilligan, William Marshall, and Barry Weingast employ a "multi-interest-group perspective" to examine the passage of the Interstate Commerce Act by focusing on the influence of two major interest groups—the railroads and short-haul shippers. Thomas Gilligan, William Marshall, and Barry Weingast, *Regulation and the Theory of Legislative Choice: The Interstate Commerce Act of 1887*, 32 J L & Econ 35 (1989). They trace the political power of these two groups through the committees in each House of Congress and the subsequent compromise bill. Although this work suggests the importance of considering many interests and their interaction in understanding political behavior and outcomes, it does not offer any basis for understanding which groups will have noticeable political power or the extent of that power.

These same themes appear in Richard Posner's critique of Stigler's theory of regulation, where he argues that it is necessary to have a broader multi-interest group approach which recognizes coalitions between producers and some of their customers. Posner, 5 Bell J Econ & Mgmt Sci at 335 (1974) (cited in n. 2). Like Gilligan, Marshall, and Weingast, Posner extols the benefits of a multi-interest group analysis as opposed to the winner-take-all (actually producer-take-all) analysis he associates with Stigler's theory of regulation. But, also like Gilligan, Marshall, and Weingast, Posner offers little insight into which groups among the many will be represented and the extent of their representation. Most importantly, we do not know why the most concentrated group (producers) is forced to share the spoils of regulation with groups of customers who are less concentrated than these producers. The two-force model indicates reasons for power in less concentrated groups. Posner's analysis does not.

Morris Fiorina constructs and employs a multi-interest-group approach to analyze the behavior of legislators on roll call votes, connecting these votes to the likelihood that a given interest group will react to a given vote and the strength of that reaction (the extent to which that support or opposition will increase or decrease the probability of re-election). Morris Fiorina, *Representatives, Roll Calls, and Constituencies* (1974). Employing this analysis, he is able to generate a number of legislative results from the interaction among interest groups. Valuable though it is, Fiorina's analysis, like those of Posner and of Gilligan, Marshall, and Weingast, does not indicate the characteristics which make a given interest group influential or which determine the degree of this influence. While his analysis helps us to understand what happens *if* various groups are strong or

theories drops the idea of constituency control and, at least in part, envisions political outcomes as the product of independent legislators on those occasions when the control of interest groups somehow slips. Unfortunately, these slippage theories do not help us understand why, when, how, and to what extent independent legislators contribute to political outcomes.[53]

The need to tie detailed description to a central analytical core, like the two-force model, can be seen in one of the most prominent works on the behavior of the political process, *The Politics of Regulation*, edited by James Q. Wilson.[54] Wilson and his followers extensively studied various forms of regulation. Critical of the narrowness of the IGTP, they argued that only a fraction of regulation is dominated by powerful concentrated interests. To organize these results, Wilson offered a taxonomy of regulation defined by a central characteristic of the two-force model — the distribution of stakes. Wilson's four categories of regulation, defined by four distributional combinations, are depicted in table 1.

Regulation described by the IGTP and the one-force model is represented in Wilson's category of "client politics," where benefits are narrowly concentrated and costs are widely distributed. But Wilson reported three other types of regulation. He used the term "majoritarian politics" for legislation where both the costs and benefits are widely distributed. He pointed to the Social Security Act and the Sherman Antitrust Act as ex-

---

likely to react, it does not tell us *when* these groups will be strong or likely to react, let alone the extent of their strength or reaction.

53. Among the best of these analyses are Dwight Lee, *Politics, Ideology, and the Power of Public Choice*, 74 Va L Rev 191 (1988); Farber and Frickey, 63 Tex L Rev (cited in n. 7); and Kalt and Zupan, 74 Am Econ Rev (cited in n. 7).

The two-force model can help to tighten the specification of slippage and, more importantly, help to better understand the connection between slippage and political outcomes. As indicated previously in the discussion of the limited relevance of motivation, even assuming all public officials are totally devoted to their ideological position, interest group patterns can prevail through the power of election and propaganda. The two-force model specifies those instances in which powerful interest groups can effectively employ the tactics of election and propaganda as well as where they are in position to entice susceptible officials. In turn, the two-force model identifies instances in which these tactics are weak and slippage is likely — most often where opposing interests equally balance each other. Efforts to replace the legislator will be balanced and propaganda will either be received from both sides or from neither. Similarly, each side is equally equipped (or unequipped) to provide material inducements. Employed in this manner, the two-force model can be considered as a complement to the slippage theory, and those still unsatisfied with the range of the two-force model in isolation can use it to add legislator ideology to the analysis.

54. James Q. Wilson, ed, *The Politics of Regulation* (1980).

TABLE I Wilson on the Origin of Regulation

	Widely distributed costs	Narrowly concentrated costs
Widely distributed benefits	majoritarian politics	entrepreneurial politics
Narrowly concentrated benefits	client politics	interest group politics

amples. He used the term "interest group politics" for regulatory legislation where the costs and benefits are both narrowly concentrated. His examples were the Commerce Act of 1886 and the Shipping Act of 1916. The last category is regulatory legislation that provides widely dispersed benefits and narrowly concentrated costs. Wilson termed this category "entrepreneurial politics." His examples were antipollution and auto-safety laws, Proposition 13, and McCarthyism.

Wilson's explanations for these political outcomes are echoed in the two-force model. For dispersed groups to win under entrepreneurial politics "requires the efforts of a skilled entrepreneur who can mobilize latent public sentiment."[55] This explanation parallels the discussion of the role of catalytic subgroups earlier in this chapter. In turn, Wilson envisioned client politics when low per capita losers "have little incentive to organize in opposition—if, indeed, they ever hear of the policy."[56] This is the basic insight of the IGTP reflected in minoritarian bias in the two-force model.

Wilson, however, never integrated these insights into a single analytic framework that employed the distribution of stakes to indicate when and where one form of politics will arise. This failure is most starkly seen in the categories of entrepreneurial politics and client politics. The distribution of stakes in these two categories, widely distributed benefits and concentrated costs and concentrated benefits and widely distributed costs, is basically the same. Both settings involve concentrated interests on one side and widely dispersed interests on the other. They differ only in their final results—from which the labels "benefits" and "costs" derive. From the more relevant ex ante standpoint, however, they are the same distributions—the skewed distribution discussed earlier.

55. Id at 370.
56. Id at 369.

Wilson's analysis provides no explanation of why the same ex ante distribution generates two diametrically opposed results—one in which the concentrated interest prevails (client politics) and the other in which the dispersed interest prevails (entrepreneurial politics). Why do concentrated interests win in one set of examples and lose in the other? Why do we see successful entrepreneurship and an activated large group in one set of instances and a passive, even unaware, large group in the other? Wilson does not provide an explanation for the prevalence of one group over another, especially in the crucial skewed distribution. Without such an explanation, Wilson's approach remains a taxonomy of government action, a set of useful descriptive categories, rather than an analytical framework.

The two-force model offers a way to determine which instances of the skewed distribution will show up as client politics and which will show up as entrepreneurial politics. The propensity for large group action varies with such factors as the absolute per capita stakes of the majority, the nonuniformity of the distribution (which also affects the possibility of entrepreneurship), the size of the majority, the complexity of the issue, and the cost of information.

Wilson, and others critical of the IGTP's simplified vision of single-group dominated politics, are correct when they call for a broad, more multiple-interest approach. Whatever their other merits, however, the various multi-interest-group analyses offered as substitutes have lacked consideration of factors that determine the relative (or absolute) political influence of any group in any given legislative setting.[57] In this chapter, I

57. The multi-interest group theories of Sam Peltzman and Gary Becker are unusual examples of this proposition. They propose a set of determinants other than the determinants of political influence in order to explain variation in the degree of minoritarian interest. Both approaches focus primarily on variation in marginal return for additional increments of investment in political influence. According to standard economic theory, they both assume diminishing marginal returns to such investment by the dominating group. The dominating group gets marginally less from its attempts to increase its gains, while at the same time increasing the marginal incentives of the losing group to invest in political activity because the losers are faced with increasing losses. Becker also focuses attention on the dissipation of the rents gained by the political victory through market activities such as non-price competition. Peltzman, 19 J L & Econ (cited in n. 3) and Gary Becker, *A Theory of Competition among Pressure Groups for Political Influence*, 98 Q J Econ 371 (1983). For an interesting recap and contemporary examination of these analyses, see Sam Peltzman, *The Economic Theory of Regulation after a Decade of Deregulation*, in Martin Bailey and Clifford Winston, eds, *Brookings Papers on Economic Activity: Microeconomics* 1–41 (1989).

The Peltzman and Becker analyses are both elegant and powerful. They allay some of the doubts about the narrowness of the one-force model because they show that "share

have proposed a form of multi-interest-group analysis that gives central attention to these determinants of political influence.

Although my analysis is stated in the form of *two* forces, it could be generalized to more. Its essential focus is on those factors that determine the power of the few and the power of the many. As such, one can imagine a whole range of interest groups concerned about any particular governmental decision. These groups may vary in size, heterogeneity, per capita impact, endowed knowledge, or any of the other factors that have been suggested in this chapter. Their political influence could be ranked according to the factors suggested in the two-force model.

Casting the multi-force analysis at least initially in terms of the tradeoff between two forces—minoritarian and majoritarian—mirrors the significant historic role of these forces. It also provides a simple spectrum that pulls together and dramatically points up the juxtaposition of factors emphasized in several literatures such as the availability of information, the costs of organization and political activity, group size, and the distributions of stakes. For these reasons, as well as to simplify exposition, I will continue to discuss this model in terms of two rather than more than two forces.[58]

---

the gain" outcomes can be expected even where concentrated groups hold most of the power and that there can be a decay in this gains as rents are dissipated. But, because they eschew concern with political parameters, these analyses cannot confront questions central to law and public policy such as which groups will be over or underrepresented in which process on which issue. Institutional analysis of political and legal reform and even positive legal analysis needs to consider these issues. Becker and Peltzman leave us with analyses that chart what will happen *if* political power of varying degrees is present, but not *when* or *why* these variations in political power will occur.

At play here may be the differences between the concerns of two branches of economic theory—the differences between the predictive purposes of positive economic analysis and the comparative institutional purposes of political economy. This distinction is raised by Geoffrey Brennan and James Buchanan: "Classical political economy was from its 18th century origins on, largely concerned with the comparison of the alternative social or institutional orders. Its main purpose was not the predicting of economic behavior for its own sake; its purpose was, instead, that of developing appropriate models of the working of alternative institutions in order that the choice between those institutions might be better informed. Modern economics, with its orientation towards empiricism and prediction, towards positivism generally defined, seems to have moved some distance from, and in the process obscured, this classical focus. The prevailing methodology is strongly oriented towards predictive analysis of choice *within* a well-defined institutional structure (or system of constraints) rather than choice *between* alternative social institutions." Brennan and Buchanan, 93 Econ J at 90 (cited in n. 15).

58. I have not directly commented on the relationship between the models of political process behavior discussed in this book and the vast and complex literature associated with the field of social choice. This book is not the place and I am not the person

THE TWO-FORCE MODEL APPLIED:
THE GROWTH OF THE BUREAUCRACY

The significance of the two-force model can be seen in its implications about such important subjects as the character of governmental bureaucracy and, even more broadly, the character of constitutions. I consider the latter in chapter 7 and the former here. The two-force model draws very different conclusions about these subjects than does the one-force model. The two-force model provides a better sense of the implications of raising or lowering the costs of political participation on the amount and the kind of political participation and, therefore, of the behavior of the political process.

Some proponents of the IGTP argue that increasing the cost of political activity will decrease the extent of rent-seeking and other special interest political action.[59] For those who view the political process as largely one of rent-seeking and implicit wealth redistribution, this decrease in activity seems particularly attractive. In the context of a single-force model and, in particular, a minoritarian bias model, the notion that increasing the cost of political activity decreases the amount of special interest activity flows from the simple notion that increased costs lead to decreased activity.

In the two-force model, however, it is no longer clear that increasing the costs of access to the political process will decrease the extent of special interest activity or even the amount of political activity in general. The countervailing effects of the two-force model mean that changes in costs

---

to attempt a summary of this field. That job is nicely done in William H. Riker and Barry R. Weingast, *Constitutional Regulation of Legislative Choice: The Political Consequences of Judicial Deference to Legislatures,* 74 Va L Rev 373 (1988).

The point of connection between this literature and the analysis presented in this chapter concerns the subject of cycling—the possibility that, with more than one issue to decide, majority rule may find no stable equilibrium but may instead cycle through alternative policy outcomes depending on how these outcomes are presented. Here policy alternative A may be preferred by a majority to alternative B, B preferred to C, and C preferred to A. Such a possibility is an image of majority rule in chaos, with no decision remaining in place any longer than it takes to restate it and vote on it again.

As social choice theorists note, such cycling is not in fact usually observed. Instead, mechanisms such as legislative committees serve to set the agenda, pose the issue in only one way, and produce relatively stable outcomes. Agenda setting then becomes the focus of analysis, and here the analyses of politics developed by the IGTP or by the two-force model come into play.

59. This is a familiar theme in the use of the IGTP in the legal literature. See, for example, Jonathan Macey, *Transaction Costs and the Normative Elements of the Public Choice Model: An Application to Constitutional Theory,* 74 Va L Rev 471, 509–10 (1988). In turn, Macey depends heavily on the work of two economists, Robert McCormick and Robert Tollison. See McCormick and Tollison, *Political Legislation* (cited in n. 34).

can operate in two distinct ways. On the one hand, the simplest application of economic theory suggests that an increase in the cost of political activity will decrease the political activity of any interest group, including special interests. This is the absolute or direct cost effect picked up by the one-force analysis. On the other hand, an increase in costs that also applies to the opposition can increase activity of any special interest group. Since the degree to which any expenditures on political action are efficacious depends in part on the extent of activity by the opposition, increased costs of political action that decrease the activity of opponents can increase the productivity of and hence the expenditure on political activity. This indirect or relative cost effect cuts in the opposite direction from the direct or absolute effect. The interplay between these two effects is particularly important where the rise in costs is less for one group than for its opponents—a likely result where majoritarian and minoritarian interests are in opposition. Whether and to what extent increases in costs will decrease political action in general or political action by any given special interest depends on the *net* impact of these two opposing cost changes.

These interacting cost effects produce complex and even seemingly perverse results. Contrary to the predictions of the IGTP, increasing the costs of access to the political process can result in increased minoritarian bias. Thus, for example, access to the political process is made more difficult by more infrequent elections. A given legislator's record becomes longer, more complex, and more difficult to evaluate. It is at least plausible that these increased costs will decrease majoritarian activity more than minoritarian activity. The low per capita interest of the majority makes less likely the increased expenditure necessary to understand the legislator's record. To the extent that this indirect effect dominates, such a change in the political process would favor special-interest legislation, and one would predict that there would be more (not less) special-interest activity and, in turn, possibly more political activity.

Similarly, in the face of majoritarian bias, decreases in the cost of access to the political process can also have perverse effects. Even such seemingly attractive reforms as the increase of information to the public require more careful examination lest they aggravate rather than alleviate an existing political malfunction. Thus, for example, it is plausible that increasing the information to the public in the racially segregated south of the United States or in Germany of the 1930s might have increased not decreased unattractive wealth redistributions from minorities (blacks and Jews respectively) to the majority.

This analysis suggests the importance of determining the direction of the existing bias and the relative impact of cost changes on the two forces to determine the efficacy of reforms that change the cost of access to the political process. In chapter 7, I discuss three examples of the tradeoff between majoritarian and minoritarian bias — the character of the original Constitution, the meaning of the famous *Carolene Products* footnote, and the role of compensation under the Takings Clause in correcting political malfunction. Each of these subjects are part of larger comparative analysis of institutional performance that requires more than the portrait of a single institution. The single institutional insights provided thus far, however, can be used to briefly examine an important issue of descriptive or positive analysis — the growth of the bureaucracy — and its treatment by several prominent social scientists.

The delegation of a significant part of governmental decision-making to administrative agencies is an important and much debated trend in the allocation of political decision-making. Although there are functional or public-interest explanations for this delegation, such as the response to complexity in decision-making and the need for greater technical expertise, these explanations seem to have fallen into general disrepute.[60] A number of theories have been advanced to replace these public-interest theories.

The most popular or at least the most discussed model of bureaucratic behavior and bureaucratic growth is that of the economist William Niskanen.[61] Niskanen's theory has been summarized as follows:

> Niskanen's view is that bureaus can be modeled in much the same way that economists model business firms, but with a few differences, such as: bureaucrats seek to maximize budgets rather than profits; their resources typically derive from lump-sum legislative appropriations rather than from selling goods in the marketplace; and, in dealing with the legislature, they have an effective monopoly over information about the true costs of supply. Incorporating these properties into a model of bureaucratic behavior, [Niskanen] demonstrates that budget-maximizing bureaucrats will put their monopoly powers to use in securing budget and outcome levels that are higher than socially optimal.[62]

60. For a comprehensive summary of the literature and the arguments see Morris P. Fiorina, *Group Concentration* at 184–87 (cited in n. 4).

61. William Niskanen, *Bureaucracy and Representative Government* (1971).

62. Gary J. Miller and Terry M. Moe, *Bureaucrats, Legislators, and the Size of Government,* 77 Am Pol Sci Rev 297, 297 (1983).

In describing the source of bureaucratic monopoly in Niskanen's model, Sam Peltz-

Although it has been influential, Niskanen's approach suffers because it is based on the questionable institutional assumption of an impotent Congress and, in turn, impotent political constituencies. It is difficult to see why Congress should give the agencies and bureaucrats all the political power Niskanen envisions. Congress chooses to allocate responsibility, and it could choose to keep matters for itself by expanding the staff and responsibility of congressional committees or by resolving the substantive details in the original legislation, thereby eliminating the need for administrative determinations. Congress could also allocate responsibility to the judiciary (which it has the power to expand) or it could increase competition among agencies, thereby decreasing the degree of bureaucratic monopoly. It is difficult to understand why Congress would give increasing power and influence (let alone monopoly power and influence) to these agencies.

Once delegation occurs, traditional principal-agent problems produce slippage in control of the agent and, therefore, bureaucratic decision-making and size may be controlled to some extent by bureaucrats. But a theory based on the assumption that this slippage is pervasive and, therefore, that it forms the complete or even dominant explanation for the growth of the bureaucracy seems extreme. Moreover, such a theory is inconsistent with the economic approach to politics that usually sees legislators and special interests as capable political actors.[63]

man places greater emphasis on Niskanen's view that competition among bureaucracies and among jurisdictions has decreased than upon the view that the rational ignorance of legislators has increased: "Niskanen's model contemplates a bureaucracy that values larger budgets and always has some power to extract budget dollars from a legislature that values bureaucratic output. An important constraint on the bureaucracy's ability to gain unproductive budget dollars is competition among bureaucrats and among jurisdictions. Thus, institutional developments that weaken competition imply growing budgets. Among these developments Niskanen cites centralization of government functions, the consolidation of governmental functions into fewer bureaus, and enhancement of bureaucratic tenure (civil service). He gives these factors greater weight than increases in the 'rational ignorance' of legislators, another source of a bureau's monopoly." Sam Peltzman, *The Growth of Government*, 23 J L & Econ 209, 214–15 (1980).

63. Sam Peltzman criticizes Niskanen's approach in similar terms: "A primary difficulty with this theory, one which Niskanen explicitly recognizes, is its treatment of centralization of bureaucratic power as an exogenous event. An obvious alternative is that the same forces generating growth of government generally produced conditions facilitating that growth. This may help explain the temptation to fall back on discrete events, like wars, to rationalize subsequent growth of government. Another difficulty stems from the model's sketchy outline of the relationship between politicians and bureaucrats. Politicians do not benefit directly from bureaucratic budgets, and Niskanen presents evidence that they lose votes for marginal budget expansions. (This is meant to

These analytical problems in Niskanen's theory have prompted a number of alternative theories which envision the growth of bureaucracy, delegation, and bureaucratic behavior as determined by Congress rather than the bureaucracies themselves. In the view of these theories, "bureaucracies are 'runaways,' and spending programs are 'uncontrollable,' because Congress made them that way."[64]

In this connection, Morris Fiorina and Roger Noll have offered a theory of delegation and bureaucratic growth based on the political benefits to incumbent congressmen produced by the existence of a complex bureaucracy.[65] Under this theory, Congress creates complex bureaucratic programs and administrative agencies so that its members can deliver guidance through this complex maze to their constituents and, in turn, gain the political support of these constituents. Although Fiorina and Noll have shifted attention from the desires of bureaucrats to the desires of politicians, their theory still slights the role of an even more basic group of political actors — political constituencies. At base, the Fiorina and Noll approach views constituents as yokels who allow their political representatives to make life difficult for them and then are grateful when these representatives lead them through the very maze the representatives have created.

This conception of constituents contains basic inconsistencies. One must wonder how many voters in a given district could actually be benefited by these facilitation services in any electoral period. At most, those aided could only be a small percentage of voters. Under the minoritarian bias model, a few may be disproportionately influential and powerful in a

corroborate the model's implication that bureaucracies are able to 'overexpand.') But the estimated size of this loss . . . is easily large enough so that modest reductions of expenditures would have changed the results of some recent elections. In that case, one has to wonder how 'rational' it is for politicians to 'ignore' bureaucratic expansion." Id at 215.

64. Charles M. Hardin, Kenneth Shepsle, and Barry R. Weingast, *Public Policy Excesses: Government by Congressional Subcommittee*, St. Louis: Washington University Center for the Study of American Business, formal publication no. 50, 22 (1982), cited in Miller and Moe, 77 Am Pol Sci Rev at 321 (cited in n. 62). Although Miller and Moe offer a powerful critique of Niskanen and establish a strong case for congressional rather than bureaucratic control over delegation, they do not offer a theory of this congressional control. They tend instead to see delegation and the growth of bureaucracy as a series of congressional mistakes.

65. Morris P. Fiorina and Roger G. Noll, *Voters, Bureaucrats and Legislators: A Rational Choice Perspective on the Growth of Bureaucracy*, 9 J Pub Econ 239 (1978) and *Voters, Legislators and Bureaucracy: Institutional Design in the Public Sector*, 68 Am Econ Assn Proc 256 (1978).

district, and services delivered to these few would matter to the legislator. But these concentrated special interest groups seem unlikely to be duped into being thankful to politicians who first make life difficult and then remove these difficulties. A concentrated interest aware of facilitation services delivered by a congressional representative would also likely be aware that it was the representative's vote that imposed the regulation in the first place.

In a subsequent work, Morris Fiorina presents an alternative theory that reflects the interaction between Congress and constituents in explaining the delegation and the growth of bureaucracy.[66] Here, Fiorina focuses on a factor important in the analysis presented in this book—the distribution of benefits and costs across interest groups. Employing the usual minoritarian bias conception of the IGTP, he argues that Congress wishes to shift responsibility for issues that involve diffused benefits and concentrated costs because these are intrinsically politically costly to members of Congress. In turn, Congress wishes to decide concentrated benefit/diffused cost issues.

Although Fiorina's analysis goes further than the others discussed in appreciating the role of constituent influence, it fails to generate the results he supposes because it relies on a one-force rather than a two-force model. If one assumes that only minoritarian influence is present, delegating issues with diffused benefits and concentrated costs to administrative agencies would not be the most profitable (or least cost) strategy for congressional representatives. By Fiorina's own logic, it would be more beneficial to simply vote against the regulatory legislation in question—a concentrated benefit/diffused cost vote. Thus, Fiorina's analysis, based as it is on a traditional minoritarian influence model, cannot explain delegation and increased bureaucracy. But the two-force model can.

If one assumes that action by Congress is likely to be more easily (cheaply) knowable to constituents than action by administrative agencies or bureaucracy, majoritarian influence is likely to be greater in the congressional than in the bureaucratic setting. In this situation, Congress sensibly passes legislation that presents the appearance of a diffused benefit/concentrated cost (majoritarian) victory while at the same time allocating the details and implementation to the less observable and more complex administrative process. In the administrative setting, the advantages of concentrated interests are greater and the likelihood of minoritarian influ-

66. Fiorina, *Group Concentration* at 175–97 (cited in n. 4).

ence increases. Here concentrated interests can frustrate the ostensible purposes and gain control. In a sense, delegation provides a way for congressional representatives to serve both influences.

Issues of environmental regulation, which form many of the examples employed by Fiorina, seem to fit this two-force perspective. One can easily envision the injury from air and water pollution as one in which victims are the general public, each of whom bears a minimal cost per each act of pollution, and the injurers are large-scale industrial polluters. This is the image I presented of the victims of pollution in the Hudson River Valley in the earlier discussion of *Boomer*. At least at the superficial level, there seems no absence of political response to control of pollution despite diffused benefits and concentrated costs from its regulation. People running for elective office often claim great devotion to protection of the environment. Victims' stakes are apparently high enough for voters to recognize a need for environmental protection and to react at the ballot box. In the pollution setting, enough possibility of majoritarian activity exists to cause office-holders to at least express support for pollution regulation.

There is reason, however, to doubt that these public expressions of support are always translated into *effective* environmental regulation. The divergence arises at the level of implementation — either at the stage of drafting the particulars of the regulations or at the administrative stage. What a politician would never do on the soap box, he or she can afford to do in the more complex, more hidden world of the bureaucracy. A politician may declare an abiding concern for the environment and even support broad (albeit vague) legislation and at the same time block implementation by halting prosecution under the guise of some procedural or jurisdictional rationale or by inhibiting particular prosecutions through pressure on the implementing agency. In turn, more sophisticated, concentrated interests may feel satisfied to know that what they appeared to have lost in the legislature they can recover in the administrative process.

The analysis depends on all the factors that determine the relative strengths of minoritarian and majoritarian influences. Thus, for example, where pollution regulation is easy and straightforward, the tactic of providing hidden minoritarian victories at the administrative level would not work so well. But, in more common, complex pollution settings where people can easily differ on strategy and approach, it is easier to hide from a low-stakes constituency not willing and able to follow all the twists and turns of administrative implementation while, at the same time, serving a high-stakes constituency able to understand these complexities and to reward efforts on their behalf. As such, passage of broad legislation with delegation of details to administrative agencies provides an attractive political strategy and, therefore, a reason for delegation and bureaucratic growth. The results follow from the existence of the two forces and the relative advantage belonging to a concentrated minority in more complex, less observed settings.

SUMMARY

In this chapter, I have presented an approach to understanding politics that builds on the interest group theory of politics by recognizing the possibility of majoritarian influence and even majoritarian bias. When combined with the minoritarian force of the IGTP, the resulting two-force model provides an analytical framework that indicates the conditions under which concentrated interests, the projected winners in the IGTP, will win, lose, or draw in their contests with more numerous dispersed interests. This two-force model can contemplate everything from special interest legislation to tyranny of the majority without leaving behind the same simple set of determinants — the distribution of stakes and the costs of political participation (most importantly, the costs of information).

I have shown that the issue of the motives of political officials — which has been so hotly debated by the opponents and proponents of the IGTP — is largely irrelevant. Whether and to what extent serious political malfunction exists depends primarily on systemic characteristics not individual motives. I have also shown the two-force model in action by examining law and public policy issues including the growth of the bureaucracy.

The analysis of a single institution — the political process — presented here was constructed to serve comparative institutional analysis and is, therefore, only the first step. In the subsequent chapters, I explore parallel participation-centered approaches to the market and adjudicative processes. In several instances, I will draw out the parallels between these institutions and the political process discussed here. The two-force model and the tradeoff between minoritarian and majoritarian bias plays a significant role in the rest of the book and, in particular, in the chapters on constitutional law.

}4{

The Market Process: Transaction Costs and Transaction Benefits

The market process serves a function parallel to the political process. It can serve as an alternative to government action in the achievement of social goals or interests. Thus, for example, in our discussion of the *Boomer* case in chapter 2, the relevant institutions included something amorphously referred to as the market. The issue there was whether the cement plant should relocate or remain. One way to make that decision was by the operation of the market process. The market process operated through transactions between the cement plant and its neighbors. Similarly, a process of transactions was seen as a way to determine whether A or B would use A's garage or whether the level of pollution in the Hudson River Valley would be changed. In these contexts, this process would again operate by transaction: B would purchase the right to use A's garage, and the cement companies would purchase the rights of all the residents of the Hudson River Valley. The market process operates via large numbers of these individual transactions to produce aggregate or social outcomes.

This is a simplified, participation-centered picture of the market process. Its focus is on participation through transactions. These transactions (or their absence), taken as a whole, produce a wide variety of results. They set price and output, allocate society's scarce resources, distribute wealth, and determine opportunity. The process in this simplified image operates without a central authority. It is atomistic, and the accomplishment of social results is inadvertent. That is, the results are produced by innumerable transactions between individuals, none of whom is concerned with aggregate results such as resource allocation efficiency or the general distribution of wealth and opportunity. This lack of specific focus on an aggregate outcome differs from the objective of most of the mass of actors in the political process — voters, lobbyists, and others. To realize any significant gain, these political actors must affect the aggregate outcome.

A participation-centered perception of the market is common. The neoclassical models of contemporary economics are based on such a perception. But, just as with analysis of the political process, the participation-centered approach to the market process is only a central core or foundation upon which to construct institutional analysis. This framework requires augmentation in some settings.

Thus, for example, not all market transactions are atomistic. Some involve parties so large that they can significantly affect or determine market outcomes. These parties operate with an awareness of their impact on aggregate results. They have some appreciable amount of monopolistic or oligopolistic power. Anyone interested in antitrust law and policy or labor law and policy would want to augment the simple participation-centered model to take account of these influential actors.

Similarly, much market activity does not take place via simple, arm's length transactions. Business arrangements are often long-term and complex and require ongoing adjustments between the parties. Most goods and services are produced within large, complex contractual arrangements called firms or corporations. Those interested in business contracting or corporate law and policy would want to augment the simple participation-centered model accordingly. I return to this subject later in this chapter.

As with the analysis of the political process, however, the participation-centered approach remains the central core of institutional analysis. No one who studies antitrust, labor, or corporate policy or any other area of law and public policy can ignore the larger participation-centered market context. As with the political process, this focus on the mass of participants hardly suggests that all participants are created equal. Some people or entities participate more or more effectively. That is the major source of variation in results. As with the political process, the extent to which the market process produces efficiency, justness, fairness, or any other goal is largely determined by the pattern of participation.

I begin this chapter with a short discussion of the dynamics of market participation. If one envisions market participation as transacting, the determinants are the benefits and costs of transacting. Here the analysis converges with Ronald Coase's famous transaction cost approach. In the second section of this chapter, I examine the similarities between the Coasean analysis and mine as well as a difference—the explicit focus in my approach on transaction benefits. This examination leads to a discussion of the difference in focus of my approach and transaction cost economics. In the next two sections, I connect the market process with the political process. First, I examine the obvious complementarity between the market

and political processes — the notion that the market does not and cannot
exist without the state. Even here the gap between theoretical and real
institutions forces much tougher choices than many analysts recognize.
Second, I examine the similarity in perceived problems in the market and
the political process by examining the parallels between rent-seeking in
the political process and some of the uses and abuses of advertising in the
market. These parallels reveal confusions in the concept of rent-seeking
and, more importantly, show that, because of the frequent parallels in
institutional behavior, it is far more difficult than commonly employed
single institutional perspectives indicate to determine what institutional
malfunctions can be remedied and how to do so.

THE DYNAMICS OF MARKET PARTICIPATION

In order to see the parallels between decision-making in the political
and market institutions and to trace out the dynamics of market participation, I return to the *Boomer* case. In that case, the dissent believed that
cement plants like the defendant caused environmental harm in the Hudson River Valley that exceeded the benefit of having such plants or at least
exceeded the costs of finding and installing pollution control devices. The
dissent also believed that socially beneficial results such as improvement
in pollution control technology or even relocation of the cement plants
required direct intervention by the courts. On the other hand, the majority
felt that these more global results would best be brought about by direct
intervention by the political process. That none of the judges relied on the
market process to resolve these issues reflects the presence of serious impediments to transacting. By examining these impediments, we can see the
dynamics of market participation and, in turn, the sources of variation in
the efficacy of the market process.

Many impediments to transacting can be traced to the numbers of participants necessary to reach a solution and, in turn, the dilution of per
capita stakes. There were several cement plants in the Hudson River Valley,
and their combined particle pollution apparently affected a large number
of residents in the area (at least tens of thousands). The possibility of a
market solution representing the interests of all was low because the possibility of participation by so many was low. Several familiar factors are
at play.

Even if there had been only one victim of the pollution and one source
in *Boomer*, it would be difficult to decide how the pollution could be most

effectively reduced by market means.[1] Because of the complexity of the problem, it would be costly to negotiate and draft a contract that detailed the relevant solution, the price to be paid, and the remedies for breach, as well as to enforce such a contract. Thus, even with a very confined distribution of impacts, the costs of transacting are not negligible and might deter either party from transacting, leaving an otherwise unattractive pollution setting unresolved. Whether the transactions will occur depends on the benefit to the transactor of removing or reducing the pollution. Put simply, if transaction benefits are greater than transaction costs, transactions take place.

Increasing the numbers of participants confounds this possibility in several ways. Even if we only increase the numbers by recognizing the presence of several polluters, while still assuming a single victim, that single victim faces greater costs of transacting since there are now more parties to negotiate with, and the situation is more technically difficult since the amount of pollution and the mechanics of solution may vary among the polluters. As we saw in the *Boomer* discussion, the possibility of any transaction virtually disappears if we now recognize that there are tens of thousands of victims as well as several polluters. A significant social benefit is now divided among thousands, thereby significantly reducing the per capita benefits to be gained from transacting. At very low per capita benefits, we run into the possibility that victims will not even recognize the benefits of transacting. If the pollution and its effects are complex, then the costs of recognizing the problem may be enough to produce no reaction and, therefore, no market participation. Even given basic recognition of the problem, the low per capita stakes in the transaction might not justify the costs of understanding technical solutions and contracting options let alone bearing the costs of negotiation and enforcement of the contract.

Where there are many victims, they are likely to vary in per capita stakes. Some individuals may suffer more pollution — for example, some may live closer to the polluters. Some individuals may suffer more injury

---

1. For convenience, I will assume throughout this hypothetical setting that the polluters have the property right. In other words, if relocation or pollution abatement or any other source of pollution control is to be achieved through the market process, the victims must purchase the right from the polluters. For the purpose of cataloging the sources of impediments to transacting, it does not matter where I assign the property right in the hypothetical setting.

from any given level of pollution either because they are physically more susceptible or because any given physical condition more greatly affects their ability to function. In the extreme, some victims may be large-scale businesses such as plant nurseries or livestock producers whose losses from pollution may be very large. Per capita transaction costs may also vary among the individual victims. Some individuals may be brighter or more sophisticated or more knowledgeable about the particulars of pollution or transacting. Some individuals may be excluded from transactions or dealt with differently because of characteristics such as race, ethnicity, or gender. In turn, the interaction between per capita benefits and per capita costs can produce size or scale effects in transacting. Large-scale victims may face proportionally lower transaction costs. For example, negotiating and enforcing a contract to improve air quality by $100,000 is unlikely to be 1,000 times more expensive than negotiating and enforcing a contract to improve air quality by $100.

How any of these variations affect the market participation of victims is further complicated because the pollution setting in *Boomer* involves a collective good. Thus, to the extent that any potential victim of pollution purchases a reduction in pollution from any potential polluter, other victims will likely also face less pollution whether or not they participate in the relevant transaction—whether or not they help defray the costs of transacting or the costs of compensating the potential polluter. As with participation in the political process, the existence of a collective good can cause less participation because the various participants will seek to free ride. They will not participate, hoping to benefit from the participation of others. This free riding often results in no transacting—no participation.

The dynamics of market participation traced out in the *Boomer* setting are sufficient to tell the story of most of what is commonly referred to in welfare economics as market malfunction or market failure. The issue of pollution is the classic version of "externalities"—effects not considered in the market's cost-benefit calculations because they are external to them. These effects are external precisely because there is no transaction to represent them. Externalities are, by their nature, failures of participation. The market failures associated with collective goods and, in the extreme, "public goods" such as national defense are extreme forms of nonparticipation in which problems of free riding play a dominant role.

The failures associated with inadequacy of information cause problems in both the quantity and quality of participation. They can defeat or distort market participation. Where low per capita transaction benefits combine with high information costs,[2] we get ignorance that can be manifested in a failure to act or in a mistaken choice that would not be made given better information. When high information costs are matched with a skewed distribution of stakes — low on one side and high on the other — we can get fraud or sharp dealing because some people will be less ignorant than others and may take advantage of the situation. The same result can occur where the distribution of benefits is uniform if the costs of information are simply lower to some than to others.

Even monopoly or monopsony, another traditional form of market failure, can be related to facets of the participation-centered approach. Monopoly is, by definition, the absence of competition and, as such, insufficient market participation. This absence most commonly results from barriers to entry — high costs of market participation. As the last chapter indicated, these costs of participation may be the product of government action such as tariffs or exclusions of competitive goods ostensibly on the grounds of health and safety. The extent to which these barriers operate to reduce competition depends on the benefits of participation. The higher monopoly profits become, the more likely it is that competition will bring about the demise of the monopoly.

Thus, the dynamics of market participation, articulated in terms of the characteristics of the benefits and costs of that participation (transaction benefits and costs), parallels the analysis used for the political process and comports with the standard list of market malfunctions employed by economists. The parallel to the political process is particularly important because our objective is institutional comparison, not just the description of the functioning of the market. The parallel to the market failure vocabulary is important because it facilitates communication. The market failure vocabulary is now widely used by law and public policy analysts.

There are, however, two limitations of the market failure constructs relative to the constructs of market participation. First, although market failure is single institutional and, therefore, incapable of yielding any normative judgments, its terminology can lead one to quite different conclusions. The market is "failing" only in the sense that it is failing to be perfect. Since all alternative responses are also imperfect, the existence of

---

2. High information costs include both the costs of acquiring basic data, such as the amount and content of emissions by each plant and the health impacts of these emissions, and the costs of understanding and assessing this data. Readily available technical information is likely to be useless or even an irritant to a population without the training to deal with it.

market "failures" cannot determine policy outcomes. Even the most able analysts, however, sometimes employ market failure as a sufficient condition for public policy.[3] Discussion in terms of market participation should avoid this misunderstanding.

Second, the market failure construct is tied to the social goal of resource allocation efficiency. The broader construct of market participation, by contrast, can be easily associated with any goal. Market participation, like political and adjudicative participation, is simply a single institutional component in a comparative institutional analysis that can be used in connection with any social goal. The market process and, therefore, market participation are relevant to the distribution of social income, wealth, and opportunities as well as to the allocation of resources.

Whether the rich get richer or the just are rewarded in the market process depends on the parameters of market participation. The costs of participation include the unwillingness of others to deal due to racial, ethnic, or gender differences. These costs are also related to education and experience gained from prior exposure to market activity and, therefore, to individual or family wealth. To the extent that per capita stakes and the costs of market participation vary according to such individual characteristics as wealth, income, education, sex, race, and birth, the analysis of participation provides important insights into the role of the market process in determining the whole range of goals.

The dynamics of market participation commonly produce far less than ideal results for any social goal or goals, including resource allocation efficiency. The tougher issue of course is whether the dynamics of participation in other institutions produce better results (however better results

3. See Harold Demsetz, *Information and Efficiency: Another Viewpoint,* 12 J L & Econ 1 (1969), discussing such mistakes in Kenneth Arrow's analysis of governmental reaction to market failures in the provision of information. For additional criticisms of the constructs of welfare economics, see Carl Dahlman, *The Problem of Externality,* 22 J L & Econ 141 (1979), and Kenneth Shepsle and Barry Weingast, *Political Solutions to Market Problems,* 78 Am Pol Sci Rev 417 (1984).

Richard Posner's single institutionalism can also probably be traced to a misunderstanding concerning the constructs of welfare economics, in particular the limits of the concept of market failure. As I showed in chapter 2 and discuss again in chapter 6, Posner ties his analysis to whether or not the market "works." In each of these instances, whether the market works is linked to the presence or absence of traditional forms of market failure. But markets are always imperfect, and market failures are always present. Thus, whether the market "works" in any meaningful sense can not be determined by the presence or absence of market failures. The concept of market failure is single institutional; it can not support an analysis of law or public policy.

are defined). Market failure (however failure is defined), like political process failure, is a single institutional notion.[4] The tougher but more relevant world of institutional choice and comparison awaits consideration in the closing chapters of this book and to some degree in the closing sections of this chapter. First I will trace through the dynamics of market participation relevant to those inquiries.

TRANSACTION COST ECONOMICS AND THE PARTICIPATION-CENTERED APPROACH

The focus on transacting and its dynamics as a means to understand the behavior of the market process is certainly not new. One of its most active contributors, Oliver Williamson, traces the field of transaction cost economics back at least sixty years.[5] Through the work of Williamson and many others, this field has contributed significantly to the study of industrial organization and business structure.

Both the fields of transaction cost economics and law and economics owe a significant debt to the work of Ronald Coase. In two famous articles, Coase contributed mightily to the origination of these two fields of study. In a 1937 article, *The Nature of the Firm,* Coase used transaction costs as the major determinant of the intra-market institutional choice between organizing production within market firms and organizing production as separate operations through contracting or transacting.[6] In a 1960 article, *The Problem of Social Cost,* Coase used the concept of transaction costs to explore the extent and source of what welfare economists termed externalities — the most basic of the market failures.[7] The first article, with its focus on intra-market choice, helped found transaction cost economics.[8] The second article, with its focus on concepts of property law, helped found law and economics.[9]

As Coase made clear in *The Problem of Social Cost,* he viewed information

---

4. Shepsle and Weingast make a similar observation: "The tensions between the public failure and market failure schools remains alive today. . . . In our opinion, insights on these controversies will not be forthcoming unless grounded in a theory of comparative performance. The analysis of both the market failure and the public failure schools entail comparisons of an institution's performance against an *ideal.*" Shepsle and Weingast, 78 Am Pol Sci Rev at 418 (cited in n. 3).

5. Oliver Williamson, *The Economic Institutions of Capitalism* 1–7 (1985).

6. Ronald H. Coase, *The Nature of the Firm,* 4 Economica (1937).

7. Ronald H. Coase, *The Problem of Social Cost,* 3 J L & Econ 1 (1960).

8. See Williamson, *Economic Institutions* at 3–4 (cited in n. 5).

9. Richard Posner, *Economic Analysis of Law* at 21–22 (4th ed 1992).

costs as the primary form of transaction costs.[10] As the costs of information vary so do the costs of transacting and, therefore, the chance that some economic impact will be external to the market processes because it has not been internalized by transacting. To Coase, externalities are not physical events, like smoke or odor; they are institutional events produced by impediments in the process of transacting. From the standpoint of institutional choice, Coase's analysis shows us the basic sources of variation in one of the important institutional alternatives of organizing economic activity — transacting.

The approach I take in this book closely parallels the work of Coase. I emphasize the determinants of market participation — transacting — as the means of understanding the relative abilities or disabilities of the market as an institution. Like Coase, I see the cost of transaction as dominated by the cost of information. Like Coase, my model of the market is constructed to answer comparative institutional questions.[11]

In one general way, however, my analysis differs from that of Coase. Coase has emphasized transaction *costs*. In the simplest sense of economics, however, an analysis of any behavior cannot depend solely on understanding its costs; one must also understand its benefits. Thus, one should understand transacting both in terms of transaction costs and transaction benefits. In my analysis, the benefit side — in the form of the distribution of stakes — has a more explicit and robust role than in that of Coase or in that of the other transaction cost economists who follow him.[12]

This difference between Coase's approach and mine may be explained by differences in the focus of the analyses. Coase and most other transac-

10. Coase writes: "In order to carry out a market transaction it is necessary to discover who it is that one wishes to deal with, to inform people that one wishes to deal and on what terms, to conduct negotiations leading up to a bargain, to draw up the contract, to undertake the inspection needed to make sure that the terms of the contract are being observed, and so on." Coase, 3 J L & Econ at 15 (cited in n. 7). I am not the first to note that the core of Coase's conception of transaction costs is the cost of information. See Dahlman, 22 J L & Econ at 148 (cited in n. 3).

11. Coase's notion of transacting and transaction costs was explicitly constructed to analyze the choice between transacting and the firm in *The Theory of the Firm*. The choice between the market and the political process is less explicitly, but still significantly, informed by Coase's transaction cost analysis in *The Problem of Social Cost*.

12. I am using the term "transaction cost economist" in the way it is used by Oliver Williamson to define that group of industrial organization economists such as Williamson who have focused on the transaction/firm choice using the concept of transaction costs. I do not mean to include every analyst who has ever employed the concept of transaction costs.

tion cost economists are concerned primarily with intra-market choice or private ordering and, in that connection, primarily with the private ordering of production—transactions between producer and producer. In such a setting, variation in the dispersion of stakes can be considered unimportant; the distribution of stakes may generally be assumed to be uniformly high per capita.[13] Where dispersed stakes appear important as, for example, in the relationship between corporate shareholders and corporate management, they can be factored in as transaction costs associated with the cost of organizing or dealing with many parties. As long as the focus is on this range of institutional choice, such a secondary role for the distribution of stakes seems acceptable. Where small numbers of parties have uniformly high stakes, the problems of collective action and the failures of recognition caused by dispersed small per capita interests are not a concern.[14]

A vast literature discusses intra-market institutional choice from this vantage. The primary institutional focus of transaction cost economics is the choice between the firm, the spot market, the long-term contingency contract, and the relational contract. Much of this literature focuses on the market firm and the choice between the firm and the spot market—the choice whether to subcontract an activity or to internalize it in a firm via vertical or conglomerate integration.[15] The study of intra-market choice

13. Although *The Problem of Social Cost* ventures into the world of extra-market choice, its analysis and examples often reflect Coase's abiding interest in intra-market choices reflected in his earlier work, *The Nature of the Firm*.

14. The narrower focus of transaction cost economics can be seen in its treatment of information. Although the modern successors of Coase have focused on the costs of information and, in particular, on the implication of differences in the endowed information positions of the transacting parties, these problems with information are not traced to low stakes or variations in stakes or, for that matter, to any well-defined source. The analysis simply recognizes that some people are exposed to and possess more information than others. Referred to as asymmetric or private information, the existence of one-sided information decreases market participation because it creates the fear that the better informed party will engage in opportunistic behavior—cheating, lying, or otherwise taking advantage of the less informed party. Parties vulnerable to opportunistic behavior may react by decreasing the market activity that involves this vulnerability or they may seek alternative methods of organizing market activity that reduce the chances of opportunistic behavior. The prominent institutional form of industrial organization used to reduce these risks is the market firm. The transaction is brought within a single hierarchical structure that helps control opportunistic behavior.

15. For overviews and discussions of this literature, see Williamson, *Economic Institutions* (cited in n. 5), and Armen Alchian and Susan Woodward, *Reflections on the Theory of the Firm*, 143 J Inst & Theoretical Econ 110–36 (1987).

also covers highly structured futures markets like commodities and stock exchanges.[16] In addition, a vast range of intra-market choices involve the distribution of goods and services such as the choice among retailing formats like department stores, supermarkets, and shopping centers.

These intra-market choices — the choice between firms, spot market transactions, relational contracting, and so forth — are not the institutional choices most immediate to law and public policy choice. The intra-market choices involve the question of how production and distribution is or ought to be organized. But the institutional choices involved in the most relevant areas of law and public policy, such as antitrust or labor policy, involve the choice of *who decides* how production and distribution is or ought to be organized. Here the institutional alternatives are the general market process and the government (the political and adjudicative processes).

To understand this point, consider Oliver Williamson's work on vertical integration, probably the most influential work in contemporary transaction cost economics.[17] Williamson demonstrated that the organizational choice to integrate additional steps of production into a market firm rather than to organize them through market transaction had significant efficiency explanations. This insight apparently contributed to the substantial softening of the Justice Department's opposition to vertical integration.[18]

The policy result, however, does not necessarily flow from a demonstration that vertical integration is likely to be efficient. Such a demonstration is neither a necessary nor a sufficient condition to wise antitrust policy. Even if most instances of vertical integration are inefficient, the correct social response would still be no regulation if the governmental regulatory process is sufficiently expensive or biased. In turn, even if most instances of vertical integration are efficient, regulation is good policy if the regulatory process could easily identify and eliminate those few instances of inefficiency.

Williamson's sophisticated examination of vertical integration is hardly irrelevant to antitrust policy. If, as Williamson argues, prior antitrust policy was based on the view that *all* vertical integration was inefficient, then the revelation that *any* could be efficient could change policy. The prior

16. For an insightful examination of the role of such markets, see Lester G. Telser and Harlow N. Higginbotham, *Organized Futures Markets: Costs and Benefits*, 85 J Pol Econ 969 (1977).

17. See Williamson, *Economic Institutions* at 85–130 (cited in n. 5).

18. Id at 99–101.

policy may also have been based on the implicit comparative institutional analysis that, so long as all vertical integrations are inefficient, the regulatory response is simple and easy — prohibit all vertical integration.[19] More subtly, Williamson's demonstration that the firm/transaction choice is highly complex impacts the institutional choice between market and regulation by raising the cost of regulation. Increased complexity raises administrative, investigative, and adjudicative costs and creates a greater chance of mistaken prosecution and conviction and an even greater chance of systemic political bias. The relevance of any of these insights, however, can only be determined by integrating them into an institutional choice different than the intra-market institutional choice upon which Williamson focused. Williamson's approach to industrial organization may be superior to the neoclassical approach he criticizes, but the insights of either approach must be passed through a different level of institutional choice in order to turn either into public policy.

Whatever the differences in emphasis, however, the work of transaction cost economists and of Coase in particular informs this book in many ways. I share Coase's sense that good economic analysis must be informed by good institutional analysis, and that institutional analysis should be pursued by understanding the determinants of institutional participation — in the case of the market, the determinants of transacting. I share Coase's perception that the cost of information is among the most important of the determinants of institutional behavior.

I also share Coase's frustration with the use made of his work and the failure of economists in general and economists interested in law in particular to see the essentially comparative institutional core of Coase's constructs.[20] In particular, the work of Coase and those other transaction cost economists interested in intra-market institutional choice strongly militates against a common misuse of a prominent feature of Coase's work, the so-called Coase theorem. In *The Problem of Social Cost,* Coase argues that, at zero transaction costs, an efficient allocation of resources would occur whatever the initial assignment of property rights. This theorem generated great interest in the "zero-transaction-cost" world. Much of this interest

---

19. Even in such a simple situation, the costs of the government program (administrative outlays, mistakes, bias) are not zero. In fact, the earlier Merger Guidelines employed a market share test to distinguish prohibited from benign vertical integration. See id at 99. Such a test, however justified, added complexity and raised cost relative to the simpler blanket prohibition.

20. See Ronald H. Coase, *The Firm, the Market and the Law* 15 (1988).

involved theoretical debates about Coase's assertion. In the main, most analysts now accept the general validity of the assertion.

Although the zero-transaction-cost world can be a powerful analytical or heuristic device, there has been a troubling tendency to argue for policy positions based on the actual existence (or near existence) of that world. This tendency has led some law and economics analysts to equate intuitions of market superiority to the existence of zero, virtually zero, or at the least very low transaction costs in the real world. These analyses, however, ignore the real tenor of Coase's work in particular and the implications of transaction cost economics in general by ignoring the pervasive presence of significant transaction costs.[21] The tough intra-market choices that are the focus of Coase's *The Nature of the Firm* and the work of such economists as Oliver Williamson, Armen Alchian, and Harold Demsetz show that transaction costs are virtually never even close to zero.

The tradeoffs among the forms of private ordering studied by transaction cost economists reveal the existence of significant costs for all forms of private ordering. As we have seen, a common means of organizing long-term, complex production relationships is to bring them within a single legal-contractual entity — the market firm. Although the pervasive nature of the market firm indicates success as an organizational form, large corporate, market-firm structures are very expensive both in terms of the labor and material necessary to operate them and the perverse incentives set up when management and ownership are separated. These firms have complex internal organizations with hierarchical management and, in the case of corporations, complex constitutions that set out the voting rights of stockholders and the procedures for election of the boards of directors. That these cumbersome, expensive arrangements are often the most cost

---

21. Robert Ellickson has carefully chronicled the significant size of transaction costs and the tendency of law and economics scholars to overstate the frictionless nature of the real world market. Referring to Coase's statement that "transaction costs . . . are large," Ellickson puts the matter succinctly: "Coase himself has said it. Field evidence shows it. Law-and-economics scholars should heed it." Robert Ellickson, *The Case for Coase and Against "Coaseanism,"* 99 Yale LJ 611, 614 (1989). Ellickson cites as examples of works that do not give transaction costs their due, John Donohue, *Diverting the Coasean: Incentive Schemes to Reduce Unemployment Spells,* 99 Yale LJ 549 (1989); Elizabeth Hoffman and Matthew Spitzer, *Experimental Tests of the Coase Theorem with Large Bargaining Groups,* 15 J Legal Stud 149 (1986); and Kenneth Vogel, *The Coase Theorem and California's Animal Trespass Law,* 16 J Legal Stud 149 (1987). As Ellickson implies, these are the most thoughtful of the offenders. The law reviews are replete with many examples that do not reflect this level of care. One recent example is Michael Bradley and Michael Rosenzweig, *The Untenable Case for Chapter 11,* 101 Yale LJ 1043 (1992).

effective means of operation indicates just how high the costs of the rejected alternatives must be.

To some degree, the tendency of law and economics people to dwell on
the world of zero (or virtually zero) transaction costs may stem from the
sole emphasis of transaction costs economics on costs rather than on the
interaction of transaction benefits and costs. If variation in transaction
costs bears the entire burden for explaining market participation, then
where analysts see successful transacting they believe transaction costs
must be low. Recognizing the interaction between transaction costs and
benefits allows the alternative explanation that market participation occurs because transaction benefits are high enough to justify bearing even
significant transaction costs.

One can see this point played out in Richard Posner's economic analysis
of law. In the *Boomer* discussion in chapter 2, we saw that Posner's single
institutional analysis links legal responses to whether the market worked
or not. Alternatively, Posner has phrased this analysis in terms of whether
transaction costs are low or high. As the subsequent discussion of tort law
shows, Posner seems to associate the existence of a working market with
the existence of frequent or regularized transacting. But the existence of
this transacting does not indicate that transaction costs are low. The choice
to transact reflects the interaction of both transaction costs and transaction
benefits. Markets work (regularized transacting occurs) even when transaction costs are high.

At first blush, the costs of transacting do seem very low in many settings. I can buy toothpaste, apples, and wine at a single location with little
expenditure of time and effort. I can purchase stocks, commodities futures,
or airline tickets by picking up the telephone.

But the market price I pay for these items already reflects a large amount
of transaction costs. The most obvious examples involve the fee I pay stock
or commodities brokers, which in turn reflects the significant costs of operating a formal market for stocks and commodities. But the price of all
the items reflect retailing, advertising, and labeling outlays, in good part
made to reduce the effort I have to put into shopping. These product and
service prices also reflect transaction costs in the form of expenditures by
the producers on accountants, lawyers, plant managers, sales representatives, and others whose major job is transacting. Without getting into the
debate over the definition of transaction costs versus other costs of production, real world settings are rare in which, even by the narrowest definition, the costs of transacting are low in an absolute sense.

That there are high costs of transacting in most settings can be seen by imagining the existence of a device that frictionlessly, instantaneously, and accurately determined the stakes and costs of all potential market transactors, made trades and agreements, produced the necessary documentation (contracts, records, and accounts) for these agreements, and accurately enforced and adjusted them. Are there many real world transactional settings in which such a device would not be in high demand?

An active market process replete with transacting reflects both the great demand for these transactions and the ingenuity of the market process in finding organizational devices that reduce the costs of transacting. The vast range of settings in which the market is clearly superior to the political or adjudicative processes is more interesting and more robustly comparative institutional than has been suggested by the standard recitations and uses of the Coase theorem. Easy victories for transacting or private ordering signal that the costs of transacting or private ordering are much lower than the costs of public ordering, not the existence of virtually zero transaction costs. Those analysts who dwell on zero or virtually zero transaction costs are mistakenly focusing on instances that are both analytically and empirically uninteresting.

As a general matter, the making of markets is a significant and complex part of the economy. A large amount of society's resources go into transacting rather than into producing goods and services. All of this says something to both market lovers and market detractors as they attempt to discuss and debate the virtues of the market. When market lovers speak about transaction costs being zero or close to zero, they are simply misstating reality. On the other hand, when market detractors characterize the vast outlays that go into packaging, retailing, and advertising as waste, they too miss the point. Neither the aesthetically pleasing world of zero transaction costs nor the vast list of alleged market wastes is useful in determining or evaluating the role of the real world market process. We live in a transaction-costly world. We live in a political-process-costly world. The issue is comparative costs, not low costs or high costs. The message for both groups is the same — the analytic reality lies in institutional comparison: low relative to what and high relative to what?

THE MARKET AND THE POLITICAL PROCESS: COMPLEMENTS AND SUBSTITUTES

The tremendous costs of transacting and the significant efforts that go into organizing markets and other activities to reduce these transaction costs also make it easy to understand the essential role of government in supporting markets. As Coase has so aptly pointed out, both the earliest forms of markets and the present organized markets like the stock and commodities exchanges involved important law functions carried out by private means.[22] Contracts were enforced, theft prohibited, and sharp dealing curtailed. These private law functions, as Coase points out, become extremely strained and perhaps impossible as we move to more complex transactions where the number of transactions, the variety of transactions, and the timing of transactions increase significantly. Here private mechanisms seem sorely tested, and it is only sensible to turn to the power of the central authority of the state to protect property and enforce contracts. Indeed, in an immense society like the United States, producing ultimate protective activities like national defense by private transactions is inconceivable.

The state, as protector of property rights, enforcer of contracts, and keeper of the peace, stands as an essential complement to the market. Without the governmental mechanisms — without the state — the cost of transacting would be immense. Most of life would be taken up with the search for and barter over goods and services and, more basically, the protection of whatever goods and services one had. Little time would be spent in the production of goods and services. Portrayals of futuristic catastrophe like those in the Mad Max movies and, unfortunately, real world catastrophe like modern day Somalia are graphic indicators of the degree to which effort would go into protection and barter rather than production. Complex market economies do not exist without significant states.

We can add to police, national defense, and contract enforcement such basic government functions as the provision of a currency. Without a generally acceptable medium of exchange, transactions are reduced to barter and sophisticated mass markets largely cease to exist. In addition, the state can promote the promulgation and exchange of information by protection of property rights in ideas, subsidization of research, and provision of education. The state can even supplement the market by simulating the outcome of market transactions where the costs of transactions (or, more exactly, the interaction of the costs and benefits of transactions) produce problems in actual market participation. These are all functions of the state that promote the conditions for a better functioning market.

We are now, however, on the brink of a familiar lapse in institutional

---

22. Coase, *The Firm* at 7–10 (cited in n. 20).

analysis—equating theoretical functions and the functioning of a real-world institution. Real states do provide an essential backdrop or setting for markets. Real states can and do function to provide greater security and certainty than one would imagine present in a stateless world—a state of nature. But real states can also be a major source of the insecurity and uncertainty that threaten markets.

Monopoly of force is a central characteristic of government. The same police and the military who provide the protection of property and person that allows the basic establishment of investment and trade can also severely threaten the security of property and person. The protection of property and person always involves both protection *by* and *from* the state and its functionaries. Whether, when, and to what extent the police or the military promote or endanger market transactions is an essential issue of institutional choice.

Similarly, as we saw in chapter 3, institutions such as administrative agencies or legislatures, put in place to enforce contracts and define property rights, can also serve to impede both transacting and the achievement of associated social goals like resource allocation efficiency. Rent-seeking flourishes in the guise of contract enforcement and property right definition. The next chapter on the adjudicative process will show limitations capable of supporting a somewhat similar tale for that institution. Whether and to what extent any of these processes and their resulting rules and laws promote or retard market transacting again raises essential and complex issues of institutional choice and constitutional and legal design.

Attempts to trivialize these issues by easy assumptions are intellectually dangerous. Whether and to what extent the structures of government thought to support the market do in fact enhance transacting, increase resource allocation efficiency, or promote any other social goal are issues too important and difficult to be assumed.

The same may be said of sweeping notions about the evolutionary tendencies of law and public policy to meet social needs. Whether and to what extent the political or adjudicative process will respond to any perceived social need—like the need for a law or a program that reduces transaction costs—depends on how that need will be represented in those processes. When the conditions for minoritarian or majoritarian bias are present, for example, these processes may be dormant or even perverse in the face of social need when that need is felt by groups who are underrepresented in these processes.

No doubt, the character of government determines the character of the market. But that realization tells us nothing about whether and to what extent governments can be expected to yield results that facilitate efficiency or transacting. The pattern of governmental behavior is not random, and it can be affected by the design of the government and predicted by an analysis that takes into account the interaction between the features of that design and the characteristics of the social issues in question. But neither prediction nor reform is easily obtained. Prediction is not well served by assuming that government will simply evolve to meet needs, and reform is not well served by calls for undefined institutional forms like the minimal state or the just state.[23]

Both the complexity of the interaction between government and the market and the importance of institutional choice for economics in general can be seen from yet another view of the implications of Ronald Coase's work. It has been suggested that the point of Coase's analysis of social cost—from which the famous Coase theorem was derived—was that the problem of conflicting uses of property could best be dealt with "through the market itself simply by a clear delineation of property rights."[24] This interpretation raises important questions about the workings of those non-market institutions that delineate property rights—the political and adjudicative processes. As the discussion of even a straightforward case like *Boomer* showed, there is nothing "simple" about the delineation of property rights by these institutions. Thus a "property rights" interpretation of Coase's work again points up that whether, when, and how the market functions is itself determined by the performance of complex, non-market processes. Understanding economic systems depends on a deep understanding of the political and adjudicative processes as well as the market process itself. In other words, economic analysis in general depends on comparative institutional analysis.

RENT-SEEKING IN THE MARKET AND POLITICAL PROCESSES

I close my discussion of the market and its parallels to the political process with a consideration of two activities, advertising and propaganda, important in the functioning of the market and of the political process, respectively. These two activities are instrumental in rent-seeking in their

---

23. In chapter 8, I return to the subject of the difficulty of defining the minimal state even when that minimal state is conceived narrowly to serve only the protection of private property.

24. This interpretation comes from a review of Coase's life and work by Steven N. S. Cheung in *The New Palgrave: A Dictionary of Economics* (1987) at 2:456.

respective institutions. I consider and compare the evils of rent-seeking in both the market and the political process, discuss the role of advertising and propaganda in this rent-seeking, and show the challenge of finding any cure for rent-seeking. In the process of this presentation, I can again exhibit the central role of information (and misinformation) in the functioning of all institutions.

As we saw in the previous chapter, rent-seeking plays a much criticized role in the functioning of politics. Where the skewed distribution provides an advantage for a concentrated, higher stakes minority over a more dispersed majority, this advantage is often used to obtain monopoly positions for producers by excluding competition through tariffs or unnecessary regulation. These rent-seeking activities have been strongly criticized for their adverse effects on competition and their waste of resources.

One form of market rent-seeking has similar attributes. Various commentators have pointed out that advertising differentiates seemingly identical products and, therefore, produces monopoly rents and decreases resource allocation efficiency.[25] The classic example is the differentiation of various brands of chemically identical medicine such as aspirin. As with political rent-seeking, these efficiency losses due to monopoly may well be dwarfed by the efficiency losses caused by the waste of resources expended on the advertising used to create these monopoly rents. Thus, although they usually appear in different journals and come from the pens of different analysts, there are parallels between rent-seeking in the market process (often achieved by advertising) and rent-seeking in the political process (often achieved by propaganda and lobbying).[26]

The parallel even extends to the connection between market rent-seeking and the skewed distribution. This connection is, in turn, tied to the connection between the skewed distribution and the dynamics of informing or, more exactly, the dynamics of misinforming. As we saw at several points in the last chapter, the connection between the skewed distribution and political rent-seeking often operates through the dynamics of information. The dispersed low per capita majority may not even have

25. For good summaries of the literature and the various positions on the role of advertising in the market, see William Comanor and Thomas Wilson, *The Effect of Advertising on Competition: A Survey*, 17 J Econ Literature 453–76 (1979) and Robert Wills, *Do Advertising-Induced Price Differences among Brands Explain Profit Differences among Products?* in Robert Wills, Julie Caswell, and John Culbertson, eds, *Issues after a Century of Federal Competition Policy* at 361 (1987).

26. The rent-seeking literature is summarized in James Buchanan, Robert Tollison, and Gordon Tullock, *Toward a Theory of the Rent-Seeking Society* (1980).

the incentives to recognize that they are harmed by a government action or even that such government action exists, and, even if they recognize the issue, they may be misled by the concentrated minority into perverse support. The concentrated minority can then work for government action favorable to them without opposition. To the extent that the dynamics of information leave the majority completely unaware of the issue, the mechanics of rent-seeking in the market differ to some degree from those of political rent-seeking. Producers seeking to convince consumers that their product is different cannot afford to be ignored. Advertising (misleading or not) requires some level of attention.

These similarities and differences can be traced out in three rough categories of interaction between per capita stakes and the possibility of informing or misinforming. Where consumers or voters have relatively high per capita stakes, it is harder to fool them because the higher stakes justify a greater willingness to obtain alternative sources of information or to obtain the sophistication necessary to critically examine any distorted information provided. On the other hand, at the very lowest levels of per capita impact, consumers or voters do not have sufficient interest to even recognize the problem or to be interested in attempting to assimilate any information (false or otherwise). They can neither be led nor misled. This complete failure of recognition produces the dormant majority in politics and unrealized or unrealizable transactions (the dormant consumers) in the market. Both these failures of recognition are problematic, but only the first leads to a potential for economic rents and rent-seeking. The second leaves a potential need unrealized in the market.

Lying somewhere between the awareness of high-stakes consumers and voters and the unawareness of low-stakes consumers and voters is a range of mid-stakes consumers and voters capable of being misled. In the political process, we get the possibility of misled majorities convinced to support legislation that is, in fact, detrimental to them. In the market process, we get misled consumers convinced to pay more for a product that is, in fact, no better than a less expensive albeit less advertised product or even to consume a product that is detrimental to them. It would seem to be these consumers and voters in the mid-range who have enough interest to listen but not enough interest to discern.

Whether consumers or voters are misled will, of course, be dictated by cost conditions as well as the distribution of stakes. Both political issues and market products and services vary in complexity and, therefore, in the amount of information or sophistication necessary to understand them. Variation in endowed positions (information already commonly possessed) and the availability of cheap information, such as media coverage, also effect the extent of understanding. These factors can even produce differential understanding about different aspects of the same issue. The two sides of a given substantive issue, whether about a product or a political position, can differ significantly in ease of recognition or understanding. Sometimes it is easier to recognize and understand the costs of a product or project than its benefits (or vice versa). Sometimes basic cultural associations or symbols can be important. It appears, for example, that the flag works well in either advertising or propaganda — sometimes overcoming otherwise meritorious but less accessible counter-positions.[27]

The interaction between the stakes and costs of information produces the overall pattern of understanding (and misunderstanding). The degree to which a symbol will be effective in convincing (or misleading) any population of consumers or voters will depend upon the per capita stakes of the relevant population and, therefore, their tendency to either critically examine or largely ignore advertising or propaganda that employs the symbol. This analysis gives us some rough indication of when there will be no reaction from consumers or voters, when consumers or voters will be misled into acting contrary to their interests, and when there will be a consumer or voter reaction that represents their basic interests. To paraphrase Abraham Lincoln, it helps us determine which people can be fooled all of the time, which can be fooled some of the time, and perhaps why they all cannot be fooled all of the time.

There may be some skepticism, especially among those who attack rent-seeking in the political process, that advertising is also insidious and that, therefore, there is a parallel universe of serious market rent-seeking. They might point out, quite correctly, that a significant portion of advertising outlays are beneficial in the sense that they increase rather than decrease competition.[28] That does not, however, differentiate advertising

27. Another example of a simple symbol is the ambulance-chasing lawyer. As we shall see in chapter 6, public reaction to the so-called litigation explosion and to tort reform is often built around this symbol even where the opposite position might in fact be more favorable to the reacting members of the public.

28. William Landes and Richard Posner, *Trademark Law: An Economic Perspective*, 30 J L & Econ 265 (1987), present such an analysis of a component of advertising, trademarks. On a more general level, they assert that "the hostile view of brand advertising has been largely and we think correctly rejected by economists." Id at 275. They cite Benjamin Klein and Keith Leffler, *The Role of Market Forces in Assuring Contractual Perfor-*

from propaganda and lobbying. The political process depends on the activities of constituents and constituent interest groups in providing the myriad varieties of information necessary to function. There is little doubt that a good part of the information provided is one-sided and intended to enhance the position of the provider. But that is equally true for market advertising.[29] As in the market, competition in providing information in the political process and the need to maintain credibility with recipients can, under the correct conditions, produce public virtue from private vice.

Contrary to the impression created in the rent-seeking literature, propaganda and lobbying activities provide important social benefits in a world in which information in general and information about constituent desires in particular is difficult to come by. This view, which would be unobjectionable in the context of advertising and the market, seems less well understood (or less clearly articulated) in the rent-seeking literature. If we were governed by perfectly informed, benevolent philosopher-kings, expensive, one-sided and potentially distortive information would be wasteful. Although propaganda and lobbying can be misleading and one-sided, a political process cut off from this information — even if such isolation could be achieved — would be too arid, removed, and dangerous to be a viable alternative.

When we turn to the subject of solutions for the problems of rent-seeking in the market and political process, we are confronted with a familiar nemesis — the skewed distribution. As we have seen, problems with propaganda and lobbying in the political process and with advertising in the market show up most dramatically when the distribution of stakes is skewed. Without the presence of a concentrated interest to produce them, neither propaganda/lobbying nor advertising would be likely. Without the

---

mance, 89 J Pol Econ 615 (1981), which, in turn, refers to economic studies supporting the non-hostile view of brand advertising.

I claim no expertise in this literature and, therefore, have a difficult time assessing the economist-counting inherent in Landes's and Posner's claim. Given even some level of disagreement about the benevolence of advertising, my point can be made on two levels. First, as the text indicates, both advertising and analogous political activities, such as lobbying and propaganda, have significant potential for benevolent effects given the significant need for and cost of information. Second, the skewed distribution may provide important hints about when there are more likely to be socially benevolent effects of either advertising or propaganda and lobbying. Wholesale characterizations of these activities may not be the best that analysts can do.

29. As we will see, it is also true for the adversarial system that lies at the heart of the adjudicative process.

presence of a dispersed interest, neither activity would be nearly as likely to be misleading and, therefore, socially detrimental. Advertising or propaganda work to mislead the general public (consumers or voters) where the low stakes of consumers or voters leave them with insufficient incentives to obtain the information necessary to check the validity of the propaganda or advertising. Lobbying, where the information is directed to political officials, is particularly distortive where only one side of the issue is presented — a result far more likely with the skewed distribution.

The presence of the skewed distribution, however, also makes it difficult to correct or remove the evils of either advertising or propaganda/lobbying. Without such plausible reforms, both market and political rent-seeking are only academic complaints without any relevance to law and public policy. One reform would be to prohibit all advertising or all propaganda and lobbying. Such an approach, if successful, would help eliminate the monopolies created by and the wasted resources expended on either market or political rent-seeking. Eliminating all advertising and all propaganda and lobbying, even if technically possible, however, is likely to be severely socially detrimental. Advertising and propaganda exist because of the great need for information in the market and in the political process.

More sensitive strategies could be focused on eliminating those forms of advertising or propaganda most likely to have derogatory effects. Only harmful advertising, propaganda, and lobbying would be eliminated. Such sifting of information would, however, require a sifting process, usually a governmental agency. Since we are in the presence of the skewed distribution, such a strategy to remove harmful advertising would run the risk of increasing political rent-seeking. The term "harmful" is subject to a wide variety of interpretations, as are terms like "false" or "misleading." Such ambiguity necessitates significant leeway in regulation. Under the guise of controlling the adverse effects of advertising, concentrated interests could and do use the political process to decrease beneficial advertising and increase the monopoly position of the concentrated interests.[30]

Any attempts to control rent-seeking within the political process must turn either to the political process itself, to a super-political process in the form of a constitutional convention, or, in the U.S. system, to the courts

30. That is the interpretation given by the U.S. Supreme Court to Virginia's bar on pharmaceutical price advertising by pharmacies in *Virginia Pharmacy Bd. v Virginia Consumer Council,* 425 US 748 (1976), the case that introduced judicial protection of commercial speech.

as constitutional interpreters. Controlling the flow of propaganda or political activity by the political process runs the risk that, rather than increasing efficiency (or any other social goal), making information less accessible may increase the biases in the political process, thereby decreasing efficiency and a wide variety of other social goods. Much of the story of First Amendment constitutional law concerns the deep and traditional distrust of governmental activities that attempt to control the flow of information either in the political or in the market process.

The issue here is not whether speech, political or market, can be misleading, inflammatory, or otherwise harmful to society, but rather whether the imperfect political process, if relied upon to curb this evil, will create even greater evil. The same question may then be asked about the imperfect institution put in place in reaction to the perceived excesses of censorship by the political process — usually the courts. As the earlier discussion of the *Pentagon Papers* case indicated, the courts have their own institutional limitations. These limitations will be explored in detail in the next and subsequent chapters. For present purposes, it is enough to note that judicial control of false advertising or false propaganda is likely to be a very limited strategy.

The story of advertising and propaganda and of their evil subsets, market and political rent-seeking, shows us that, especially in the context of the skewed distribution, the two most important institutions — the political process and the market — have a desperate and continuous need for information and that the filling of this need creates serious distortions in the same institutions. The story also shows us the difficulty of establishing valid, sensible, or trustworthy strategies to correct these problems because lying behind each strategy is the same skewed distribution and, therefore, similar difficult institutional questions for the reform. Addressing these tasks makes comparative institutional analysis both more difficult and more relevant than single institutional analysis.

SUMMARY

In the market process, social results such as setting market prices and outputs, allocating resources, and determining the distribution of wealth and opportunity are usually produced by a virtually uncountable number of transactions and exchanges, each of which is carried out without concern for the aggregate result. The ability of the market process depends on the quality of this market participation. How many people potentially affected by transactions will represent these impacts through market participation? Understanding the sources of variation in this participation is the backbone of understanding variation in the efficacy of the market process.

The transaction cost economics approach first advanced by Ronald Coase provides a view of the market broadly useful for comparative institutional analysis. The participation-centered approach to institutional behavior employed in this book closely resembles Coase's analysis of transacting. It differs, however, in its greater emphasis on the role of the distribution of stakes — the role of transaction benefits.

This chapter examined the differences between intra-market and extra-market institutional choices. It discussed the necessary role for government action in support of market activity. But the inevitably imperfect nature of both market and political processes quickly reminds us that any supportive role will necessarily involve difficult institutional choices. In this connection, I examined the difficult institutional choice between market and political processes in the context of the troubling skewed distribution by looking at the comparison between political rent-seeking and market rent-seeking. This comparison again showed both the importance of information and the parallel nature of institutional problems. More examination of the market-politics comparison awaits more specific contexts and the consideration of the third institutional alternative — the judicial process.

}5{

The Courts as an Institution:
The Structure and Scale of Justice

Compared to the political process and the market, the judicial or adjudicative process exhibits three distinctive structural elements that shape how it functions. First, the adjudicative process is more formally defined and has more formal requirements for participation than do the other two institutions. In most instances, in order to participate, litigants must meet and overcome more obstacles than either voters or consumers. Second, the adjudicative process is much smaller — its physical resources and personnel are far fewer — than the political process. More importantly, it is far more difficult to increase in size. By contrast, the more amorphous market is the most easily expanded or contracted of the three institutions and, although difficult to measure precisely, by far the largest. Third, judges, the central officials of the judicial process, are more independent from the general population than either their market or political counterparts. These three basic characteristics — higher threshold access cost, limited scale, and judicial independence — interact with each other and with the conditions of participation that are the subject matter of the participation-centered approach; together they produce the comparative advantages and disadvantages of the adjudicative process versus the market and political processes.

In the first section of the chapter, I examine those characteristics of the adjudicative process that enhance judicial independence and evenhandedness. Independence and evenhandedness come at significant cost. The second section traces out the implication of this cost on the pattern of adjudication. The interaction of this cost with the various configurations of stakes can operate to bar important social issues from the courts, thereby creating significant systemic comparative disadvantages for the adjudicative process. The third section examines two sources of significant comparative advantages for the adjudicative process. The fourth section examines two additional dimensions of the adjudicative process — judicial competence and the scale or size of the adjudicative process — that affect both the character and the ability of the adjudicative process relative to the other institutions.

The Structures of Independence

Judges play several roles in the adjudicative process. As trial judges, they oversee the initial stages of disputes and, in the absence of juries, operate as determiners of facts as well as arbiters of law. As appellate judges, usually sitting in groups of three to nine, they determine whether an error occurred in the trial process. Appellate courts articulate the rules that most people consider judge-made law.

The independence of judges stems primarily from their terms of employment. The connection can be seen most dramatically in the federal judiciary. Federal judges serve for life and cannot be removed except by the cumbersome impeachment process. Compensation is set for judges as a class, and Congress cannot single out individual judges.[1]

In addition, federal judges traditionally come to the bench as a final vocation. The longevity and high average age of federal judges attest to a limited interest in job mobility. Although judges are not completely indifferent to alternate job opportunities, the range of alternatives attractive to judges appears to be more limited than for political and market actors. Job security and the general disinterest in other positions makes it difficult to influence judges by replacement or inducement. Replacing judges is a longer term strategy than replacing legislators. Financial inducement of judges is more difficult to arrange than with elected officials both because elected officials have a more pressing need for campaign contributions and because contributions to elected officials carry fewer sanctions.

Juries are similarly walled-off from outside influence or at least more so than comparable decision-makers in the market and political processes. Sitting in groups of from six to twelve individuals, jurors determine basic factual elements, often rendering ultimate verdicts on guilt, liability, damages, and sentences. They are chosen at random from the population and serve for only short periods—in general, for only a few trials or indictments. Their anonymity and continuous turnover as well as the difficulty of predicting which case any individual juror may hear makes them a difficult target for influence. Unlike bureaucrats who hear many cases of a specialized type, a given juror will hear only one or two cases. Any long-term or subtle efforts aimed at gaining favor with jurors—such as educating them to favor a given position—would have to be aimed at the general population. Jurors are a vast, diffuse, and moving target.

1. Even state court judges serve for longer terms and are otherwise more insulated from the general electorate than are comparable legislative and executive officials.

Independence, or at least insulation from unequal influence, is also increased by the manner in which information comes to judges and juries. Information reaching both judge and jury is largely funneled through the courtroom and the adversarial process. Obviously, neither judge nor jury is immune to pretrial sources of information; they were not born on the day of trial. But informal, ex parte discussion is, at least formally, precluded and is, in reality, much more difficult to accomplish than in the less formal political process let alone in the highly informal market. The requirements of written complaints, service, and notice along with pretrial discovery and the rules of evidence are designed to give all parties to a lawsuit equal access both to information and to official decision-makers.

These features of the adjudicative process reinforce the popular image that the judicial process is more evenhanded and its officials more independent than political officials. To a considerable extent, this image is valid. However, the same structural elements and safeguards that produce independence and evenhandedness produce systemic biases in adjudication and limitations on the competence and physical capacity of the adjudicative process. Like independence and evenhandedness, these attributes must be recognized in any rendition of the adjudicative process intended to serve institutional comparison.

These systemic effects result primarily from the high costs of litigation — costs produced by the same structural elements thought to produce independence and evenhandedness. The adjudicative process has many more formal requirements for participation than either the market or the political process. Resulting differences in the costs of participation cause significant differences in the range of issues seen by the courts relative to these other institutions.

Although these expensive formalities in general produce greater judicial independence, in at least one important sense they decrease the independence of judges. For all their greater insulation from the forces of replacement and inducement, judges are far less able to initiate decision-making than legislators. Legislators can resolve a social issue without anyone officially and formally bringing the issue to their attention. They can glean the public will, or the likelihood that the public or any part of the public will react favorably with votes or contributions, and act without any formal complaint or proceeding. Judges must await action brought by moving parties, often private parties. Although voters, lobbyists, and interest groups are important actors in the political process, they are not indispensable. By contrast, even the most aggressive judge is forced to limit his or her efforts in initiating action to sending subtle signals or invitations to those who can bring action. As we shall see, these invitations often go unaccepted.

Whether and to what extent invitations to litigate are accepted, as well as which issues are litigated, is significantly affected by the high costs of meeting the formal requirements for adjudication. A wide variety of criteria condition and control admission to the adjudicative process. Standing determines who can bring action based on a given wrong. Jurisdiction determines which court can hear the action. Choice of law determines which state's law will be employed. Justiciability and ripeness determine when wrongdoing can come to the courts.[2] The difficulty of understanding and meeting these requirements raises the cost of litigation.

A complaining party is also required to put the complaint in writing, file the writing, and serve the writing on the individuals or entities against whom the complainant seeks remedy. The harms must be specific; and they must be linked to specific wrongs committed by a finite set of specified defendants. Again, the law controlling these aspects of litigation is complex and uncertain.

Before any trial is held, litigants can expect contests before judges testing the sufficiency of the complaint or of its service as well as raising issues such as standing, jurisdiction, choice of law, justiciability, and ripeness. Litigants can also expect to spend a long period before trial in a process of discovery used to elicit information and evidence. This discovery often involves extensive examination of witnesses in person (depositions) and in writing (interrogatories). Unlike fact gathering in the political process,

---

2. Justiciability "limits the Courts to cases presented in an adversary context and in a form historically viewed as capable of resolution through the judicial process." *Flast v Cohen*, 392 US 83, 95 (1968). Arising out of the restrictions on the judiciary in Article III of the Constitution, application of the doctrine has restricted the judiciary from issuing advisory opinions, from examining moot issues, and from examining issues where the parties have no standing to maintain the action. Id at 95.

Ripeness determines when an issue may be heard before the court. The purpose of the ripeness doctrine is to insure that courts avoid entangling themselves in abstract or theoretical considerations until a concrete event has taken place, leading to an actual controversy between litigants. *Abbott Laboratories v Gardner*, 387 US 136, 148 (1967). The basic notion of the ripeness doctrine is that courts do not have jurisdiction to examine an issue unless a substantial controversy of "sufficient immediacy and reality" exists between parties of adverse legal interests. *Maryland Cas. Co. v Pacific Coal and Oil Co.*, 312 US 270, 273 (1941). This allows courts to avoid considering matters involving future events that may or may not occur. The controversy in a case must be immediately present and involve a real, and not speculative, injury to a party. *Carstens v Lamm*, 543 F Supp 68, 76 (D Colo 1982).

this factual investigation is funded primarily by the parties, not the public. If trial follows, the arguments and the evidence presented to judges and juries must fulfill extensive rules of procedure, decorum, and evidence. These rules are complex and, therefore, expensive to understand and fulfill. This expensive presentation is again made and funded primarily by the litigating parties.

The costs of participation in the adjudicative process, like the costs of participation in the market and political processes, are largely information costs. In the adjudicative process, the formalities and complexities require such a significant accumulation of knowledge and experience that the virtually universal manner of dealing with them is to hire an expert — the lawyer. Thus, although litigants can, in theory, represent themselves in court, few litigate their interests without the significant, indeed often dominating, presence of a hired lawyer with expertise in the particular area of law. Lawyers are hired as the least expensive (but certainly not inexpensive) way to deal with the daunting information costs of litigation.

By contrast, consumers and voters often face a far less expensive road to registering their needs in the market or the political process. The market and the political process offer many informal inroads. In many circumstances, voters and consumers do not even have to act in order to have their views reflected in the relevant process. Where either producers or politicians believe that significant consumer or voter interest exists, they shape their behavior accordingly. Even if these consumer or voter interests are dispersed and small per capita, even a modicum of willingness to purchase goods or to cast ballots is often sufficient for producers and politicians to discover this willingness and serve it. Pollsters are employed by politicians and producers alike. Through the use of propaganda or advertising, politicians and producers can stimulate or articulate a need only subconsciously felt by consumers or voters. As we have seen, they may also create or manipulate such needs. The market and political processes are geared to aggressively react to consumer or voter needs (real or created) because producers and politicians, unlike judges and juries, depend for their livelihood on responding to these needs.

In effect, the market and the political processes invite anyone with a problem to stop by and let their interest be known — sharpening demand with sales pitches and media exposure and meeting it with twenty-four-hour service, drive-up windows, or even home delivery. On the other hand, the standoffish courts, operating at remote locations, require anyone with a grievance to bring along someone who speaks the language of the judges and who knows how to meet all their difficult requirements. Even if no one stops by, the political process can act through the independent legislator, perhaps motivated by his or her perception of the public interest, but the similarly motivated judge can do nothing until a litigant takes the initiative.

From a social standpoint, the greater insulation of judges from the various pressures, produced in part by the presence of all the formalities, provides an important source of comparative advantage for the adjudicative process. This independence provides judges with the opportunity to shape social decisions without some of the biases and pressures that distort other institutions. But the threshold costs of litigation, interacting with the distribution of stakes, can keep the courts from a given social issue or from large sets of social issues. Although issues of competence and physical capacity may also significantly proscribe judicial activity, these factors often pale in importance to the impact of the dynamics of litigation in determining whether and to what extent any social issue will be considered by the adjudicative process.

PARTICIPATION AND INDEPENDENCE

To better understand how the dynamics of litigation affect the type of social issues that reach the adjudicative process, I look to the same participation-centered approach that was used to understand politics and the market. I use the simple typology of the distribution of stakes employed in the previous chapters — uniform high stakes (concentrated), uniform low stakes (dispersed), and the skewed distribution (part concentrated, part dispersed). For present purposes, I focus primarily on litigation between private parties. The unique qualities of the adjudicative process, especially relative to the political process, show up most clearly in private litigation since litigation instituted by the government is itself an aspect of the political process.

Uniform Low Stakes

Issues characterized by the uniform low stakes distribution would be very unlikely to find their way into the adjudicative process. The uniform low distribution means both dispersed defendants and dispersed plaintiffs — or, more exactly given the high probability of inaction, dispersed *potential* plaintiffs and dispersed *potential* defendants. As we shall see in the discussion of the skewed distribution, even where the interests are dispersed on only one side, the by-now familiar problems of information and collective action aggravated by the high costs of litigation severely reduce the chances of litigation. Where the interests are highly dispersed on all sides, litigation disappears.

Various forms of pollution where both the sources and the victims are widespread are familiar examples. These forms of non-point pollution can be contrasted with forms of pollution where the impacts are more concentrated on both sides, such as the situation in *Boomer,* or where they are at least more concentrated on one side, such as the point-source pollution of the Hudson River Valley by a few cement plants. As we saw in the discussion of *Boomer,* even in the latter case, litigation is unlikely. Private litigation of non-point pollution, especially where the adverse effects are also widespread, is nonexistent.

Non-point-source pollution with widespread effects, however, is not the most important or most dramatic example of a uniform low stakes issue. That honor goes to classic public goods issues like the establishment and funding of national defense. Public goods involve interests dispersed over most of the population. Although the social (aggregate) benefits can be vast, the per capita benefits are small — especially in comparison to the costs of production. In addition, excluding noncontributors from enjoying the good is impossible. The costs of litigation and enforcement are so high, the per capita stakes so small, and the free riding associated with the funding of the litigation so endemic that it is impossible to even imagine resolving public goods issues in the adjudicative process. Although issues of law and order and even national defense are litigated, this litigation takes place only after another institution — the political process — has made the basic public goods decisions. In such a situation, the government becomes a concentrated interest consolidating the low stakes on at least one side of the issue. We will come to this case subsequently. The basic lesson, however, is that, even if judges wanted to resolve public goods issues, they could not do so without radically changing the incentives for litigation. The dynamics of adjudication place an important range of social issues far beyond the reach of the adjudicative process.

Uniform High Stakes

We can turn now to the uniform high stakes distribution — small numbers of actors with high per capita stakes. At least at first blush, one would expect that private litigation is likely where the stakes are uniformly high (where there are a few highly impacted potential plaintiffs and a few highly impacted potential defendants). The higher the stakes of potential plaintiffs, the more likely that each will be willing to bear the high costs. Litigation is more attractive and easier in the uniform high distribution than in the uniform low distribution. That does not mean, however, that high stakes issues are most likely to be adjudicated as opposed to being resolved by some other institution. All the institutions are most responsive in the context of a uniform high distribution and, therefore, at least in theory, the relationship between high stakes and adjudication is equivocal.

In fact, most high stakes issues are not resolved in the adjudicative process because, although the adjudicative process is at its best in the presence of high stakes, the market often works even better. Sometimes parties avoid controversies that might result in litigation by working out their problems through a series of intra-market arrangements. They can avoid litigation through complex contracts that detail contingencies and set out specific responses. More commonly, high stakes parties who have continuing relationships work out any unforeseen differences through informal negotiation or informal governance mechanisms, without any thought of litigation.[3] As a general matter, the market firm can be considered as an attempt to mitigate or channel potential controversies by bringing them into a hierarchical arrangement that disposes of them internally by fiat. As we saw in chapter 4, uniform high stakes is primarily the bailiwick of intra-market institutional choice.

This analysis certainly does not mean that high stakes issues are less likely to be litigated than low stakes issues. Most issues that are litigated are high stakes issues. The implication of the analysis is that, as a general matter, we can expect a large percentage of high stakes issues to be resolved through market arrangements even though, without these arrangements, they would be prime candidates for adjudication. The parties will arrange their affairs so as both to avoid litigation and to minimize the impacts of legal directives. Again, a range of issues is kept from the courts by the dynamics of adjudication and institutional choice. Judges will not be able to closely control the outcomes in these settings.

Skewed Distribution of Stakes

Having discussed the uniform low and uniform high stakes issues, we are left with the skewed distribution — dispersed on one side and concentrated on the other. Here judges through their control of the rules of class action can affect the extent to which the adjudication process will see these

---

3. See Stewart Macaulay, *Non-Contractual Relations in Business: A Preliminary Study,* 28 Am Sociological Rev 55 (1963); Thomas Palay, *Comparative Institutional Economics: The Governance of Rail Freight Contracting,* 13 J Legal Stud 265 (1984).

cases. The propensity to litigate is more likely to be affected by the availability of class actions where the dispersion is among potential plaintiffs rather than among potential defendants. The problems of effectively enforcing at least injunctive relief against dispersed defendants are severe because enforcement costs such as monitoring and litigating violations of the injunction rise with the number of defendants covered.[4] The rules of class action do not much affect these problems. The cost of controlling thousands of non-point-source polluters is very high no matter what the procedural rules of adjudication.

Where there are concentrated potential defendants and dispersed potential plaintiffs, the class action mechanism can be more effectively employed to increase the chance of adjudication. The class action promotes litigation by providing a way to pool or cover litigation expenses from some source other than the pocket of a single member of the plaintiff group. The expenses of the class action are paid from the collective award before the remaining amount is distributed to the larger group. Where there is only injunctive relief, the courts are often empowered to order the losing defendant to pay the plaintiffs' litigation expenses.

Although in theory the class action mechanism could compensate for the decrease in litigation due to the dispersion of stakes, in reality it often will not do so. More important for our purposes, the shortfalls in litigation and the inadequacies of the class action mechanism to solve them become more pronounced as dispersion and numbers increase. As we have seen, the prospect of inaction and, therefore, of no response from any member of the class increases as dispersion increases. Very dispersed claims with no concentrated subgroups of higher stakes often go unrepresented in the adjudicative process because the members of the low stakes group do not even recognize the existence of the injury or the availability of the class action recovery. Even where an individual or small subset possesses sufficient stakes to recognize the injury and the availability of the class action mechanism, they may free ride, waiting for others to bring the action.

4. Even for damage actions, where the injurer group is very widely dispersed, collection costs are immense. Although these can be reduced by arbitrarily allowing the collection of all or most of the damages from a few of the most accessible injurers, there are problems of both fairness and effectiveness. Thus, to use the non-point source pollution example, where each polluter contributed a small fraction of the total impact on the plaintiff, it would seem disproportionate to force one injurer to bear all the damage award. It would also be unlikely to have much affect on future pollution because most polluters would not be faced with much danger of paying such awards, especially where most such polluters would be unable to pay and would, therefore, be immune from ever bearing such a concentrated judgment. I return to the issue of the choice of defendants for collection in the discussion of tort reform in the next chapter.

Greater dispersion can greatly increase the costs of bringing a class action. Greater numbers increase the likelihood of heterogeneity in the class and, therefore, increase the chance of problems with representativeness which, in turn, increase the expenses of litigation to deal with these problems.[5] In addition to increasing the costs of defending the validity of the class, concerns about representativeness and fair treatment for those class members not actually active in the litigation increase the likelihood that judges will require individual notice to each of these inactive members. This notice, whatever its importance, increases the costs of litigation — a cost that obviously increases with the number in the class. Because risk and expense go up as the dispersion and numbers go up, any shortfalls in the cost reimbursement mechanism, such as the insufficient allowance for risk in the award of expenses, are magnified, making class actions less likely as size and dispersion increase.[6]

5. The issue of representativeness concerns whether or how well the interests of the dispersed group will be represented by the representative plaintiffs and their lawyers. To the extent that the lawyer for a class or the class representative have different incentives than the dormant class members, litigation results may not be in the best interests of the class. Lawyers may settle too easily in order to maximize the lawyer's fee component of the settlement. Class representatives, who have different agendas than other members of the class, can undermine class interests. One can even imagine fraudulent actions in which would-be defendants manufacture a plaintiff class that generously settles the action in the defendant's favor and precludes real plaintiffs from subsequent action. The usual safeguards of the adversarial process weaken in the face of the dormancy of dispersed interests.

These concerns about representativeness, however justifiable, inevitably increase with the size and dispersion of the class. Challenges to the representativeness of named plaintiffs are likely to increase as the group size increases and, therefore, the possibility of differences among class members increases. These challenges add to litigation costs and threaten the success of the action. For a discussion of the impact of increasingly restrictive representativeness requirements on class actions in the employment discrimination area, see Judith J. Johnson, *Rebuilding the Barriers: The Trend in Employment Discrimination Class Actions,* 19 Colum Human Rts L Rev 1 (1987).

6. The Supreme Court of the United States seriously restricted class actions, especially for highly dispersed interests, in three central cases, *Snyder v Harris,* 394 US 332 (1969) (holding that separate and distinct claims presented by and for various claimants in a federal diversity action may not be added together to satisfy the requisite jurisdictional amount in controversy), *Zahn v International Paper Co.,* 414 US 291 (1974) (holding that individual notice must be sent to all class members whose names and addresses can be ascertained through reasonable effort despite a prohibitively high cost of such notification), and *Eisen v Carlisle & Jacquelin,* 417 US 156 (1974) (holding that each plaintiff in a Rule 23(b)(3) class action, not just named plaintiffs, must satisfy the jurisdictional amount requirement and that any plaintiff not meeting that requirement must be dropped from the lawsuit). For a discussion of the status of class actions following these decisions, see American Bar Association Section of Litigation, *Class Actions: In the Wake of Eisen III & IV* (1977).

The significant expenses associated with notice and representativeness, which increase with dispersion, make the adjudication of highly dispersed claims unlikely. The much trumpeted decline of class actions in general seems to indicate an increasing deterioration in the representation of highly dispersed interests in private adjudication.[7] With the exception of occasional "public interest" actions, widely dispersed interests seem largely absent from the courts.

In summary, the interaction of stakes with the high costs of participation molds the character of adjudicative decision-making. A wide range of social issues, roughly described as "public goods" issues, will never be adjudicated because they involve a uniform low (highly dispersed) distribution of stakes. Such issues reach the courts only when the political process has already shouldered most of the decision-making responsibility and, by its presence, provided a concentrated interest. Even where stakes are uniformly high, many issues will be settled by transaction rather than adjudication. In the world of skewed distributions, the chance of adjudication depends on the rules for class action. The chances of such litigation seem small where either side is highly dispersed. Although the independence of judges is important, systemic forces, paradoxically magnified by the structural features that produce independence, significantly constrain the influence of judges on social policy. Judges and legal commentators must integrate this understanding into their choices and proposals or suffer unexpected and often unwanted results.

The dynamics of litigation and the systemic exclusion, or at least underrepresentation, of important social issues in the adjudicative process forces some doubt about the validity, or at least the robustness, of the basic assertion of Posnerian law and economics that "judge-made rules tend to be efficiency-promoting while those made by legislatures tend to be efficiency-reducing."[8] Even if one were to accept uncritically the evidence Richard Posner marshals to support this assertion,[9] the evidence does not establish the efficiency of the adjudicative versus the political process or, as some

7. See Douglas Martin, *The Rise and Fall of the Class Action Law Suit*, New York Times (Jan. 8, 1988), quoting remarks of Paul Carrington, official reporter of the Federal Rules of Civil Procedure, that "class actions had their day in the sun and kind of petered out." See also Johnson, 19 Colum Human Rts L Rev (cited in n. 5) and John J. Donohue and Peter Siegelman, *The Changing Nature of Employment Discrimination Litigation*, 43 Stan L Rev 983 (1991).

8. Richard Posner, *Economic Analysis of Law* at 523 (4th ed 1992).

9. I critically examine an earlier version of this assertion and the evidence marshaled for it in Neil Komesar, *In Search of a General Approach to Legal Analysis: A Comparative Institutional Alternative*, 79 Mich L Rev 1350, 1356–62 (1981).

seem to suggest, the substitution of the adjudicative for the political process.[10] It only shows that, in a few instances, adjudicative decisions improved efficiency and legislative determinations decreased efficiency (at least relative to some ideal). Although the substitution of the adjudicative process for the political process might well improve efficiency and other important social goals in some situations, a proposition I will consider subsequently in several specific contexts, any wholesale declaration of adjudicative superiority seriously ignores the inherent systemic capabilities of the two processes.

As the earlier discussion showed, no matter how poorly the political process handles basic public goods determinations, those decisions could not be handled better by the adjudicative process — not without altering the very character of adjudication. The same adjudicative inertness associated with classic public goods is, to a significant degree, present for a broad range of issues involving uniform low stakes distributions (such as non-point-source pollution with widespread damage) and even for issues involving skewed distributions (such as point-source pollution with widespread damage). When we add the problems of judicial competence and scale, addressed subsequently, it is impossible to associate resource allocation efficiency with courts and inefficiency with legislatures in general.[11] Contrary to the assertions of Posner and others, a large range of legislative rule-making promotes efficiency *relative to the alternatives* — the only relevant way in which efficiency can be determined.

Adjudication and the Shifted Distribution

The previous discussion showed the adjudicative process faring badly in several institutional comparisons. As a general matter, where the adjudicative process is compared to the market or political process, one or the other alternative processes is often superior because of the dynamics of institutional participation. In some settings, however, these dynamics provide the adjudicative process with significant comparative institutional advantages relative to the political and market processes.

The most straightforward examples of this advantage involve the social

10. Robert Cooter and Daniel Rubinfeld, *Economic Analysis of Legal Disputes and their Resolution*, 27 J of Econ Lit 1067, 1093–94 (1989).

11. In chapter 8, I consider analogous overreaching claims for the judiciary outside the context of resource allocation efficiency, in particular in connection with Richard Epstein's position on the Takings Clause and the general position of the fundamental values analysts.

goal of safety or prevention of accidents, where the adjudicative process, operating through private actions for damages, sometimes faces a different and more favorable distribution of stakes than does either the market or the political process. The adjudicative process faces a more favorable distribution because of the retrospective focus of private damage actions as opposed to the prospective focus of the market and political processes.

This favorable difference occurs where a potential injury has a very low probability of occurring but carries with it significant loss if the event occurs. Before the injury, there may be many low stakes, potential victims. Each potential victim has low stakes because the probability of the bad outcome is so low. After an injury has occurred, however, the class of victims is no longer the same as the large class of potential victims with their small per capita stakes. There is now a small class of actual victims with large per capita stakes.

The crucial distinction here is between ex ante and ex post distributions of stakes — the distributions of stakes before and after the injury. In most institutional settings, the relevant actors are potential victims and injurers. In the market, they are the parties that buy and sell safety or insurance. In the political process, they are the parties who seek or oppose safety or insurance regulation.

In the adjudicative process, however, damage actions are largely retrospective. It is actual victims and injurers who are the litigants. A plaintiff must actually have suffered damage to bring damage actions, and the damages measured are actual not potential. As we shall see, these damage actions can have significant prospective effects as their threat affects *potential* injurers and, thereby, increases the safety of *potential* victims. But *actual* not potential victims and injurers litigate and produce the signal to potential injurers. Where we have high stakes actual victims, we have an increased possibility of triggering the adjudicative mechanism or process because the large individual stakes justify individual private actions (often as joint ventures with contingent-fee lawyers).

This comparative advantage exists, however, only where there is a "shifted distribution" — where the victims' low distribution ex ante becomes a high uniform distribution ex post. This shift does not always accompany actual injury. A low distribution ex ante may remain a low distribution ex post. The actual damage done, as well as the potential damage, may affect many victims but at a relatively low per capita level. Many examples of air or water pollution have this configuration of damage. *Boomer*'s victims of pollution in the Hudson River Valley — both actual and potential — fit this configuration. Here all the problems of adjudication in the face of dispersed stakes remain for damages actions as well as injunctive actions.

This existence of the shifted distribution provides a powerful advantage for the adjudicative process relative to both the market and the political process.[12] In chapter 6, I argue that the configuration of stakes in the shifted distribution creates both a significant comparative advantage for private damage actions in settings like product and service safety and, in turn, a potential need for judicial protection of that advantage against the political process — protection that might even produce strict constitutional judicial review of tort reform legislation.

A more subtle and qualified form of shifted distribution operates in some types of public law adjudication — adjudication that questions the validity of government actions such as statutes or administrative decisions. Where the shift occurs, it is more likely that government action will be challenged in litigation, and, therefore, subject to judicial review, than when the shift does not occur. As such, this shift can affect the configuration of both constitutional and statutory interpretation.

As we saw in chapter 3, when faced with a skewed distribution, the political process can manifest severe distortions of two opposite kinds — severe majoritarian or minoritarian bias. Where the skewed distribution produces majoritarian bias, the resulting action by the political process converts the skewed distribution into a uniform high distribution. The side that wins in the political process does not have to muster the resources to litigate the constitutionality of the resulting legislation. The state will bear the burden of defending the legislation in court. Where a dispersed majority prevails in the political process at the expense of a concentrated minority, the state is confronted with concentrated interests; as a result, there are well-represented positions on both sides of the legislation. In effect, political victory converts the dispersed majority into a single concentrated entity — the government that passed the legislation — and, in turn, converts a skewed distribution into a uniform high distribution.

12. As we shall see in chapter 6, if the social goal sought is increased safety or prevention, the advantages for the courts may exist only where a skewed distribution is converted into a uniform high or concentrated distribution. Where an ex ante uniform low distribution is converted into a uniform high distribution, we get the increase in adjudicative activity. To achieve the goal of prevention, however, the deterrence signal must not only be sent by active private prosecution. It must also be received. Low stakes for potential injuries (the target of the deterrent signal) decreases this prospect.

The same conversion does not occur, however, where the political process suffers from minoritarian bias because the losers are the dispersed majority. In effect, the distribution has not shifted. When the concentrated interest wins in the political process, the resulting distribution of stakes facing the adjudicative process is still skewed rather than uniform high. It is less likely to be litigated because we have a dispersed interest on one side.

This analysis has some important implications for constitution making and constitutional law. Judicial review of legislation can serve as a means to counteract or deal with political malfunctions such as majoritarian and minoritarian bias. The effectiveness of such review, however, depends on whether the government action will be challenged in court. The courts cannot review what they do not see. The analysis of litigation presented in this book strongly suggests that concentrated high stakes victims are more likely to litigate than dispersed low stakes interests. Thus, roughly speaking, if the courts offer protection to both harmed majorities and harmed minorities, the harmed minority is more likely to actively seek that protection. On this basis, majoritarian bias is more likely to be corrected by judicial review than is minoritarian bias.

A more subtle examination of the characteristics of the underlying distributions qualifies the degree, though not the existence, of this difference between the propensities to adjudicate the effects of majoritarian and minoritarian bias. The existence of higher stakes subgroups within the low stakes majority creates the possibility that the interests of the dispersed majority will find some representation in constitutional litigation. The degree to which such subgroups will litigate depends on factors we discussed earlier such as the tendency to free ride (which in turn depends on the number of higher stakes members within the majority and how high these stakes are) and the rules of class action (in particular the adequacy of awarded lawyers fees). Even in the most favorable case, however, there will be less chance of adjudication and less effort expended on that litigation where the losing interests are more dispersed than where they are more concentrated.[13] The implications of this form

---

13. The same insights apply to judicial activities outside of constitutional law, such as statutory interpretation. For example, Guido Calabresi has suggested that courts should review and eliminate "obsolete" legislation. Guido Calabresi, *A Common Law for the Age of Statutes* (1982). Such an expansive strategy for statutory interpretation may have surprising results when filtered through the dynamics of litigation. Many of

of shifted distribution for the judicial role in constitutional law will be examined more closely in chapter 7.

COMPETENCE AND SCALE

Any discussion of the advantages or disadvantages of the adjudicative process must include consideration of two other institutional dimensions—competence and scale. By competence, I mean the ability of trials and of triers (judges and juries) to investigate, understand, and make the substantive social decisions that may come to them. By scale, I mean the resources or budget available to the judiciary and the constraints on the expansion of the size of the adjudicative process. Scale and competence interact with each other and with the determinants of litigation (stakes and costs) to determine the institutional ability of the adjudicative process. Thus, for example, the comparative advantages of the shifted distributions associated with protecting political minorities and granting private damages may be less attractive when these shifted distributions occur in the context of substantive issues that severely strain the abilities of judges and juries or require disproportionately large allocations of scarce judicial resources. Institutional choice involves tradeoffs between competence, scale, and the systemic biases associated with the interaction of stakes and costs.

Competence

Various doubts have been raised about the competence of judges and juries as decision-makers: doubts about the competence of juries to understand highly technical issues and evidence in complex, large-scale litigation;[14] doubts about the ability of judges to handle complex and sensitive

---

Calabresi's examples of obsolete legislation appear to be instances of minoritarian bias. Because the losers in such legislation are often dispersed majorities, less of this legislation may be reviewed than Calabresi supposes. Instead, legislation by which concentrated minorities have been adversely affected would be overrepresented in the sample of legislation that the Calabresian program would face. To the extent that instances of majoritarian legislative victories would be overrepresented in the Calabresian program, the courts would either be picking up instances of majoritarian bias missed in constitutional judicial review or, more likely, perversely reviewing instances in which majority influence was finally able to overcome minoritarian bias. Concentrated minorities may, in effect, get another bite at an apple of which they have already had more than their share. Contrary to Calabresi's hopes, his proposal for judicial statutory review might well aggravate rather than cure minoritarian bias in the production of statutes.

14. Serious criticism of juries has been around for quite a long time. See, Jerome Frank, *Law and the Modern Mind* 178–85 (1936). For more contemporary discussions concerning jury competence, see William J. Luneberg and Mark Nordenberg, *Specially*

issues concerning subjects such as foreign affairs or national defense;[15] and doubts about the ability of the adjudicative process to deal with large-scale social policy issues where there are many conflicting interests and a continuing need for implementation and oversight.[16] There is little doubt that juries have very limited technical expertise and sophistication. Jurors are randomly chosen from the general population, and individual jurors are often chosen in the voir dire explicitly to avoid expertise in the specific technical issue of the case. These inexpert juries are then asked to listen to the technical and complex testimony of conflicting expert witnesses and decide difficult substantive issues. Similarly, trial and appellate judges formally trained only as lawyers and coming from a wide variety of practice backgrounds are regularly asked to judge the facts in and fashion the rules for complex litigation. These judges, both trial and appellate, usually are not asked to specialize in one type of controversy and, therefore, do not obtain the expertise that such frequent exposure would bring.

Juries and judges can easily be unfavorably contrasted with the technically more expert bureaucrats of administrative agencies who, like juries and judges, serve as fact-finders and implementers of rules and standards. Similarly, recent suggestions for specialized courts and for limitations on large-scale interventions into political process decision-making are reactions to the limited technical ability of generalist judges.[17]

Qualified Juries and Expert Nonjury Tribunals: Alternative for Coping with the Complexities of Modern Civil Litigation, 67 Va L Rev 887 (1981); Peter Huber, *Liability: The Legal Revolution and its Consequences* 41–44, 50–51 (1988); Committee on the Federal Courts of the New York State Bar Association, *Improving Jury Comprehension in Complex Civil Litigation,* 62 St John's L Rev 549 (1988). For a thoughtful discussion of the issues involved in the critique of jury performance, see Stephen Daniels, *The Question of Jury Competence and the Politics of Civil Justice Reform: Symbols, Rhetoric and Agenda Building,* 52 L & Contemp Probs 269 (1989). In general, see Symposium, *Is the Jury Competent?* 52 L & Contemp Probs (1989).

15. We saw this issue in the context of the *Pentagon Papers* case discussed in chapter 2. See also Fritz Scharpf, *Judicial Review and the Political Question: A Functional Analysis,* 75 Yale LJ 517 (1966).

16. See Donald Horowitz, *The Courts and Social Policy* (1977).

17. For some suggestions concerning specialized courts, see Richard L. Revesz, *Specialized Courts and the Administrative Lawmaking System,* 139 U Pa L Rev 1111 (1990); Ellen R. Jordan, *Specialized Courts: A Choice?* 76 Nw U L Rev 745 (1981); Daniel J. Meador, *An Appellate Court Dilemma and a Solution through Subject Matter Organization,* 16 U Mich J L Ref 471 (1983). For a thorough discussion of the differing views concerning specialized courts, see Richard Posner, *The Federal Courts: Crisis and Reform* 147–60 (1985); Daniel P. Currie and Frank I. Goodman, *Judicial Review of Federal Administrative Action: The Quest for the Optimum Forum,* 75 Colum L Rev 1, 63–85 (1975); Paul D. Carrington et al., *Justice on Appeal* 168–72 (1976).

From a comparative institutional standpoint, this lack of expertise may be discomforting, but the criticism is, as it stands, only a parade of horribles. It is single institutional. Comparative institutional analysis requires the parallel consideration of the institutional alternatives — in this case, more expert administrative agencies and specialized courts. From the perspective of technical expertise, these agencies with their narrower scope and more specialized staffing are superior to generalist trial court judges and randomly chosen juries. In turn, trial court judges who see many trials and the resolution of at least some similar issues and who are in general highly educated can be seen as superior to the less educated, less experienced, and less permanent jury.

These same factors, however, provide advantages to admittedly less expert juries, particularly in the world of the skewed distribution. The very characteristics that make juries less expert make them less subject to systematic influence and bias. The transient jury is not a good target for one-sided efforts at influence associated with the skewed distribution. The constantly changing jury is difficult to influence through continuous long-term contact and propaganda. The parties are forced to sway the jury by advocacy in the more formally confined adversarial process, where opposing parties have more equal opportunities to present their viewpoints. In addition, the random jury selection process makes any attempt to staff the jury with cronies extremely difficult if not impossible. Although inducement — most likely in the form of bribes — is not unknown, it is difficult both because juries are, to some degree, separated from the general public during deliberation and because the costs of bribery, including possible criminal sanctions, are seldom justified when the bribery will cover only one case rather than a set of cases. Administrative agencies, in contrast, are fixed targets hearing many cases, and are easier and more worthwhile to influence via education, bribery, or restaffing.[18]

In their random choice from the general population and their greater resistance to minoritarian bias, juries provide a form of majoritarian influence within the adjudicative process; therefore, their use must be considered in terms of the character of the social issue to be decided. As a general matter, where the conditions for strong minoritarian bias may be present, the jury's advantages are significant and may outweigh lack of expertise

18. Somewhat the same factors are present, albeit in a much more subtle fashion, in the choice between trial court and jury. Trial courts are more fixed targets for influence than are juries, and their expertise, though greater than juries, is not so great as that at least pretended for administrative agencies.

even in a complex setting.[19] I return to this tradeoff between degree of bias and degree of expertise in the next chapter.

The majoritarian character of the jury is sometimes unattractive. Consider for example the resolution of legal claims that members of a targeted minority have been discriminated against by the majority. A randomly chosen jury may be a subset of the injuring group. Here the more distant judge or even the somewhat more distanced administrative agency may be less subject to bias as well as more technically expert.

A less noticed but more troubling and important tradeoff between information and independence in the adjudicative process is that insulation separates judges from a great deal of information about the desires and needs of the public. In politics, public officials must understand the wants and needs of the general public or at least powerful parts of the general public to remain in office or obtain higher office. These interests link political officials to the populace and provide them with the most robust and dramatic information on the central question of desires and needs. This information is essential to public policy; it provides the "weights" to be given the various opposing public policy positions or options. The problem with all this informality and interdependence is that under the wrong conditions — particularly, the skewed distribution — these informal channels for presentation or revelation of desires can carry a severely distorted view of public needs.

By contrast, judges and juries stand aloof. They depend on others to convince them by evidence and reason, but they do not depend on these others for their jobs and livelihood. The adversarial process attempts to equalize the representation of positions and the delivery of information by assuring that both positions are at least formally represented and that information reaching judge and jury is confined to that brought them by opposing advocates.

The tradeoff is between a political process that integrates far more information but with a more significant risk of bias and an adjudicative process that suppresses information but decreases distortions in its presentation. The adjudicative process hears and considers less, but is more evenhanded in what it hears and considers. The price of evenhandedness is most dramatically revealed in that important range of social issues where

19. It is common to associate the jury's "political function" only with criminal cases. See Posner, *Economic Analysis* at 549 (cited in n. 8). But as the text indicates, the jury's role as an institutional counterweight may be as important in civil actions where minoritarian influence might bias more permanent decision-makers.

the adjudicative process hears nothing—a significant disability traceable to the high cost of participation.[20] This tradeoff between information and evenhandedness is among the most difficult issues in institutional choice.

Scale

The implications of increasing or decreasing the physical capacity (the scale) of any institution are important in determining the ability of that institution. However, considerations of size, in particular the implications of severe constraints on growth, play such an important role in the adjudicative process and so strongly affect inter-institutional choices that they require special consideration. The constraints on the size of the adjudicative process and the implications of these constraints on judicial choices are more obvious and dramatic than any comparable constraints on the size of the market and political processes. In fact, it is the relative ease with which the market and political processes expand that creates the demands that strain the physical capacity of the adjudicative process.

Embedded in the expansion of these other institutions are several factors that drive the demand for judicial resources. General demographic changes, such as increased population and increased gross national product, often operating through the market and the political process, increase the demand on the judiciary. Increased population means more people to be injured. Increased gross national product means increased commercial transacting and with it the chance for more disputes and litigation.

Increases in population and GNP also increase governmental activity, and with it, the demand for adjudicative activity. Growth in legislation or in public enforcement of existing legislation increases the role of courts as implementers of legislation. This growth also increases the demand for the courts as reviewers of governmental action—either by their statutory

20. These modes of gathering information can also be contrasted with the more robust, self-interested, less formal world of the market. In the market, the exaggeration of the adversarial process is controlled in part by the need to put one's money where one's claims are. Claims that something is more or less valuable must be matched with offers and acceptances. In the perfect market, all necessary information is provided by those value-backed transactions. In the real market, opportunism and bounded rationality allow for significant manipulation and obfuscation. But market decision-makers are driven to get through these smoke screens by the very self-interest from which the adjudicative process attempts to insulate its officials. Independent investigation and search are common characteristics of market decision-making. The comparable distortions occur where transaction costs (and their interaction with transaction benefits) prevent representation of some interest in existing transactions.

authority over administrative agencies or by their constitutional authority over legislation. The number of governmental transactions and even more narrowly the number of governmental regulatory decisions have reached a virtually uncountable level (and these, in turn, are quite likely very small in number when compared with the total number of private transactions taking place periodically).

Broad demographic factors like increased population and economic activity or broad changes in political outputs do not, however, translate simply or linearly into increased demand for judicial activity, because many institutional interactions confound this translation. Thus, for example, increased population and increased economic activity may manifest themselves in improvement in some of the market mechanisms that lower transaction costs and, therefore, increase the attractiveness of market versus adjudicative solutions. Technological changes, such as the advent of information gathering and presentation in the computer age, can make prevention or resolution of disputes easier in some contexts. Alterations in the underlying parameters of the political process may also decrease disputes about political outcomes. For example, some equalization in political influence across groups or regions may operate to decrease political tensions or, at least, make them less dramatic and more complex to monitor.[21]

For all of these qualifications, however, a significant increase in demand for adjudication is inherent in the sizable growth in the market and politics. The existence of this demand, however, does not necessarily translate into increased litigation. Whether and to what extent this demand manifests itself in increased litigation depends on the capacity of the courts to process more litigation and the methods the courts employ to accommodate the supply of and demand for adjudication.

One obvious means for dealing with the increased demand for adjudication is to increase the size or capacity of the adjudicative process. The federal and state judiciaries have increased in size. The numbers of judges and in particular of non-judge personnel have increased significantly. The

---

21. Consider here the conflicting possibilities associated with greater population mobility. Mobility in its simplest sense may decrease the use of the court system by allowing an alternative of simply moving away from an offending political jurisdiction. This is an example of the substitution of exit for voice. See Albert O. Hirschman, *Exit, Voice and Loyalty* (1970) and Charles M. Tiebout, *A Pure Theory of Local Expenditures*, 64 J Pol Econ 416 (1956).

judiciary, however, has been unable to expand to keep up with the increases elsewhere, and, more importantly, it is unlikely to do so in the future.

The most important constraint on the expansion of the adjudicative process stems from the central role of judges, particularly of the appellate judge.[22] Independence and competence make substitution of non-judges for judges difficult. To some degree, such substitution does occur. Judicial clerks and, to some degree, clerical help ease the load of judges. In addition, creative trial judges have called upon such substitutes as masters and magistrates to help them; indeed, "managerial" judges have created various helpers such as plaintiffs' committees or community advisors to aid when large-scale litigation requires an ongoing role for the trial court in the oversight of important public functions.[23] Whatever these successes, however, the central role of the independent judge makes it very doubtful that adjudicative capacity—the size or scale of the courts—can be expanded as easily as the capacities of the market and the political process without seriously changing the character of the adjudicative process.

The main bottleneck here is the appellate court structure. This central component of the adjudicative process, meant to articulate the rules under which adjudication takes place and to define the rights that trigger litigation, is difficult to expand. Each judicial system within the United States has at its apex a supreme court. These courts are staffed by a small set of judges, often nine like the Supreme Court of the United States. The most obvious reform, increasing the number of judges on these high courts, does not easily or even necessarily increase the output of this court. While

22. A more subtle constraint on the expansion of the adjudicative process is its dependence on public funding. In order to expand, the courts must receive additional funding from the political process. Courts, especially in their role as constitutional reviewers of legislation, are in significant tension with the political process. This tension creates a source of constraint on judicial size or at least on judicial capacity to oppose the political process.

Although judges individually may be independent of the political process, the judiciary as a whole is not. Where some judicial functions such as constitutional judicial review are antagonistic to the political process, this dependence can translate biases in the political process into systemic biases in the adjudicative process. By constraining the size of the judiciary while at the same time increasing the amount of judicial activity in non-antagonistic areas (for example, by passing legislation that requires more activity of the courts), the political process is in position to decrease the ability of the adjudicative process to confront the political process.

23. For a detailed description of the use of these devices in the area of school desegregation, see Michael Rebell and Arthur Block, *Educational Policy Making and the Courts: An Empirical Study of Judicial Activism* (1982).

an increase in judges would decrease the per judge load of opinion writing, it would not decrease the time and effort necessary to reach a collective decision by this body. In fact, increasing the numbers would probably make such collective decisions more difficult and time consuming.[24]

Increasing the number of intermediate courts of appeals can serve to decrease the strain on these supreme courts. Here again, however, expansion of these intermediate courts is limited. At some stage, conflicts among the views taken by these separate courts begin to create greater uncertainty and greater demands for resolution by the higher supreme court. The adjudicative process depends on hierarchical review and formal procedure as a means to insure that judges do not abuse their independence. These needs make the removal or resolution of conflicts and errors by higher courts a necessary component of the adjudicative process.

To some degree, subject matter specialization might also ease the strain on the highest courts. But to achieve any significant improvement, two problems must be dealt with. First, there is the problem of allocating by specialty. It is not easy to cabin or categorize most of the legal and public policy issues now subject (or potentially subject) to adjudication. Contracts, commercial law, constitutional law, and tort law litigation can each cover such a wide range of substantive subject matter that little would be gained in expertise by setting up courts for each category. These categories also overlap so often that specialized jurisdiction would produce a great deal of disputation about the coverage of each tribunal. As a general matter, broadening the categories would dilute the gains of specialization and narrowing the categories would lead to overlap in jurisdiction.

Second, and more important, specialization increases the potential for the bias associated with substituting "expert" judges for "general" judges. Like the substitution of administrative agencies for inexpert juries discussed earlier, specialized courts substituted for general courts are more likely to be subject to long-term influence by information provision and even by replacement than general courts. Courts become more attractive targets for special interest groups as their jurisdiction is narrowed. Investment in either propaganda or replacement is more productive for these interest groups when these efforts can be focused on a more narrowly defined group of judges. Where the conditions for serious minoritarian bias (or even majoritarian bias) are present, the movement from general to expert decision-makers can come at significant social cost.

---

24. See Richard Posner, *The Federal Courts* at 14 (cited in n. 17).

The failure to adequately expand the size of the adjudicative process produces the prospect of demand for adjudicative services greater than the existing capacity can meet. Such excess demand hardly supposes queues outside courthouse doors—although the much discussed and controversial litigation explosion often creates such an image.[25] The judicial process has a number of methods to deal with any excess demand on its capacity.[26]

25. The following are typical of the popular descriptions of the litigation explosion: "[J]udges . . . are now faced with . . . a virtual tidal wave of litigation. . . . [C]ourts have been burdened with ever-increasing numbers of both criminal and civil cases. Skyrocketing caseloads are stretching courts beyond their limits. In the federal district courts alone, over 228,000 cases were filed between June 30, 1981 and June 30, 1982, an increase of nearly 40 percent in only five years that a judge must decide. In human terms, this translates into an annual caseload approaching 450 cases per judge—more than one case every day. I ask how it is possible to keep this system from faltering under such conditions. . . . The strain on judicial resources is rapidly becoming a crisis of brobdingnagian proportions. A judge with too little time to consider carefully the merits of a case before him runs the risk of being transformed from a minister of justice into a stereotypical 'paper pusher.' We all react deeply to inefficient or overcrowded hospitals, but a certain lethargy sets in when the courts are overloaded, when rights are not being enforced because the cases cannot be heard, when decisions do not reflect the same individual care that we demand of a physician at all times." Irving Kaufman, *The Courts in Peril,* Miami Herald, Feb. 13, 1983.

"Look at the sheer number of disputes now flowing through our judicial system. . . . In 1989 alone, more than 18 million civil suits were filed in this country—one for every 10 adults—making us the most litigious society in the world. Once in courts, many litigants face excessive delays, some caused by overloaded court dockets." *Remarks by Vice President Dan Quayle before the American Bar Association,* Washington Post, Aug. 15, 1991.

"[T]he current [litigation] system is cruelly slow. Last year the backlog of personal-injury, product-liability and other civil damage suits in the Law Division of the Cook County Circuit Court reached 67,776 cases, 20 percent of them 5 years or older. Delays of 6 to 10 years between filing and trial are common." John McCarron, *Too Many Lawsuits Spoil Torts, Courts,* Chicago Tribune, May 19, 1991.

"The backdrop for Quayle's speech was the widely documented litigation explosion in the United States in recent decades. This frenzy of filings (18 million new lawsuits a year) has clogged the nation's courts, added a liability premium to the costs of products and health care, and burdened the competitiveness of American business." *The Costs of Lawyering,* The Christian Science Monitor, Aug. 19, 1991.

26. One theoretical method of rationing is to charge a "demand-clearing" price for judicial services. This increase in price might begin with charging litigants the "full" cost of litigation. Litigants do not pay the full costs of the adjudicative system they use. These costs are borne by the general taxpaying public. The failure to charge these costs eliminates a rationing device that could help balance demand and supply. The absence of these "full charges" in part reflects a desire to make the adjudicative process available to all—a lofty goal that we have seen largely goes unfulfilled. It is also rationalized by the existence of external social benefits usually in the form of the production of prece-

Each of these methods, however, has its own implications for the function-ing of the adjudicative process. These implications involve an interplay of competence, independence, and bias; in turn, each has implications for institutional choice.

Courts can control the extent and type of common law litigation by decreasing the chance of plaintiff's success or the amount of damages awarded if successful. Lowering these stakes decreases the number of claims where the stakes will exceed the threshold costs of litigation. In a parallel fashion, the courts can reduce the number of requests that they review governmental activity by setting out standards that increase the def-erence given to the reviewed entity. On the constitutional level, they can employ standards like "minimal scrutiny" that provide great deference to legislative outcomes. In reviews of administrative agency determinations, they can set out standards that provide greater deference to an agency's interpretation of statutes. These alterations in standards decrease the stakes of plaintiffs — in this instance usually by decreasing the probability of suc-cess — and, therefore, decrease the number of instances in which stakes exceed the threshold costs of litigation. Similarly, the courts can decrease litigation by requiring more forms and procedures, by narrowing the types of cases acceptable for adjudication, by narrowing standing or by increas-ing the requirements for class action. In part, such a narrowing of case type can also be seen as confining the judicial process to issues with which judges are more familiar or to issues more likely to have better defined litigants and more straightforward and thorough presentations.

Finally, the courts can decrease the demand on their resources by articu-lating and imposing simpler rules and more sweeping solutions. Here the courts can resolve more disputes at lower cost. Simpler rules mean that the opposing parties are more likely to have similar views on the probability of winning or losing and are hence more likely to settle sooner in the

---

dents (broader judicial pronouncements applicable to all). For an example of these sorts of arguments, see Posner, *Economic Analysis of Law* at 539–42 (cited in n. 8).

In fact, as we have seen and as we will see more strongly in the discussion of safety and health in the next chapter, adjudication can have significant external social benefits beyond the production of precedent — a view consistent with the image of the adjudica-tive process as a major social decision-making institution. One prominent example is the role of private tort damage actions in regulating safety and health. The existence of these external benefits in combination with the severe underrepresentation of dispersed interests caused by the already high threshold costs of litigation suggests that, from a comparative institutional standpoint, a simple pass through of the systemic costs of the adjudicative system could aggravate rather than ameliorate existing social problems.

litigation process. There will, therefore, be fewer hearings, trials, and appeals given the same level of disputes.[27]

Each of these existing approaches to controlling the strain on judicial resources and capacity is accompanied by a range of institutional and comparative institutional consequences. Narrowing common law rights and remedies may eliminate judicial involvement in social issues that are particularly badly handled by the alternative market and political institutions. As we shall see in the next chapter on tort reform, for example, comparative institutional considerations indicate that decreasing rights and remedies in the context of the shifted distribution may come at a particularly high cost to society.

Similarly, increasing deference to political entities comes at high social cost when the decision-making processes of these political entities are particularly defective — where, for example, the skewed distribution is manifested in either extreme minoritarian or majoritarian bias. Raising the cost of litigation, especially by decreasing access to standing or class action, means that serious social problems involving dispersed interests are excluded from the judicial process even though these problems are handled very badly elsewhere. As a general matter, it is poor strategy to cut social costs without regard to the severity of the associated cuts in social benefits.

Accommodating excess demand by increasing the certainty of the law (thereby decreasing the amount of litigation per controversy) raises particularly subtle dangers. Increasing certainty is attractive because it does not necessarily require a decrease in the number of claims or disputes handed by the adjudicative process. It operates instead by increasing the prospect that any dispute will be resolved earlier in the process and with less expenditure both private and public. The existing adjudication process can handle more claims.

Problems arise, however, if this strategy is pursued too single mindedly. Greater certainty is easier to achieve for substantive issues about which judges have strong technical competence and for issues that can be resolved by a simple and specific rule rather than a complex and vague standard. For these reasons, it is obviously tempting for courts to limit their activity to issues with which they feel comfortable. They can be more confident that they are making the correct decisions, and they can more confidently propose the sort of sweeping solutions that will settle cases at

27. For a general discussion of the dynamics of settlement, see id at 554–60.

earlier stages. Such comfort with a subject matter is a valid consideration in institutional comparison. But it cannot be controlling.

Judges must be particularly careful to avoid the siren-song of single institutionalism. Valid institutional comparison calls upon courts to function when they can do a better job than the alternatives. Sometimes that comparison can require courts to jettison issues with which they are comfortable (because the market or political processes handle these even better) in favor of issues with which they will have to struggle (because the market or political processes handle these even worse). Courts must consider their own abilities and the impacts on their resources, but they must consider more. In the relevant comparative institutional world, courts may be called upon to consider issues for which they are ill equipped in some absolute sense because they are better equipped to do so in a relative sense.

As a general matter, judges are faced with a unique (and uniquely difficult) task. More than other decision-makers, they can be expected to even-handedly and carefully weigh and balance social needs. But this weighing and balancing requires them to carefully consider essential institutional realities. Judges must balance the need for a given adjudicative activity, often defined by the severity of the malfunction in the usually more dominant market or political processes, with the costs of that activity, defined by the severity of the strain on limited judicial resources and on judicial abilities constrained by systemic biases and limited expertise. The courts must continuously juggle a series of important and credible claims on severely constrained judicial resources. The extent to which a claim requires judicial resources, including the extent to which it can be handled by simple rules or be litigated before judges who are comfortable with the subject matter, are important factors in both a normative and positive analysis of adjudication. But, especially on the normative level, they cannot be the only factors considered.

SUMMARY

Judicial independence, which characterizes the beginning and end of many institutional analyses of the courts, comes at a high price. In search of independence and fairness and to constrain the worst evils of a judiciary unbeholden to the people, rules, procedures, and practices raise the costs of participation in the adjudicative process so high that many important issues, although handled badly elsewhere, will not be adjudicated. The same rules and procedures decrease the expertise of adjudicative decision-makers relative to officials in the political process and constrain the courts' access to important information. The formal and hierarchical adjudicative process is difficult to expand and the resulting strains on size produce rationing devices that have problematic comparative institutional implications.

This expensive independence, however, provides important comparative advantages for the adjudicative process. Severe biases in other institutions, in particular the political process, are sometimes avoided or reduced in the adjudicative process. This comparative advantage should tell judges that they should employ the limited resources of the adjudicative process by substituting adjudicative decision-making for political decision-making or market decision-making only when the balance of bias, competence, and scale favors that substitution.

Independence comes to judges at a significant cost to society. With the luxury of contemplation and deliberation comes the responsibility to use their limited resources in the most effective way. More than the officials in any other institutions, judges have the freedom and the responsibility to decide based on broad social considerations. At the core of these difficult but essential decisions is institutional choice. In the chapters that follow, I employ the analyses of politics, markets, and courts thus far set out to examine some proposals for institutional choice by judges.

}III{

Applications: Weighing the Relative Merits of Institutions

}6{

Safety, Tort Law, and Tort Reform

This chapter focuses on the subjects of tort liability and tort reform. It examines these subjects by analyzing the relationship between institutional choice and the social achievement of safety. It compares the advantages and disadvantages of achieving safety through private tort damage actions in the courts as opposed to through market transactions or through regulation in the political process.

The achievement of the optimal level of safety is an important social goal. Injuries from traffic accidents, workplace activities, and the consumption of products and services alone cost society hundreds of billions of dollars annually.[1] Yet reducing serious injury is expensive, and excessive concern for safety can cause serious social loss by unduly diminishing the availability of useful and important products and services. Because of these important competing considerations, the stakes in achieving the optimal level of safety are sizable.

Advocates of tort reform have repeatedly argued that the current tort system is costly and cumbersome. The calls for tort reform have been accompanied by an impressive listing of the costs of tort liability — both the administrative costs of running the systems and the general costs to productivity and resource allocation.[2] Yet the best of institutions are highly

---

1. According to one source, the so-called "economic loss" resulting from motor vehicle accidents in 1987 was $85 billion. Insurance Information Institute, *1988–89 Property and Casualty Insurance Facts* 81 (1989). The same source estimated comparable "economic loss" figures for workplace accidents in 1987 at $40 billion. Id at 98. Similar costs for "injuries from products used in and around the home may well exceed $5.5 billion" in 1970 dollars or over $20 billion in 1987 dollars. *Final Report of the National Commission on Product Safety* 68 (1970). These figures do not reflect the nonpecuniary costs of injury and death, which may dwarf the pecuniary costs of motor vehicle, workplace, and consumer products accidents. See the discussion of nonpecuniary losses in the section "Institutional Function and the Measure of Damages" in this chapter.

2. See, e.g., Peter Huber, *Safety and the Second Best: The Hazards of Public Risk Management in the Courts,* 88 Colum L Rev 277 (1985); Symposium, *Alternative Compensation Schemes and Tort Theory,* 73 Cal L Rev 548 (1985) (collection of articles describing problems with tort system and proposing tort reform); George Priest, *Modern Tort Law and its*

imperfect and expensive. Whether and to what extent tort liability plays a valuable role in the achievement of safety cannot be adequately determined by a parade of horribles — no matter how long or horrible the parade. Examining the role of tort liability in achieving safety graphically shows the difficulty of institutional choice and, therefore, of law and public policy choice in real world settings.

Tort liability can play only a small role in the achievement of safety relative to either the political process or the market. The scale of the judiciary as well as the dynamics of litigation dictate the size of this role. Yet although the role is relatively small, it can be important. In some settings, tort liability — associated with the shifted distribution discussed in the last chapter — may have significant comparative advantages over the alternative arrangements. Perversely, these are the very settings where efforts at tort reform are most active. This perversity suggests that tort reform needs reforming, and it raises the possibility that the courts may have to decide who decides about tort reform.

In the first section of the chapter, I discuss the law and economics treatment of tort liability. In the second, I examine the institutional features of tort liability in three different distributions of stakes roughly representing three important injury settings — automobile injury, air and water pollution, and product injury. In the third, I compare tort liability with other institutional responses. In the fourth, I consider a series of proposed tort reforms in terms of institutional choice. I close with a brief consideration of the need for judicial protection of tort liability — a natural transition to the next chapters on constitutional law.

SAFETY, RESOURCE ALLOCATION EFFICIENCY, AND TORT LAW

Law and economics scholars have a long-standing interest in tort liability. This interest can be traced directly to the work of Guido Calabresi, particularly to his book *The Costs of Accidents.*[3] Calabresi saw in torts a connection between liability and safety. He understood the existence of the tradeoff between the costs of unprevented harm and the costs of preventing that harm. This connection between economics and tort law has been expanded greatly by the work of Richard Posner, who has written extensively about the connection between negligence law and the goal of

---

Reform, 22 Valp U L Rev 1 (1989); Stephen Sugarman, *Doing Away with Personal Injury Law* (1989).

3. Guido Calabresi, *The Costs of Accidents: A Legal and Economic Analysis* (1970).

resource allocation efficiency.[4] In his view, the logic of negligence law could be found in balancing the benefits and costs of prevention and, in turn, in creating the incentives for cost-justified prevention of mishaps. In other words, he argued that the logic of negligence law could be found in resource allocation efficiency and economic analysis.

Others may differ as to whether tort liability and negligence should be analyzed in terms of safety and resource allocation efficiency.[5] I do not. Like Calabresi and Posner, I accept an important connection between tort liability and the goals of safety and resource allocation efficiency. But this connection does not tell me much.

Safety is a goal choice; tort liability is a law or public policy choice. No goal choice standing on its own dictates law or public policy choices. The goal of safety is consistent with a wide variety of law and public policy choices. Depending on the institutional setting, negligence liability, strict liability, or no liability are each consistent with safety and resource allocation efficiency. Put in institutional terms, depending on the setting, optimal safety might be achieved by tort liability through the adjudicative process, by regulation through the political process, or by transactions through the market process. The link between goals and law and public policy results is institutional choice.

The connection between tort law and safety is captured in the famous Hand formula — a judicial formulation of the negligence doctrine that defines negligent behavior in terms of the costs and benefits of prevention. According to the formula, there is negligence when $B < p \times L$, where B stands for the burden of taking the safety step in question, p stands for the probability of the mishap, and L stands for the loss if the mishap occurs.[6] In his attempt to reduce his sense of reasonable care to a formula, Judge Learned Hand provided a significant boost to law and economics. In one short formula, he linked negligence liability, resource allocation efficiency, and safety.

4. See, e.g., Richard Posner, *A Theory of Negligence*, 1 J Legal Stud 29 (1972); Richard Posner and William Landes, *The Economic Structure of Tort Law* (1987); Richard Posner, *Economic Analysis of Law* ch 6 (4th ed 1992).

5. See, e.g., George Fletcher, *Fairness and Utility in Tort Theory*, 85 Harv L Rev 537 (1972); Richard Epstein, *A Theory of Strict Liability*, 2 J Legal Stud 151 (1973).

6. Judge Hand presented his famous formula in *United States v Carroll Towing Co.*, 159 F2d 169 (2d Cir 1947). Since most safety steps only reduce the chance of mishap not eliminate it, the Hand formula better captures Hand's meaning if "p" stands for the *reduction* in the probability of mishap associated with the safety step. See Posner, *Economic Analysis of Law* at 164–65 (cited in n. 4).

But as the Hand formula starkly lays out the important balance between the costs and benefits of safety steps, it also reveals how much more there is to tort law and tort reform. Few would differ with this general balance of cost and benefits. Few would differ with the desirability of cost-justified safety. The controversial issues of law and public policy choice in this area are issues of institutional choice — choosing which imperfect institution is to balance the costs and benefits of safety presented by Judge Hand. Tort reform controversy is not about whether safety is an important goal or whether achieving safety requires the balance of social costs and benefits. It is about which institutional alternative best achieves safety.

One does not need to leave the narrower world of negligence liability itself to see a significant range of institutional choices and, therefore, a significant range of law and public policy choices. Even within the world of negligence for which Hand proposed his formula, a large amount of law involves the choice of who decides. In the adjudicative process in which American negligence liability is determined, the presumptive balancer of the costs and benefits of safety is the civil jury. As the usual trier of fact, the jury is assigned the duty of determining whether or not the conduct of the parties constitutes reasonable care. Juries listen to evidence presented about safety steps both taken and not taken. They usually hear defendants argue that the costs of doing any more would be prohibitive and the likelihood of preventing harm very remote. They usually hear plaintiffs argue that defendants could have significantly reduced the chance of serious mishap without much effort. Juries then decide whether the defendant failed to take due care and assess damages if the defendant is liable.

At least at first glance, institutional choice associated with negligence liability seems simple — the jury decides. On closer inspection, however, the institutional choice is far more complicated and important. Discomfort with the jury as a decision-maker has prompted a number of instances in which other decision-makers are substituted. Trial judges substitute themselves for juries when they direct verdicts. Appellate courts substitute themselves for juries when they impose specific rules meant to determine negligence liability in a range of cases.[7] Judges substitute legislative determinations for jury determinations of negligence when they decide on the weight to be given to the violation of penal or regulatory statutes in determining lack of due care.[8] Judges even substitute markets for juries when

7. See Neil Komesar, *In Search of a General Approach to Legal Analysis: A Comparative Institutional Alternative,* 79 Mich L Rev 1350, 1381–83 (1981).

8. Id at 1375–81.

they use the pattern of behavior or custom as evidence of negligence. Thus, even within the narrow realm of negligence liability, there are a number of important institutional choices — choices of which institution will make the due care balance.

In his usually encyclopedic textbook on law and economics, Richard Posner discusses only one of these institutional features of negligence law — custom. As we saw in the discussion of *Boomer*, Posner's theory of the common law focuses on variations in the characteristics of the market. There the issue was the general shape of property law. Not surprisingly, Posner focuses on the role of market custom in negligence law. His single institutional analysis — the market works or doesn't work — proved to be inadequate in the context of the *Boomer* case. Its inadequacies are even more dramatically evident in connection with the issue of custom.

Custom substitutes for the jury's separate or independent assessment of the advantages and disadvantages of a safety step. Instead of weighing and balancing the benefits and costs of given safety steps, the jury is told how people in the defendant's position usually behave — what safety steps they usually take. The judge can control the impact of this custom evidence by excluding the evidence as irrelevant, varying the jury instructions, or by directing verdicts on the basis of unchallenged custom evidence. This range of legal reactions is reflected in the leading treatise on the subject:

> In a particular case, where there is nothing in the evidence or in common experience to lead to the contrary conclusion, this inference may be so strong that it calls for a directed verdict on the issue of negligence. . . . Some few courts formerly made the effort to treat all customs in this manner, and to enlarge the normal inference into an "unbending test" of negligence, under which the ordinary usages of a business or industry became the sole criterion as to what the actor should, as a reasonable man, have done.
>
> Such an arbitrary rule proved in the long run impossible to justify. . . . Customs and usages themselves are many and various; some are the result of careful thought and decision, while others arise from the kind of inadvertence, carelessness, indifference, cost-paring and corner-cutting that normally is associated with negligence.[9]

The passage reflects the state of conventional legal analysis, which simply restates the issue, along with long lists of factors none of which is linked to any clear conception of when these factors are important. Posner

9. William Prosser, *The Law of Torts* 166–67 (4th ed 1971) (footnotes omitted).

offers an analysis of custom that goes beyond the vagueness of this conventional approach.[10] He argues that the custom defense will be available where there is a market incentive, independent of the threat of liability, to take safety precautions. Situations where the potential victims are customers of the potential injurers provide the principle examples. The sellers of a good or service may have an incentive to make the product or service safe even if they face no threat from courts or regulatory agencies because their failure to take the necessary steps will cost them business from customers who demand such services. To the extent that such transactional discipline exists, the sellers internalize all the factors in the Hand formula and their behavior exemplifies reasonable care. In such a situation, the activities of the usual seller can be taken as the indicator of reasonable safety to which the activities of an allegedly wayward seller can be compared.

Posner's perspective makes it easier to understand important features of the pattern of custom cases. Most prominently, the cases in which custom evidence is seriously used almost invariably involve instances in which the victim and injurer were in some prior relationship. The most extreme use of custom is the area of medical malpractice where, in general, an injured patient cannot establish a case of negligence without establishing that the defendant physician failed to follow the custom in the industry. Here the defendant and plaintiff were clearly in a prior relationship.

Although Posner's institutional analysis says significantly more than the vague non-institutional analyses that preceded it, it is once again single institutional. It asks only about variation in the ability of the market. The market is never perfect; transaction costs are never zero. The incentives to take safety steps will always be imperfect, and, therefore, the custom observed can never be a foolproof indicator of due care. To see the point, consider the treatment of custom in medical malpractice. Under existing law, standard jury instructions in medical malpractice cases are cast in terms of custom. The jury is to decide not whether the defendant health care provider failed to take reasonable precautions but only whether the defendant failed to follow the relevant custom. Posner argues that this strong reliance on custom is explained by the "buyer-seller relationship" between patient and physician.

But the market for health services hardly ranks among the best functioning markets. Patients generally are unsophisticated and unknowledge-

---

10. Posner, *Economic Analysis of Law* at 168–69 (cited in n. 4).

able consumers of this complex service.[11] Although there is a market relationship between physician and patient, the great differences in information between the parties would hardly recommend the market for medical services as a prime example of the perfect or nearly perfect market. The market may work here, but not splendidly.

The market for safety in the delivery of health care can be contrasted with the much smoother running market for safety in the simpler setting of a well-known custom case, *T. J. Hooper*.[12] *T. J. Hooper* involved the loss of barges in a storm. The plaintiff barge-owner argued that the defendant tug-owner was negligent in failing to have a radio that would have warned of the impending storm. The evidence indicated that such radios were not customarily employed in the industry. The possibility that all the parties to transactions for towing services and towing safety are sophisticated and knowledgeable and that, therefore, the observed custom would already be disciplined by market factors seems much greater than the same possibility for the parties in medical transactions. Yet despite the fact that a buyer-seller relationship existed and that all the parties seemed sophisticated and knowledgeable, the court in *T. J. Hooper* held that the custom evidence was unnecessary and affirmed the decision for the plaintiff.

The *T. J. Hooper* decision violates Posner's analysis and remains a mystery to him. The mystery is all the more galling since the author of the opinion was none other than Judge Learned Hand. Hand's seeming betrayal of the principles of law and economics leaves Posner nonplussed: "It is therefore ironic that the classic statement of the principle that compliance with custom is not a defense to a negligence action should have been made — and by Judge Hand! — in a case in which the plaintiff was the defendant's customer."[13]

But the problem here lies not in Hand's analysis but in Posner's. As always, where the issue is institutional choice — the choice between custom in the market and the jury as the determiner of safety — the analysis must be comparative institutional. The question is not how well the market works in two different settings (barge towing and medical), but how well the market works relative to the jury (or judge) in the barge towing or medical malpractice settings. When Posner asks the wrong question, he gets the wrong answer. Using Posner's analysis, the market works better in

---

11. See William Schwartz and Neil Komesar, *Doctors, Damages and Deterrence: An Economic View of Medical Malpractice,* 298 New Eng J Med 1282 (1978).

12. *The T. J. Hooper,* 60 F2d 737 (2d Cir 1932), cert denied, 287 US 662 (1932).

13. Posner, *Economic Analysis of Law* at 168 (cited in n. 4).

the *T. J. Hooper* setting than in medical malpractice and, therefore, a fortiori, if custom is preferred in medical malpractice it should be preferable in *T. J. Hooper*. But that is the wrong analysis.

The correct question is whether, in either the medical malpractice or the *T. J. Hooper* setting, the market works better than the alternative — the jury (or judge). Judges and juries are also imperfect decision-makers, and, more importantly, their ability varies with the setting. As we have seen, juries and judges are not expert. Their determinations of adequate safety are likely to be less trustworthy the more complex and technically difficult the safety steps in question.

The different role for custom in *T. J. Hooper* as compared to medical malpractice becomes more sensible when one considers that medical malpractice presents the judge or jury with a much more difficult and complex issue than did the simple safety question in *T. J. Hooper*. In *T. J. Hooper,* the question was merely whether ships should be equipped with radios to hear weather reports. Judge Hand considered the issue relatively straightforward and capable of decision by the normal trier of fact.[14]

From a comparative institutional perspective, we have a familiar pattern. The abilities of the relevant institutions usually move together, and they are affected by the same variable — the costs of information. In the medical malpractice setting, we have the choice between two highly imperfect decision-makers. The highly technical nature of medicine that makes it difficult for consumers of medical services to transact for sufficient safety and to police such transactions also makes it difficult for juries to determine whether the failure to take a given safety step is reasonable. The institutional choice is between two highly imperfect alternatives — the best of bad alternatives must be chosen. On the other hand, with *T. J. Hooper,* we have the more pleasant choice between two relatively sound alternatives. As is often true, in each instance, the institutions are close in ability. Slight variations in factual setting can produce exceptions to what

14. Interestingly, the lists of factors employed by traditional torts scholars to explain custom include consideration of the technical expertise of the jury. Thus, after trying a number of factors, in connection with the role of custom in medical malpractice, William Prosser makes the following observation: "It seems clear, in any case, that the result is closely tied in with the layman's ignorance of medical matters and the necessity of expert testimony." Prosser, *The Law of Torts* 165 (cited in n. 9).

However, these analyses not only slight consideration of variation in the attributes of the market but also generally fail to construct a succinct framework that integrates the factors that they suggest and the facts of the case.

seem to be rules, as they do, for example, in those rare medical malpractice settings where custom is ignored.[15] Judges Posner and Hand might differ on whether the market or the courts is the better determiner of safety in the *T. J. Hooper* setting. But neither view is obviously inconsistent with safety, efficiency, or economic analysis.[16]

Law and economics analysts need to recognize and explicate the comparative institutional core of their discipline. I believe that that core is far more important to the discipline than is the goal of resource allocation efficiency. Recognizing the importance of comparative institutional analysis and examining its implications can do a great deal for law and economics. More broadly, given that Posner's single institutionalism mirrors the single institutionalism of the market failure constructs of welfare economics, the same advice applies to economic analysis of public policy in general.

The analyses of custom or of the other intra-negligence institutional choices presented in this section are only a microcosm of a broader world of institutional choices inherent in the analysis of safety and tort liability. But the issues and lessons are similar in the broader contexts to which I now turn.

THE ADJUDICATIVE PROCESS IN THREE SETTINGS

Beginning in this section, I examine the institutional choices involved in achieving optimal safety or prevention in contexts broader than the negligence cases discussed in the last section. To facilitate this analysis, I turn more explicitly to the determinants of the participation-centered approach to institutional analysis. In this section, I examine the functioning of tort liability in three injury settings defined by differences in the distribution of the impacts or stakes of the injury and its prevention. In the next section, I focus on the relative workings of the adjudicative, market, and political processes in one of these settings — product liability.

Consistent with the analysis set out in the earlier chapters, the institu-

15. See *Helling v Carey*, 83 Wash 2d 514, 519 P2d 981 (1974).
16. The difference between Judges Posner and Hand over the outcome in *T. J. Hooper* may stem from their implicit institutional presumptions or default positions. To Posner, if the market works relatively well, the market gets the job. To Hand, if the courts work relatively well, the courts get the job (or, more accurately, retain the job). There is no a priori reason on comparative institutional grounds to choose one or the other of these default positions.

tional analysis presented in this chapter examines the dynamics of participation and, in particular, the behavior of four groups of participants who
play important roles in all the various systems — potential victims, potential injurers, actual victims, and actual injurers. Depending on the institutional setting, these actors are litigants, lobbyists, voters, consumers, and
producers. The analysis traces the response of these various actors to the
different per capita impacts or stakes involved in different types of injuries
such as automobile accidents, product injuries, and pollution.[17]

The participation-centered approach with its emphasis on both the
benefits and costs of participation — and, in particular, the benefits and
costs of information — allows me to address several subjects of interest in
law and public policy choice such as deterrence, insurance, litigation,
prosecution, and politics. I associate deterrence, litigation, prosecution, or
political response with the participation of these various groups of actors.[18]
These subjects are often either treated exogenously (assumed to exist at
some level or levels determined outside the analysis) or ignored in analyses
of tort reform. Here I treat them as variable and part of a comparative
institutional framework.[19]

17. This lineup of institutional players also includes judges, juries, prosecutors, bureaucrats, and legislators — the "officials" in the various institutions. To a considerable
extent, the behavior of these officials is related to those of the primary actors. But separate consideration of these other actors and their responses will be considered as we
go along.
18. The institutional analysis presented here focuses primarily on one of several major goals which dictate a social response to injury — prevention. Prevention must play an
important part in any social response to injury. Preventing serious injury, where feasible,
is inherently attractive. The goal is feasible, optimal, or cost effective prevention, not
prevention at any cost. In Calabresi's terms, the concern is "primary accident cost reduction." See Calabresi, *The Costs of Accidents* at 237 (cited in n. 3).
19. No one, so far as I know, has attempted to integrate consideration of all these
various roles and institutions into one framework. There have been calls for a comparative institutional approach, as in Richard Stewart, *Crisis in Tort Law? The Institutional
Perspective*, 54 U Chi L Rev 184 (1987), but no responses.
I do not mean to suggest that the tort literature is bereft of creative institutional and
systemic analyses. Guido Calabresi, who has long focused on the systemic nature of tort
liability, has given particular attention to the behavior of injurers and victims as potential avoiders or preventers. See, for example, Calabresi, *The Costs of Accidents* (cited in
n. 3). See also Guido Calabresi and Jon Hirschoff, *Toward a Test for Strict Liability in Torts*,
81 Yale LJ 1055 (1972); Guido Calabresi and Alvin Klevorik, *Four Tests for Liability in Torts*,
14 J Legal Stud 585 (1985). Similarly, several law and economics scholars have given
sophisticated attention to the question of potential victims as bargainers and, therefore,
to the efficacy of the market alternative. Alan Schwartz, *Proposals for Products Liability
Reform: A Theoretical Synthesis*, 97 Yale LJ 353, 371–84 (1988) provides an excellent summary and analysis of the literature here. Even the issue of victims and injurers as litigants

In this section, I examine the ability of the adjudicative process and in particular its private damage actions to produce prevention in three different injury settings. These settings are defined by the per capita impact of an injury on our primary actors—actual victims, actual injurers, potential victims, and potential injurers. As these configurations of impacts vary, the behavior of primary actors varies and, in turn, the performance of basic institutions like the adjudicative process varies. In the next section, I will examine the implications of variation in the impact of injuries on the functioning of the market and political processes as well.

Each distribution of impacts considered here is depicted in a simple two-by-two table. The per capita impacts are described as high or low. This binary characterization of impacts is meant to provide a simple starting point; in the various discussions, I will consider the question of variations within these categories—how high and how low. Per capita impact, not total social impact, varies here. Thus, for the purposes of this discussion, assume that the total impact on society in all the settings is the same amount (e.g., $100 million per year). The three settings differ in the distribution of this social injury among the relevant victim and injurer populations. Thus, for example, low per capita impact for actual victims means that there are many actual victims (e.g., 10 million) each of whom suffers a small loss (e.g., $10), while high per capita impact per actual injurer means that there are a few injurers (e.g., 10) each of whom is responsible for a sizable amount of injury (e.g., $10 million each).

Describing potential injury is somewhat more complicated than describing actual injury although it is similar in conception. Potential injury can be described by a probability and a resulting injury. Thus, for example, imagine a population of 10 million potential victims facing an injury that has a probability of .0001 (1/10,000) with a loss of $100,000 (1,000 actual injuries are expected). The expected loss would then be $10 per victim per year. (Note that this is a low per capita potential loss but a high per capita

---

has been considered in terms of variation in behavior based on the stakes involved. Consider here Marc Galanter, *Why the "Haves" Come Out Ahead: Speculations on the Limits of Legal Change,* 9 L & Soc Rev 95 (1974), and the literature on the evolutionary models of common law efficiency. The role of victims and injurers as actors in the political process has generally been ignored in the tort context. An exception here is Fred Zacharias, *The Politics of Torts,* 95 Yale LJ 698 (1986), which argues that "courts should decide limited categories of negligence cases with a view to the possibility of a 'political' response." Id at 698.

I do mean to suggest, however, that missing from the tort literature is a systematic and careful comparison of these institutions across relevant injury types.

actual loss). The same person rarely will be victimized more than once. Low per capita impact among potential injurers has the same characteristic—large social injury spread among many injurers. High per capita impact among potential injurers involves a smaller number of potential injurers usually exposed to a high frequency of significant injury. In the extreme, one can imagine a single producer of injury. The expected potential loss would be the full $100 million.[20]

Distribution 1

	potential	actual
victim	low	high
injurer	low	high

We can imagine this injury as one where there are many potential injurers and victims each of whom has a low probability of injuring or being injured. The potential social (aggregate) impact can be very high, but it is distributed widely. On the other hand, although few will actually be injured or will injure, each occurrence of injury will be severe. An example of this distribution is forest fires started by carelessly thrown matches or cigarettes. Many such matches or cigarettes are thrown without starting a fire. But, very infrequently, major fires devouring both forests and surrounding communities may be started. The probability of being a victim of such carelessness is very low ex ante, but the impact, should the improbable occur, can be very large (for example, having your home destroyed). A more common example, though, as we shall see, a more controversial one, would be automobile accidents between drivers each of whom has a low ex ante probability of being a victim or injurer, but each of whom can be involved in a significant injury ex post.

This distribution would likely produce active prosecution in the tort setting. The high per capita actual victims (and their contingency fee

20. Depending on the choice of time period, we could have a large *potential* social loss with no *actual* social loss in a given period. Thus, for example, a $100 million per year expected social loss could be associated with a Chernobyl nuclear accident which might occur only once in 10 or 20 years. Here we have very low probabilities but very large losses per actual victim and astronomic actual losses for society as a whole. For the purposes of the present discussion, the analysis envisions more conventional losses in which the social loss will be realized in each year; in our example, there would be approximately 1,000 injuries involving $100,000 in any given year.

lawyers) have the incentive to bring action.[21] But the large number of cases (and the associated large administrative costs) may not buy much prevention. Low per capita impact on potential injurers (and even potential victims) may mean that signals from the system will not be received. Information on potential tort liability is hardly free, especially in the context of a vague standard like negligence as opposed to a simpler rule that proscribes specific conduct. A vague standard, which allows substantial variation in outcome case-by-case, makes the pattern of potential liability more complex and difficult and, therefore, more costly to understand. Low per capita potential impact provides little reason to expend the resources necessary to acquire this understanding. High costs and low returns for understanding the signal limit the chance that the signal will be received and responded to.

I am treating deterrence as a matter of gradation determined by the costs and benefits of understanding the signal. Rather than taking the usual approaches that assume either that all signals are frictionlessly and costlessly received or that people in general do not respond to legal signals, I focus on the degree of response and, more importantly, on the determinants of the degree of response. The larger the per capita stakes created by tort law for potential injurers the more likely they are to expend the efforts necessary to perceive, understand, and react to the sanctions. The lower the stakes the lower the chance that the message sent by the tort system will be received by potential injurers. Low stakes for potential injurers do not bode well for deterrence.[22]

The low deterrability potential in distribution 1 can be exacerbated by liability insurance. If liability insurance is available to everyone at the

21. In our forest fire example, the actual victims may have problems identifying the cause of the fire (the actual injurer). But they will have the incentive to do so and to bring action if the identification is made.

22. Debates about deterrence easily devolve into debates about human rationality. Critics of deterrence argue that at least in certain circumstances humans do not operate in a calculating rational manner; proponents of deterrence refute these claims by pointing to empirical studies that, they argue, show such responses. See, for example, the exchange between Howard Latin and Richard Posner. Howard Latin, *Problem-Solving Behavior and Theories of Tort Liability*, 73 Cal L Rev 677 (1985), and Richard Posner, *Can Lawyers Solve the Problems of the Tort System?* 73 Cal L Rev 747 (1985).

The analysis presented here, however, does not associate lack of deterrence with limited rationality. The issue here is optimal expenditure on knowledge and sophistication. It does not pay to understand certain events and risks. There is, in effect, optimal ignorance. For a classic discussion of "optimal ignorance" in the context of political behavior, see Anthony Downs, *An Economic Theory of Democracy* 207–19 (1957).

same price without regard to their efforts to prevent and that price does not induce self-insurance, then insurance at least reduces and may even eliminate the incentive to prevent.[23] With potential liability spread over many potential injurers, differential pricing (what is called "experience rating") is unlikely. The culprit again is the balance between the cost of information and the incentives to acquire it.

There are market forces pressing toward experience rating. It would profit insurance companies to pick out only the low risk customers, given the same premium. In turn, this selection process would promote differential rates in a competitive insurance industry and provide the incentive for injurers to take safety steps. The information necessary to make these differentiations, however, is not costless. Where we have a large number of potential injurers, identifying important differences and investigating to determine where and when those differences exist can be very expensive. At the same time, the low per capita liability means low average premiums and a low return per capita to the insurance provider for differentiating among customers. It simply may not be worthwhile for the provider to differentiate carefully among many low stakes (low premium) potential customers. In this sense, rate differentiation and in turn the effect of liability insurance on deterrence, like the receipt of the tort system's deterrence signal, is subject to variation that can be tied to variation in the distribution of injury impacts.

Thus, in the setting of distribution 1, low per capita stakes limit the possibility of injurer response both because the returns to understanding and responding are low and because individual liability insurance rates are unlikely to respond to any preventative efforts a potential injurer might make. Under these circumstances, the tort system may produce many cases and their associated costs without much change in injurer behavior. We have high potential for prosecution (the signal will be sent), but low deterrability (the signal will not be received).

---

23. Elimination would require complete coverage of *all* losses including psychological loss. One may still observe a form of prevention since the higher insurance costs associated with the failure to take individual safety steps may induce a reduction in the injurious activity in general. See Landes and Posner, *The Economic Structure* at 10–11 (cited in n. 4). Such a reduction in accidents, however, could as easily be associated with a system of no fault or no liability in which people insured against the resulting impacts. This would be especially true for the auto accident context discussed by Landes and Posner. The higher rates of accident and injury they discuss would likely reduce driving whether these rates were translated through negligence liability, strict liability, no fault, or no liability.

Distribution 2

	potential	actual
victim	low	low
injurer	high	high

This second distribution produces the possibility of high deterrability for potential injurers associated with high stakes for these injurers. But now actual victims have low per capita stakes, and as a result there will be problems with private prosecution in the tort system. The pecuniary stakes are not present for either individual actual victims or their contingency fee lawyers. Here we have a situation just the opposite of that in distribution 1. We have high deterrability (the signal would be received), but low potential for prosecution (the signal will not be sent).

This setting is exemplified by the Hudson River air pollution setting of the *Boomer* case and was the subject of considerable discussion in chapter 5. If victims would organize and pool their interests, then they might have the necessary incentive to spend the resources required for private prosecution. But organizing requires resources. At very low per capita stakes, incentives may be too small for victims even to recognize that they have been injured. Even if the injury were recognized, the victims still face the difficult task of getting others to contribute to litigation. The natural tendency to free ride would defeat the endeavor. As we have seen, the problem could be overcome, to some extent, in the tort setting if pooling mechanisms like class actions are employed. Here one litigant or a lawyer is the central moving party, and the pecuniary incentives can come from a share of the recovery or payment of lawyers fees. As we have also seen, however, recent trends have diminished the general effectiveness of class actions.[24]

Distribution 3

	potential	actual
victim	low	high
injurer	high	high

24. See the discussion of class actions in chapter 5.

At least as a rough approximation, distribution 3 fits the common conception of product injury — numerous consumers as potential victims, large-scale manufacturers as potential injurers causing low probability but serious injuries.[25] The bursting pop bottle and the exploding gas tank at issue in two famous product injury cases are mishaps consistent with this distribution.[26] This distribution is the central focus of the next section — as well as the central focus of tort reform.

Distribution 3 takes the best features of distribution 1 and 2. Because there are high stakes actual victims, the chances of sending the signal are increased relative to distribution 2. The prospects of significant damage awards provide greater incentives for actual victims (and their contingency fee lawyer-partner) to bring action. This greater possibility of litigation makes credible the threat of liability for failure to prevent. Distribution 3 is the "shifted distribution" discussed in chapter 5.

Because distribution 3 results in high stakes potential injurers, the chances of receiving this signal are now increased relative to distribution 1. Higher per capita stakes for potential injurers improve the chances for receipt of the signal on several fronts. Deterrability for injurers is now more feasible. Higher potential liability per capita provides greater incentives to expend the resources necessary to understand the signal. More complex signals associated with complex case-by-case liability rules can be sent because large-scale potential injurers have the incentive to decipher these complex signals.[27] Signals sent have a higher probability of being received.[28]

25. A recent study of product liability actions in federal courts reveals a pattern of both substantial concentration and substantial dispersion: "half of all cases filed between 1974 and 1986 named fewer than 80 lead defendants, whereas the other half involved more than 19,000 defendants." Terry Dungworth, *Products Liability and the Business Sector,* Rand Corp., Institute for Civil Justice, R-3668-ICJ vii (1988).

26. See *Escola v Coca Cola Bottling Co.,* 24 Cal 2d 453, 150 P2d 436 (1944) and the Pinto case discussed subsequently in the section "Targeting High Deterrability" in this chapter.

27. For the same reason, the low per capita stakes for potential victims tends to make them unlikely targets for tort liability (usually manifested in the form of a contributory negligence defense). This point is explored at greater length in the section "Targeting High Deterrability" in this chapter.

28. A recent study of corporate responses to product liability showed significant concern for and reaction to potential liability — far greater, for example, than concern for and reaction to regulatory efforts in the same industries. This response was not focused on particular legal outcomes; the signal received was general — "Be careful, or you will be sued." This study found that product design decisions were affected by the threat of such liability. G. Eads and P. Reuter, *Designing Safer Products: Corporate Response to Product Liability Law and Regulation,* The Institute for Civil Justice, Rand Corp. (1983) (R-3022-ICJ).

As we saw in the discussion of distribution 1, tort deterrability can also be blunted by the presence of liability insurance. High per capita stakes for potential injurers will tend to dissipate this impediment to deterrence as well. As we saw, insurance companies have the incentive to identify and compete for potential injurers with the lowest probability of mishaps. To the extent that this identification and competition exists, potential injurers have an incentive to take safety steps that lower the chance of mishap. This differentiation among potential injurers by insurance companies, like all the activities studied here, is not free and requires insurance companies to expend resources to obtain the necessary information.

Differentiation becomes more cost justifiable as the stakes of the individual policy rise. Thus, for example, an insurance company that identifies and insures a given injurer who is less likely than average to incur a given form of liability will save 100 times more if the average expected liability for the insurance period (the total expected insurance payout) for that injurer were $1,000,000 as opposed to $10,000.[29] If a large-scale injurer capable of reducing the probability of mishaps cannot get insurance companies to recognize this ability through experience rating, there is a strong incentive to self-insure.[30]

29. This analysis supposes that the costs to the insurance company of identifying the lower risk insured is the same for the higher scale mishap as for the lower scale mishap. It is difficult to know whether and to what extent this is true on a per capita basis. Injury data about a large scale injurer will accumulate more rapidly, and deviations among large scale injurers will become evident more quickly than deviations among small scale injurers. On the other hand, these large scale injuries may often be caused in a more complex way, requiring more study per injurer. As to *total* costs of acquiring information (rather than per injurer cost), there can be little doubt that the costs are much lower to understand and differentiate the behavior of a few than of many injurers. The total transaction costs of bargaining over and establishing separate plans for a few potential injurers should also be much lower than for many potential injurers.

30. Self-insurance is more likely for large scale potential injurers for two reasons. First, their ratio of total potential liability to total costs of understanding liability and discovering how to reduce it by prevention is much higher, giving them greater incentives to understand the signal and produce the prevention. Second, the greater frequency of mishaps per time period makes it more likely that actual liability over time will be constant, thereby lowering the costs associated with risk aversion. On these two scores, the costs of risk management are lower per incident for large scale than for small scale injurers.

Throughout this discussion, high per capita potential injurers are being associated with entities that have many injuries in a given year. The same analysis does not apply nearly as well for high per capita potential injurers who have very infrequent but catastrophic injuries such as the Chernobyl mishap; see note 20. As such, the analysis of self-insurance and preventative reaction presented in the text does not apply straightforwardly to such nuclear mishaps and perhaps, therefore, to the nuclear industry. This is not to say, however, that the unique position of the members of this industry in the

Again, I am treating the issue of the possibility of experience rating (or self-insurance) as a matter of gradation dependent upon the stakes involved. "Ratability" like deterrability is not constant across all tort situations. In fact, the rapid rise in all insurance rates that produces the various "insurance crises" and the accompanying calls for tort reform actually make ratability and, therefore, deterrability more likely. As the scale of rates go up, the benefits from either experience rating or self-insurance increase. The observation that more manufacturers are self-insuring[31] that seems so troubling on other scores may, in fact, signal an improvement in deterrability.[32]

Thus, in summary, the adjudicative process and private damage remedies work best in distribution 3. Both the sending of the signal and the receiving of the signal seem to work well especially when compared to distribution 2 in connection with the sending of the signal and distribution 1 in connection with receiving the signal.

The observant reader will have noted, however, that I have not yet asked the correct question. It makes no difference for law and public policy whether the adjudicative process is at its best in distribution 3. What is important is whether, in any given distribution or setting, the adjudicative process is better than the alternative institutional possibilities — the market and the political process. Distribution 3 will be the focus of this comparison of institutions because tort reform is most active, has its greatest effect, and is least appropriate in that setting. As we shall see, the tort process is not only at its best in distribution 3; it is, more importantly, likely to be better than its institutional alternatives. Institutional analysis presents the disquieting possibility that the workings of tort reform will perversely undermine tort liability and its comparative advantage in providing safety in this context.

----

chain of information might not lead to self-insurance or superior avoidance for other reasons. That is simply an extension of the analysis not attempted here.

31. See Interagency Task Force on Product Liability, *Final Report*, III-17 (1978); George Priest, *The Current Insurance Crisis and Modern Tort Law*, 96 Yale LJ 1521 (1987).

32. On the general subject of the role of insurance, a recent study of corporate responses to product liability found a significant trend toward liability insurance arrangements like self-insurance and increased deductibles that make it more likely that these potential injurers will receive the tort liability signal: "Our interviews suggest that the insurance industry is likely to play a declining role with respect to the large manufacturers who produce most of the consumer goods in the nation. These manufacturers have shifted largely to either self-insurance or policies involving high deductibles and significant coinsurance." Eads and Reuter, *Designing Safer Products* at 8 (cited in n. 28).

DISTRIBUTION 3 AND THE COMPARISON OF INSTITUTIONS

The product liability configuration (distribution 3) that is seemingly favorable for the courts and tort liability is problematic for the other institutions because of the significant differential between ex ante stakes for
injurers and victims. The other institutions have significant ex ante features that cause serious distortions in their performance. This is the tale of
the "shifted distribution" told in the previous chapter.

In distribution 3, voluntary transactions (the market) can provide a viable institutional response to the extent that consumers (potential victims)
appreciate the existing level of risk. This appreciation will vary with the
size of the potential victims' per capita stakes. As was the case with distribution 1, per capita stakes for distribution 3 potential victims are low. The
issue now becomes how low "low" is. Very low stakes can defeat serious
recognition of the danger and willingness to purchase safety; the benefits
gained from outlays to understand or even recognize the risk may be too
low. On the other hand, as per capita stakes for consumers rise, the potential for market-produced prevention increases. The ability of potential
victims to recognize the existence of the risk will also vary with the complexity of the risk—with how much it will cost to acquire the necessary
information. A complex product may have risks that are remote and difficult to understand. This analysis suggests that product and service injury
settings where the technology is highly complex and the stakes for victims
are very low ex ante are poor candidates for market provision of safety.[33]

In distribution 3, the significant difference in stakes between potential

33. The tort literature contains numerous discussions of the potential for private
transactions. Two thoughtful recent articles have quite different views on this subject.
Alan Schwartz reviews recent data and concludes that, though the data are thin, they
support the conclusion the consumers do not misperceive risk and, therefore, that market transactions deserve significantly more respect as an alternative in the product liability setting. Schwartz, 97 Yale LJ at 378–84 (cited in n. 19). Two other respected
commentators hold quite a different viewpoint of the available data and their implications. Calabresi and Klevorick, 14 J Legal Stud at 617 (cited in n. 19).

These articles reflect a common treatment of the question of consumer understanding. They conclude either that consumers do or do not understand. They do not treat
consumer reaction as a continuum whose character is defined by basic determinants and
which, therefore, may vary from one form of potential product injury to another. From
the vantage of the analysis proposed in this book, one might examine these data and
these views from a perspective informed by the correlation between transactability and
consumer stakes. How likely was the bad event? How traumatic? How complex? Variation in consumer response may reflect different forms of injury configurations and,
therefore, different stakes.

injurers and potential victims can cause serious distortions in the criminal and administrative systems. We are now dealing with public rather than private prosecution. In the tort system, the private prosecutors (actual victims and their lawyers) are motivated at least in part by the possibility of substantial pecuniary recovery. But public prosecutors do not directly benefit from any fines or other sanctions extracted from offenders.

To the extent that public prosecutors can be affected by the activities of persons outside the official process, there may be a bias toward the injurer group. Members of that group with its high per capita potential stakes have a better chance of recognizing the dangers to themselves of active prosecution and of organizing the efforts necessary to affect the activity in their favor (i.e., to decrease it). Such activities might take the form of graft, political contributions, political pressure on legislators or executives, or more subtly in the form of careful lobbying and propaganda efforts influencing the attitude of the agency in their favor.

As we move toward administrative regulation where liability is determined as well as prosecuted by government employees (bureaucrats), these distortive tendencies strengthen. Now we have replaced the jury with expert boards of bureaucrats as well as moved from private to public prosecution. Society gains, in some ways, from this shift. Unknowledgeable, unsophisticated juries are replaced by more knowledgeable, more sophisticated bureaucrats who gain knowledge and experience as they decide more cases. Juries are part-time, amateurs. Bureaucrats are full-time, professionals.

In the face of significant differentials in ex ante stakes, however, these characteristics can have quite different implications. Fixed decision-makers are better targets for such activities as graft, political pressure, and propaganda. They are responsible for determining the outcome of many cases; a given jury is usually responsible for one. It is easier to identify these permanent decision-makers and to influence them over time. More importantly, any investment in influence covers more cases and, therefore, yields a higher return. Even public-minded and honest civil servants are capable of being influenced by concerted educational (propaganda) activities.

Lobbying and propaganda are necessary and socially valuable components in large-scale political systems that deal with a large variety of complex social issues — in other words, much of public decision-making. They provide information and insights about the implications of these issues on various groups in society. Problems arise, however, when one group's views are overrepresented. Such overrepresentation is inherent in the significant difference in ex ante stakes in the product liability setting.

In theory, the legislature controls the tort as well as the criminal and administrative responses to injuries. In practice, the tort system has evolved and changed through judicial rather than legislative decisions.[34] As tort litigation has increased and jury awards have grown, however, the stakes for changing the tort system — for tort reform — have grown. But the institutional picture presented in this chapter suggests a serious tort reform paradox inherent in the product injury configuration. The very mishaps least in need of removal from the tort system because of the high potential for deterrability associated with high per capita potential injurers are most likely to be removed because of the political effectiveness of the same high per capita injurers. The same high per capita stakes that make potential injurers deterrable targets for tort liability also make them politically active and quite probably overrepresented in the political processes of tort reform relative to low per capita stakes potential victims. Here reform may be demanded most where it is needed least.[35]

This overrepresentation of concentrated potential injurers in the tort reform process is not without qualification. There are some sources of representation for dispersed potential victims in the political process.[36] In

34. Even if appellate courts control torts, however, some potential still exists for overrepresentation of the injurer in the torts system. Appellate judges are usually not as directly subject to political influence as legislators or administrators. But that does not make them immune from the influences of propaganda. High stakes potential injurers can take part in campaigns to educate judges to their way of thinking. They may accumulate war chests for litigation and appeal that are disproportionate in the context of any individual case but sensible in view of the large number of potential cases facing each injurer (or small group of potential injurers). See Galanter, 9 L & Soc Rev (cited in n. 19).

These efforts are most effectively aimed at appellate courts, where appellate judges are fixed targets analogous to the bureaucrats in administrative agencies. Appellate determinations can control a large set of cases, and those defendants who will face a large number of cases will find it advisable to invest in influencing these determinations. This "repeat players" effect creates some bias within the torts system analogous to that within the more directly political criminal-regulatory system, although one would expect this bias to be more limited since avenues for influence are more limited.

35. As chapter 3 showed, the skewed distribution can be consistent with either minoritarian or majoritarian bias. In the context of product liability, however, the complexity of the subject matter and the absence of safe targets makes majoritarian bias very unlikely. I discuss this point at length and contrast the political response to product liability with the political response to another issue of safety and health, AIDS, in Neil Komesar, *Injuries and Institutions: Tort Reform, Tort Theory, and Beyond*, 65 NYU L Rev 23, 44–47 (1990).

36. In some instances, high per capita potential victims may be present to represent the victims' viewpoint. In addition, the presence of unions may provide some victim representation for workplace product-related injuries. More pervasively, there is the possibility of representations by the plaintiff's bar, those lawyers who represent plaintiffs in

addition, manufacturers and insurance companies are not monolithic, and the category of product liability is not homogeneous. Not all product liability injuries are characterized by distribution 3. Products and services can be produced on a small scale with an accompanyingly smaller per capita stake per potential injurer. But, as a general matter, the interests of potential victims in safety and prevention are poorly represented in the political process, the important institutional issues of tort reform seem particularly poorly understood, and, accordingly, the elimination of tort liability has become too easy an out for many.

Before examining the implications of this discussion for tort reform, I want to briefly explore the comparative institutional implications of the other distributions—the other injury settings. The seeming strength of the adjudicative process in the product safety setting depends on the existence of the shifted distribution—the shift from skewed distribution ex ante to a uniform distribution ex post. As we have seen in the consideration of distribution 2, when there is no shift from an ex ante to an ex post situa-

---

personal injury actions. There are, however, significant differences between the interests of the plaintiff's bar and potential victims associated with the working of contingency fees and the difference between the interests of potential victims and the interests of the actual victims with whom the plaintiff's bar is allied. These differences distort the representation of the interest of potential victims by the plaintiff's bar. I discuss this issue in Komesar, 65 NYU L Rev at 43–44 (cited in n. 35).

More importantly, the political dynamics of tort reform handicap political efforts by the plaintiff's bar. Not only are the interests of potential victims likely to be underrepresented in the political process, but it is likely that, to the extent they play any role, potential victims will end up perversely supporting tort reform. In other words, we may see a misled majority. This outcome is the product of the very low per capita stakes of potential victims, the complex nature of safety in the tort system, and greater simplicity or accessibility of one side of the story. Usually, this means the presence of a simple symbol and, in the case of tort reform, there is a traditional one—the ambulance-chasing lawyer.

From time immemorial, or at least since we have had lawyers, lawyers have proven to be invaluable targets for popular and political displeasure. The present day is no different. In 1992, a president and vice president in desperate need of a domestic agenda and a Congress in desperate need to deflect attention from its own tattered image once again raised the image of greedy ambulance chasers duping yokel juries into irrational and excessive awards. The tort reform bandwagon, whatever the merits of the substantive issue, is fueled by powerful and traditional simple symbols. It is easier to sell the case that tort liability and private damage actions are just a method for already rich and selfish lawyers to become richer than it is to sell the case that these rich and selfish lawyers may play an important social role in the achievement of optimal safety. Understanding that tort liability can serve an important prevention role in settings like distribution 3 requires a level of consideration and sophistication that is simply not justified by the low per capita stakes of potential victims.

tion and the adjudicative process faces a skewed distribution, it works significantly less well. Indeed, it not only functions badly relative to its ability in distribution 3; it may also function badly relative to the political process in distribution 2. At very low per capita stakes for actual victims, the private damage remedy may well grind to a halt. The political process with its greater informality has a greater chance to respond to low stakes voters (albeit a distorted and poor one) than the more expensive adjudicative process has to respond to low stakes litigants (in particular low stakes plaintiffs). Here we have the Hudson River Valley pollution variant of the *Boomer* case.

Even where a shift to uniform high stakes occurs, if that the shift came from a uniform low rather than a skewed distribution ex ante, the political process may be superior to the adjudicative process. This is distribution 1. With this distribution, low per capita stakes limit the possibility of injurer response to the deterrent signal both because the returns to understanding and responding to that signal are low and because the potential injurers' liability insurance rates are unlikely to respond to any preventative efforts that potential injurers might make. Under these circumstances, the tort system may produce many cases (and their associated costs) without much change in injurer behavior (the associated benefits). In other words, there is high potential for prosecution (the signal will be sent), but low deterrability (the signal will not be received).

At least at first blush, the shift from private to public prosecution does not promise any significant advantages. Deterring low stakes potential injurers is still a problem. The criminal law system and administrative regulation, however, do offer three potential advantages over the tort system in connection with deterrability: the possibility of shifting the focus of prosecution to specified bad acts, rather than the bad act/bad outcome combination that characterizes tort liability; centralized decision-making, which allows for the rationing of prosecutorial resources; and the absence of liability insurance.

The fact that administrative regulation and criminal prosecution can target individual bad acts may increase prevention in two ways. First, by specifying particular acts for prohibition rather than using a vague standard like negligence, such a system makes the liability signal clearer and easier to understand (cheaper to acquire). Second, such a system defines a broader base for liability and, therefore, allows more frequent prosecutions. More frequent prosecution means that more people are likely to have direct, visible exposure to liability and, with it, easier (more accessible) awareness of the legal liability signal.[37] In addition, the criminal and regulatory systems allow a centralized decision that can explicitly balance the cost of suits and the benefits of deterrability for society as a whole. In theory at least, public prosecutors can choose to decrease prosecution (thereby saving the administrative costs) where there is little chance for inducing preventative behavior. The tort process with its decentralized, private prosecution decisions does not easily allow for this sort of social calculation.

These are largely "technical" institutional advantages. The political process often allows for more flexibility and expertise than the adjudicative process, in theory. However, as we have seen throughout this book, what the criminal and regulatory systems or any other institution might do in theory can be quite different from what they do in practice. As always, we need to consider the behavioral incentives of the public officials who make these decisions and, in turn, the incentives and behavior of victims and injurers whose actions as lobbyists, voters, or propagandists help determine the decisions of these public officials. The low per capita stakes for both potential victims and potential injurers in distribution 1 suggests the absence of organized political activity by either group and, therefore, the absence of the systematic overrepresentation of one group. In distribution 1, the image of an objective political process that evenhandedly balances the costs and benefits of prosecution — impermissibly simplistic in other settings — may approximate reality.

One can play these themes out with the example of auto accidents. Scholars have long criticized fault-based tort liability for auto accidents. The advocates of no-fault plans have vociferously attacked conventional tort liability with some success.[38] These calls for the demise of tort liability, while questionable when generalized to all areas of tort liability,[39] may fit

---

37. Often, these advantages of criminal liability come with higher social costs. More frequent prosecution means more cases and, usually, higher administrative expenses. To the extent that more prosecutions result in greater deterrence, the number of bad acts and thus the number of future prosecutions is reduced. In addition, clearly defined offenses for which the punishment is not great will tend to decrease the incentives for protracting litigation. Opposing parties are more willing to settle cases at low levels of litigation the closer their perceptions of the likely outcome of litigation and the lower the stakes involved. Clearly defined liability rules make it likely that the parties will have similar perceptions of the outcome of litigation. See Posner, *Economic Analysis of Law* at 559–61 (cited in n. 4).

38. The classic work in this area is Robert Keeton and Jeffrey O'Connell, *Basic Protection for the Traffic Victim: A Blueprint for Reforming Automobile Insurance* (1965).

39. I address this point in the next section.

where deterrability is weak in the tort setting and the political process alternative is relatively unbiased.

The criminal system induces auto safety through the use of licensing provisions and a code of traffic regulations. The regulations focus on bad acts, and their violations are defined by simple criteria such as speed limits. Although bad acts are common (far more than bad results), the cost of the system is minimized because simply defined violations and relatively low penalties limit the propensity for the parties to belabor the litigation.[40]

TORT REFORM AND INSTITUTIONAL CHOICE

Consistent with the message of this chapter — and, indeed, of this book — I see tort reform as a complex problem of institutional choice in which the relative ability of institutions can vary from context to context. As such, what may work in one context will not work in another. In this section, I will show that often neglected institutional implications make tort reform proposals that are sensible in one context highly questionable when transferred to another context. In particular, when distribution 3 is involved, many of the proposals can have unattractive, unforeseen consequences and tort liability can have strong comparative advantages. This result stems from the significant potential for prevention or safety gains from tort liability in distribution 3. As the last part of this section shows, these gains can even make sense of one of the most criticized features of tort liability — punitive damages.

The Issue of "Who Decides?"

Although the institutional choice — the issue of "who decides?" — is central to the analysis employed in this chapter, even the more sophisticated considerations of tort law and tort reform commonly neglect this subject. In some instances, important changes in institutional decision-making go unnoticed. In others, substitute decision-makers are often simply assumed to operate in a flawless manner — a "black box" analysis.

---

40. Whether and to what extent auto accidents actually fit the distribution 1 profile is open to debate. Clearly, there are deviations from the prototype. There are high stakes potential injurers such as taxicab companies and trucking firms. More generally, low stakes indicate low deterrability, not zero deterrability. A recent study shows an increase in automobile accidents associated with the shift from fault to no-fault auto systems. William Landes, *Insurance, Liability, and Accidents: A Theoretical and Empirical Investigation of the Effect of No-Fault Accidents*, 25 J L & Econ 49, 59–65 (1982). But see Jeffrey O'Connell and Saul Levmore, *A Reply to Landes: A Faulty Study of the Effect of No-Fault on Fault?* 48 Mo L Rev 649 (1983).

The proponents of the no-fault system employed for auto accidents, for example, have suggested that the no-fault principle should apply to product and service liability cases.[41] However, auto accidents and product accidents are quite different, and neither reforms nor calls for reforms have the meaning or validity in the second category of cases that they have in the first.

In a world of very limited deterrability, such as exists in distribution 1, a no-fault system that compromises or downgrades deterrence may reduce cost with little loss in prevention, since there may be little prevention to lose.[42] Because of the low per capita stakes for potential avoiders, the tort system is arguably unlikely to induce potential injurers to take the necessary safety steps. Also, the low per capita stakes of both potential injurers and potential victims reduce the likelihood that these groups will manipulate public enforcement. In this context, the tort system may offer little prevention, and public enforcement in the criminal or regulatory system may be a more trustworthy source of prevention.

The configuration of impact is quite different for the product liability setting than it is for the automobile accident setting. In distribution 3, the product liability setting, the prospects of deterrence through tort liability are generally much higher. The high per capita stakes for potential injurers make them more responsive to tort liability incentives to prevent accidents. These high stakes also provide greater incentive for experience rating and self-insurance, which reduce the problems for deterrence caused by liability insurance. At the same time, the public enforcement mecha-

41. Jeffrey O'Connell has discussed his proposals to apply no-fault principles to the areas of product liability and medical malpractice in several articles. See, for example, Jeffrey O'Connell, *Balanced Proposals for Product Liability Reform*, 48 Ohio St LJ 317 (1987); Jeffrey O'Connell, *Neo-No-Fault Remedies for Medical Injuries: Coordinated Statutory and Contractual Alternatives*, 49 L & Contemp Probs 125 (1986). This idea was influential in the federal tort reform legislation proposed by Senator John Danforth. See S 2760, 99th Cong, 2d Sess §§ 201, 204 (1986).

42. Although no-fault proposals and plans vary even in the context of automobile accidents, they all share a singular focus on providing insurance and a disregard for prevention. This lack of concern for prevention is reflected in such features as liability without regard to who was in the best position to prevent, limits on the amount of recovery (especially for "noneconomic" losses), and the elimination of compensation for losses caused by the mishaps but not borne by the immediate victim. In pursuit of the last objective, payments of medical expenses by third parties and income taxes are eliminated from recovery even though these medical outlays and lost taxes are important social costs that should be reflected in any deterrence signal.

nisms of the criminal and regulatory processes are now more suspect because these high per capita stakes also make potential injurers an active
political force capable of dominating the politically dormant low stakes
potential victims.

Advocates for no-fault insurance have made sweeping assertions about
the lack of deterrence in the tort system. Such pronouncements may be
acceptable when the potential for tort deterrence is low and that deterrence can actually be obtained elsewhere. But they may be ill-suited for the
product liability setting, both because the prospects for inducing safety
through the tort system are strong and the prospects for inducing it elsewhere are weak. Proposals for movement toward alternative liability systems in that context must be accompanied by more careful considerations
of the alternative mechanisms for prevention.

Even otherwise sophisticated law and economics treatments of tort law
ignore essential institutional issues inherent in basic changes in decision-
makers. Thus, for example, Pat Danzon, an economist who has extensively
studied tort liability in general and medical malpractice in particular, has
suggested that a schedule of damages be substituted for individualized
case-by-case damage determinations by juries.[43] Danzon includes in this
proposal a schedule for pain and suffering awards.[44] Danzon's proposal
parallels actual tort reforms that have set caps on aspects of damages such
as "non-economic" loss.

In evaluating the use of schedules and caps, the important institutional
question is, who will set and review the schedule of damages or the caps
on damages? If, as is likely, the legislature or an administrative agency is
in charge of creating and reviewing these schedules and caps, the political
process has been substituted for the jury as the determiner of damages,
and the cast of characters who will influence these outcomes changes. The
actions and activities of *potential* victims and *potential* injurers become the
central focus of the analysis rather than the activities of *actual* victims and
actual injurers. In a contest for influence between potential victims and
injurers in an area like product and service liability (the context in which
these reforms are most often offered), the position of the high stakes potential injurers is likely to be significantly overrepresented, and those schedules or caps will be biased downward—a bias likely to worsen as inflation

43. See Patricia Danzon, *Tort Reform and the Role of Government in Private Insurance
Markets,* 13 J Legal Stud 517, 533 (1984).
44. Id

reduces real awards and necessary adjustments are blocked by the greater influence of these potential injurers.[45]

This analysis does not mean that scheduled damages or capped damages are a bad idea. They can create increased stability and certainty.[46] All else being equal, this certainty and stability can increase the potential for prevention by sending a signal that is easier to understand. But the analysis suggests that any advantages resulting from greater stability and certainty may be offset by reduced prevention. The diminution in prevention results from the fact that such reforms reallocate the setting of damages from a case-by-case jury determination, which is harder to influence ex ante, to general decision-makers such as legislatures and administrative agencies, where concentrated interests have a greater chance to prevail. Reformers need to be sure that uncertainty and instability are serious — not simply an extrapolation of a few aberrations — because there are significant risks inherent in obtaining certainty and stability through these reforms.

Similarly, in connection with a proposal that reduces damages and, therefore, the deterrent signal in product liability law, Alan Schwartz proposes that the lost deterrence can be made up by the use of "tort fines."[47] Under Schwartz's proposal, these fines would be determined by the criminal-regulatory system rather than the tort system. The governmental agency in charge of determining the fines could consider a wide variety of sophisticated and complex factors, such as the implications of diminishing marginal utility on the value of increments in safety, which would likely be beyond the competence of a lay jury. Here Schwartz offers an institutional argument for his proposal. But it picks up only part of the institutional picture. His analysis reflects the technical aspects of institutional choice: administrative agencies would have more expertise than juries. However, it ignores important behavioral aspects of institutional choice.

---

45. In the context of "noneconomic" loss, the legislatures of several states have imposed caps. Some of the jurisdictions that have capped noneconomic loss put in place mechanisms that adjust damage awards to compensate for inflation. See Idaho Code § 6–1603 (1987); Mich Comp Laws Ann § 600–1483 (West 1987 & Supp 1989); Mo Ann Stat § 538.210 (Vernon 1986); Wash Rev Code Ann § 4.56.250 (West 1988). Other jurisdictions have included no inflation-adjusting mechanisms at all, leaving the political process responsible for adjustments for inflation. See Alaska Stat § 9.17.010 (1988); 1987 Colo Rev Stat § 13.21–102.5; Fla Stat Ann § 768.80 (West 1986 & Supp 1989); Md Cts & Jud Proc Code Ann § 11–108 (1988); Neb Rev Stat Ann § 44–2825 (1987); NH Rev Stat Ann § 508:4-d (Equity 1987); NM Stat Ann § 41–5–6 (1986); Or Rev Stat § 18.560 (1987). I discuss the general issue of limiting noneconomic loss in the next section.

46. See Danzon, 13 J Legal Stud at 527–30 (cited in n. 43).

47. Schwartz, 97 Yale LJ at 410 (cited in n. 19).

The agency that determines tort fines is part of the political process, and important biases can distort its determinations, especially in the area of product accidents where the interests of potential injurers can be significantly overrepresented in the political process.[48] The analysis presented here suggests that tort fines for product accidents may well be set too low and that apprehension and enforcement of these fines may be infrequent.

The message here is a familiar one. No matter how sage the analysis in other respects, it can be seriously flawed if it is not attentive to institutional considerations. Even where assumptions of frictionless or unbiased systems are tolerable in the abstract, they are questionable when manifested in actual proposals for reform. To see the fallibility of assuming frictionless alternatives, one only has to note that if the tort system were assumed to operate without cost or mistake, there would be no need to reform it.[49]

As a general matter, institutional change of great significance is hidden in the folds of many proposals for reform. Many proposed reforms of the tort system, and indeed many legal reforms in general, target the jury as a source of problems. Juries are inexpert and this lack of expertise can impose significant social costs, especially as the matters in controversy become more complex and technical. An often unobserved tradeoff occurs, however, when experts are substituted for the jury. These experts, usually an administrative panel within the tort system[50] or more generally an

48. Early on in his article, Schwartz disclaims any consideration of problems of political malfunction. Id.

49. In a book published after the article that forms the basis for this chapter, W. Kip Viscusi calls for an analysis of products liability that compares and chooses institutions. W. Kip Viscusi, *Reforming Products Liability* (1991). But, whatever its other merits, Viscusi's analysis takes a technical and sometimes largely superficial approach to institutional analyses. Thus, for example, he suggests the following reform to product liability based on his view of "institutional interactions": "Firms should be exempted from potential liability in design defect cases if they can demonstrate . . . compliance with specific government regulation. . . ." Id at 128. The analysis presupposes that when the political process acts it is a priori superior to the product liability system. In the context of product liability and, therefore, the skewed distribution, assuming blanket superiority for the political process largely assumes away the problem. Were Viscusi's reform adopted, we could expect large-scale potential injurers to seek regulation of a minimal sort, thereby insulating themselves from more serious inquiry in the tort system. It may be wise to substitute regulation for tort liability. But that is not a conclusion one should reach by assuming a perfect or near perfect regulatory response, especially in the context of product liability.

50. See, e.g., Alaska Stat § 09.55.536 (1983); Ariz Rev Stat Ann § 12–567 (West 1987 & Supp 1988); Title 18 Del Code Ann §§ 6803–6814 (1987 & Supp 1988); Hawaii Rev Stat § 671.11–20 (1985 & Supp 1988); Idaho Code § 00–1001 to 1013 (1987); Ill Ann Stat ch. 110, § 2–1013 (Smith-Hurd 1988 & Supp 1989); Ind Code Ann §§ 16–9.5–9–1 to

administrative agency outside it, tend to serve for long periods of time. These decision-makers see many similar cases and render many decisions. The stability, specialization, and experience achieved by this durability in decision-making enhances expertise. But durability also makes decision-makers much easier targets for lobbying, propaganda, graft, and influence. Juries, by contrast, are moving targets, constantly changing in composition and, as such, generally more difficult to lobby or bribe.

Juries also operate in an institutional process in which *actual* victims and *actual* injurers are the relevant participants. Administrative agencies and legislatures, on the other hand, operate in an institutional process where *potential* victims and *potential* injurers are the relevant participants. Thus, the shift from a jury to administrative experts means a great deal more than increased expertise. It also means a shift in the configuration of interested parties and, depending on the injury context, the distinct possibility of increased bias. Moreover, the possibility for this bias increases as the complexity of the substantive issues and of the administrative process increases. As it becomes more difficult and expensive for the public to police these systems, it becomes easier for unscrupulous bureaucrats to hide biased decisions and more difficult for even scrupulous bureaucrats to avoid relying on outside sources for information. The importance of the tradeoff between technical and behavioral institutional features makes substituting away from juries far trickier than most calls for that substitution seem to recognize.

Institutional Function and the Measure of Damages

Tort reformers have frequently attempted to eliminate compensation for nonpecuniary damages, especially pain and suffering.[51] These reformers criticize the awarding of pain and suffering damages because these

---

16–9.5–9–10 (West 1987 & Supp 1989); La Rev Stat Ann § 40.1299.47 (West 1988 & Supp 1989); Md Cts & Jud Proc Code Ann § 3–2A–01–06 (1987 & Supp 1988); Wis Stat § 655.42 to .68 (1988).

51. The term used for these damages by most tort reformers and legislatures is "noneconomic." The term is a serious misnomer. There is nothing noneconomic about the concerns that underlie damage categories such as pain and suffering or mental distress. Economic theory distinguishes them from other damages only in the unimportant sense that these concerns are not commonly realized in pecuniary form. But the former are as important a determinant of economic behavior as are the latter. For an economic treatment of the nonpecuniary elements of tort damages, see Neil Komesar, *Toward a General Theory of Personal Injury Loss*, 3 J Legal Stud 457 (1974).

forms of damages are not subject to exact measurement, give juries significant leeway, and provide a source of instability or uncertainty in the tort
system.[52] More generally, many reformers question the conceptual validity
of nonpecuniary claims, which they view as unworthy of compensation.
Limits on "non-economic" loss have been imposed by several jurisdictions and are being considered by others.[53]

Recently, the voices of some law and economics scholars have been
added to those opposing these nonpecuniary elements, especially in the
context of product liability. These scholars argue that although the knowledgeable insurance purchaser faced with the prospect of severe injury
might want to purchase insurance to replace pecuniary losses that occur
in such forms as lost earnings and medical bills, he or she would be far
less interested in purchasing insurance for nonpecuniary losses because
money received from the insurance company would substitute poorly for
nonpecuniary losses. When a catastrophic physical injury such as severe
paralysis or loss of sight stops someone from enjoying the pleasures of life,
money from the insurance company is a poor substitute. According to the
prevailing view, these nonpecuniary losses would play a less significant
role in a knowledgeable consumer's purchase of insurance. Because the
costs of tort recovery in the product liability area are likely to be borne by
consumers of the product, the allowance of recovery for nonpecuniary
damages in effect forces consumers to purchase more insurance than they
would want. Therefore, the argument goes, nonpecuniary losses ought not
be part of damage awards.[54]

These arguments are sensible so far as they go. However, optimal insurance is not the only or even the most important aspect of society's attempt
to cope with injuries. Prevention is also important. It may be that the hypothetical knowledgeable purchaser of insurance would not consider nonpecuniary losses in the purchase of insurance, and, therefore, that the tort
system ought not consider these losses when it structures damages for insurance purposes. However, the hypothetical knowledgeable purchaser of

52. See, for example, O'Connell, 49 L & Contemp Probs at 125 (cited in n. 41); Jeffrey
O'Connell, A "Neo-No-Fault" Contract in Lieu of Tort: Preaccident Guarantees of Postacci-
dent Settlement Offers, 73 Calif L Rev 898, 899–900 (1985); Jeffrey O'Connell, Offers that
Can't be Refused: Foreclosure of Personal Injury Claims by Defendants' Prompt Tender of
Claimants' Net Economic Loss, 77 Nw UL Rev 589, 591–92 (1982).
53. See note 45.
54. These arguments are summarized and well presented in Schwartz, 97 Yale LJ at
362–67 (cited in n. 19).

prevention would consider these losses in the purchase of prevention, and, therefore, the tort system ought to consider these losses when it structures damages for prevention purposes.

Insurance, in effect, purchases replacement dollars for a future already crippled by the injury. Prevention purchases the preservation of an uninjured way of life. Unlike insurance, the focus of the prevention choice is not on the post-accident world; rather it is on the preservation of the pre-accident world. In that setting, nonpecuniary elements are highly relevant. They quite likely dominate the pecuniary elements. Avoidance of pain and of loss of the pleasures of life are central in the impetus to prevent serious mishap.

Income and wealth are only in service of those myriad activities that make up life and living. These activities are the primary elements of life; pecuniary elements are secondary. It turns reality on its head to give ascendancy to the pecuniary.[55] We prevent to avoid all the consequences of injury, often the least of which is pecuniary. Any determination of the desirable level of prevention that ignored nonpecuniary losses would grossly underestimate the desire for prevention. When the tort system attempts to induce the correct level of prevention, a signal sent to potential injurers that reflected only the pecuniary aspects of loss would induce far too little prevention.

Analytically, we are faced with a quandary. If nonpecuniary losses are included in tort awards, we may get too much insurance.[56] But if they are excluded, we may get too little prevention. To help resolve this quandary, we can turn to the institutional analysis set out earlier in the chapter.

Where the configuration of institutional factors in a given context shows little potential for deterrability in the tort system or where there are well-functioning alternative prevention strategies, the elimination of non-

55. For a fuller treatment of this subject, see Komesar, 3 J Legal Stud (cited in n. 51).

56. Excess insurance would be at most a temporary occurrence under a perfectly functioning negligence system. In theory, negligence only allows awards for avoidable mishaps. If, therefore, there are no errors in liability or damages by juries and judges, all or at least enough claims are brought, and potential injurers understand and respond to the signal sent, there will soon be no avoidable injuries and no damage awards that include the excessive insurance components. Quite obviously, such a perfect system does not exist.

Strict liability, however, even in theory, imposes all loss on the targeted injurers and would always involve the excessive insurance problem. I discuss these and other aspects of the negligence/strict liability choice in Komesar, 65 NYU L Rev at 70–75 (cited in n. 35).

pecuniary elements for whatever reason comes at low cost in prevention. Thus, for injuries characterized by distribution 1, where there is little deterrent potential, elimination of the nonpecuniary elements comes at low cost. But such an elimination comes at much higher cost for injuries characterized by distribution 3, such as many product and service injuries, where deterrability is high in the tort system and serious problems arise in alternative institutional means of achieving prevention. Unfortunately, tort liability for product and service injury is most often the target for eliminating nonpecuniary damages.[57]

To the extent that prevention is desirable and, more importantly, obtainable, reforms that cap or limit nonpecuniary loss are counterproductive.[58] Reform of damage rules should take into account the prevention potential of a given area of tort liability and tailor the reforms accordingly.[59]

57. Many states have placed limits on "noneconomic" loss have done so only in the context of medical malpractice. See Ala Code § 6–544 (1988 & Supp 1989); Calif Civ Code § 3333.2 (West 1986 & Supp 1989); Ind Code Ann § 16–9.5–2–2 (West 1975 & Supp 1989); La Rev Stat Ann §§ 40:1299.39 & 42 (West 1977 & Supp 1990); Mass Gen Laws Ann ch. 231, § 6014 (West, 1987 & Supp 1989); ND Cent Code § 26.1–14–11 (1987 & Supp 1989); Ohio Rev Code Ann § 2307.43 (Baldwin 1987); SD Cod Laws Ann § 21–3–11 (1987); Utah Code Ann § 78–14–1–7.1 (1987); Va Code Ann § 8.01–581.15 (1984); W Va Code § 55–7B–8 (1987 & Supp 1989); Wis Stat Ann § 893.55 (West 1987 & Supp 1988). Along the same lines, Schwartz's analysis of nonpecuniary damages focuses on product liability reform. See Schwartz, 97 Yale LJ (cited in n. 19).

58. For a quite different view, see Priest, 22 Valp U L Rev at 37 (cited in n. 2).

59. Existing tort damage rules, as well as proposed reforms, may too severely limit nonpecuniary recovery and, thereby, inhibit prevention. The traditional tort treatment of wrongful death damages, for example, involves a sweeping elimination of important nonpecuniary losses. For a long period of time, wrongful death statutes virtually excluded nonpecuniary elements. See William Prosser, *The Law of Torts* at 905–7 (cited in n. 9). The basis of measurement was limited to the pecuniary contributions or savings of the deceased. Over time, usually through expansive interpretation of the statutes by the courts, the definition of wrongful death damages has grown to include greater recognition of nonpecuniary elements. Id at 908.

Despite these changes, however, the basic focus of wrongful death damages remains on post-injury insurance or compensation rather than pre-injury prevention. Losses to survivors, such as spouses, children, and parents, determine recovery in most jurisdictions. Id at 905–10. Those jurisdictions that focus on the decedent measure most damages in terms of the lost accumulation of funds to the decedent's estate (lost savings) that might otherwise have been available to his or her heirs. Id. The wrongful death system reflects the worldview of a person purchasing life insurance—concern for the care of survivors given the death of the principal.

Prevention, however, is concerned not with the post-death state but with the pre-death state. For prevention of death, the focus is not exclusively or even primarily on survivors. It is ludicrous to suppose that people avoid being killed simply to maintain a

Targeting High Deterrability: An Alternative View of Punitive Damages and Contributory Negligence

There has been a recent trend toward significant punitive damages awards in tort cases in general and in product liability cases in particular. This tendency has been met with substantial criticism and with legislative changes that have either eliminated punitive damages or made them more difficult to obtain.[60] Critics paint the image of juries wildly imposing siz-

support of their families or even to keep their families from sorrow and grief. Such concerns are important, but they do not normally exceed the basic concern for continuing one's own life.

From a prevention standpoint, the resulting tort system contains serious distortions because of these damage rules in wrongful death damage cases. It is common knowledge that damage awards for serious injury are greater than those for wrongful death. The difference may reflect the fact that money can do more for the living victim than for the dead victim—an insurance-compensation focus. But from a prevention standpoint, it suggests that death is usually preferable to injury—a counterintuitive notion. The system tells potential injurers that it is less important to prevent death—usually the most serious of consequences. As we shall see, when injurers in fact operate in this way, such behavior can produce social outrage. See the discussion of the Pinto case in the next section (discussing *Grimshaw v Ford Motor Co.*, 119 Cal App 3d 757, 174 Cal Rptr 348 (1981)). From a prevention standpoint at least, desirable tort reform might call for more generous definitions of wrongful death damage.

60. For a good summary of the debate concerning punitive damages see David Owen, *Punitive Damages in Products Liability Litigation*, 74 Mich L Rev 1257 (1976); David Owen, *Problems in Assessing Punitive Damages against Manufacturers of Defective Products*, 49 U Chi L Rev 1 (1982). In the earlier work, Owen strongly defends the role of punitive damages, while in the later work, he expresses serious misgivings about the recent trend in punitive damage awards.

Many states have enacted legislation limiting punitive damages. In some states, for a plaintiff to win punitive damages he must meet a higher burden of proof than if he does not claim punitive damages. See Ala Code § 6–11–20 (1988); Alaska Stat § 09.17.020 (1988); Idaho Code § 6–1604 (1987); Ind Code Ann § 34–4–34–2 (West 1987); Iowa Code § 668.A.1 (1987); Ky Rev Stat Ann § 411.184 (Michie/Bobbs-Merrill 1988); Or Rev Stat § 41.315 (1987); SD Cod Laws § 21–1–4.1 (1986). Other states have adopted restrictive formulas and procedures for determining punitive damages. See Ala Code § 6–11–21 (1988) (limiting punitive damages to $250,000, unless there is malice or pattern of negligence); 1988 Colo Rev Stat § 13.21–102 (1988) (limiting punitive damages to less than or equal to amount of compensatory damages awarded); Fla Stat Ann § 768.73 (West 1986) (limiting punitive damages to three times amount of compensatory damages awarded); Kan Stat Ann § 60–3702 (1987) (providing for bifurcated proceedings in which judges decide punitive damage awards; punitive damages limited to $5 million or 1½ times profits); Minn Stat Ann § 549.191 (West 1987) (establishing strict timetable for punitive damage trials); Mo Rev Stat § 510.263 (1988) (providing for bifurcated proceedings in which judges determine punitive damage awards); Okl Stat § 23.9 (1986) (limiting punitive damages to less than or equal to amount of compensatory damages awarded). New Hampshire has eliminated punitive damages. See NH Rev Stat Ann § 507:16 (1986).

able punitive damage awards on large corporations merely because these corporations balanced other factors against safety and concluded that certain increments of safety were unwarranted. Perhaps these corporations were mistaken in their calculations and should compensate those they wronged, suggest the critics, but there is no justification for sizable additional punishment. While it might seem evil for individuals to act in a calculating manner, the argument continues, it is socially beneficial that large business entities that manufacture complex and important products act this way; these manufacturers are merely making the careful cost-benefit analyses that consumers and the nation should expect of them.[61] To critics of the tort system, this trend in punitive damage awards is just another manifestation of jury hostility to large-scale or wealthy defendants — another example of jury decisions based on the presence of "deep pockets."[62]

The most dramatic, most publicized, and most criticized of the very large punitive damage awards returned by American juries was the $125 million punitive damage award granted by a jury against Ford Motor Company in connection with its design of the Pinto gas tank.[63] It is very difficult to tell whether highly publicized awards, such as that in the *Grimshaw* case just mentioned, are part of a significant national trend or are only isolated instances.[64] Clearly these awards greatly concern manufacturers and their insurers. This concern has some merit. Whatever sympathy a severe injury might produce — in *Grimshaw,* a thirteen-year-old boy was severely burned over 90 percent of his body[65] — such incidents will occur in any society that does not wish to eliminate important and beneficial activities such as driving. It would be a mistake to induce manufacturers

61. See Owen, 49 U Chi L Rev at 17 n 83 (cited in n. 60).

62. Critics argue that juries grant awards to plaintiffs against "deep pockets," merely because "deep pockets" are wealthy. This is said to epitomize the jury's disregard for legal rules, irrational sympathy for injured plaintiffs, and antipathy to large enterprises and other wealthy defendants. The term "deep pockets" is employed in this fashion many times in a recent article written by a large law firm at the behest of a group of 140 associations of potential defendants. Joint Statement, *The Need for Legislative Reform of the Tort System: A Report on the Liability Crisis from the Affected Organizations,* 10 Hamline L Rev 345, 345–48 (1987) (Joint statement prepared by Sidley and Austin law firm).

63. The case was *Grimshaw v Ford Motor Co.,* 119 Cal App 3d 757, 174 Cal Rptr 348 (1981).

64. See generally Mark Peterson, Syam Sarma, Michael Shanley, *Punitive Damages: Empirical Findings* 14–18 (1987) (determining that size of punitive damage awards in Cook County, Illinois and San Francisco County, California increased significantly from 1960 to 1984).

65. 119 Cal App 3d at 771, 174 Cal Rptr at 358.

to consider only safety while ignoring comfort, service, and affordability. Punitive damages set too high might stop production of valuable products or, at the least, force prices unnecessarily higher. In addition, higher punitive damage awards can increase claims and cases and, in turn, increase society's litigation expenses.

Yet, despite these arguments and the widespread criticism of punitive damages, sizable punitive damage awards against these manufacturers, especially ones based on the calculating behavior of these manufacturers, serve a beneficial purpose in the tort system. Increased awards and the accompanying increased tendency to sue are useful when the signal sent without these increases is too small because there are too few cases brought or because compensatory damage awards are too low to produce the appropriate levels of prevention. Punitive damages — damages in excess of actual damages — can correct these signals and create the incentive to prevent.

In product and service accidents, empirical evidence indicates that the number of successful claims by victims is significantly below the number of injuries justifying such claims.[66] Also, serious product injuries will likely involve significant undervaluation in compensatory damages. Because death is a distinct possibility from some forms of product malfunction, problems in the statutorily controlled wrongful death rules alone create a serious shortfall in the damage signal sent by the tort system. Wrongful death rules often eliminate damage awards for most pain and suffering and

66. Available empiricism indicates that the percentage of claims (let alone successful claims) may be less than 10 percent of awardable injuries. See United States Department of Commerce, Interagency Task Force on Product Liability, *Final Report,* VII–212 (1978); United States Department of Health, Education and Welfare, *Report of the Secretary's Commission on Medical Malpractice* app. at 50, 62 (1973).

It appears that only a very small fraction of injuries result in claims, let alone full awards. A federal report concluded that, for the period 1973 to 1975, 6.7 million product-related injuries occurred with fewer than 70,000 (approximately 1 percent) resulting in claims (not necessarily awards). *Final Report* at VII–212. These figures are rough and do not show what fraction of these injuries would justify claims. See id. A more detailed study of medical mishaps indicated that only 6.7 percent of those incidents designated by experts as serious medical malpractice even were brought as claims (let alone resulted in awards). See Pocincki, Dagger, and Schwartz, *The Incidence of Iatrogenic Injuries,* in United States Department of Health, Education and Welfare, Report of the Secretary's Commission on Medical Malpractice app. at 50, 62 (1973), discussed in Schwartz and Komesar, *Doctors, Damages and Deterrence,* 298 New Eng J Med 1282, 1286 (1978).

For an excellent summary of studies showing that only a small fraction of actionable injuries are claimed, let alone successfully prosecuted, see Richard Abel, *The Real Torts Crisis: Too Few Claims,* 48 Ohio St LJ 443, 448–52 (1987).

all value of life.[67] Most focus on the losses to survivors rather than the loss to the deceased. As such, they are geared to the consequences of injury, not the prevention of injury.

The emphasis on the shortfall in the deterrent signal in the product liability context, however, may seem to be in tension with the analysis presented in section 2 of this chapter. According to the institutional analysis employed earlier, this shortfall in the product liability context should be less severe than elsewhere. If not all cases are brought, at least the high per capita stakes for actual victims make such suits more likely than in other areas. If the deterrent signal is incomplete, at least the high per capita stakes for potential injurers make it more likely to be received. Why then focus punitive damages on product liability?

The apparent irony disappears, however, when one considers the advantages of targeting deterrable potential injurers in a strategy to increase prevention effectively. The tort system is expensive and, therefore, any attempt to stimulate more tort cases requires justification in the form of a significant potential for increased prevention. High stakes injurers are the appropriate target for the incentives created by punitive damages because they are a target likely to respond—more bang (injurer response) for the buck (the costs of more litigation). Calm, calculating manufacturers are particularly attractive targets for punitive damage awards, not because they are more evil than other injurers or because they are wealthier, but because they are more deterrable.[68] Moreover, because manufacturers calculate, it is especially important to send them the correct signal.[69]

67. See note 60.
68. In traditional punitive damages law, wealth is used to judge ability to pay. Owen maintains that serious problems result when total sales are used to measure the wealth of a corporation. Owen argues that corporate wealth is more complicated than individual wealth and that total sales provide a poor measure of ability to pay. See Owen, 49 U Chi L Rev at 19–20 (cited in n. 60). But, from the standpoint of the analysis in this book, even if total sales do not measure ability to pay, they do closely approximate scale of operations—an important approximation of deterrability.
69. It is possible to question whether corporations, presumably the most common form of business organization for large-scale activity, really are capable of responding to the signal the tort system sends. Large corporations have complex decision-making structures involving many people with mixed incentives. Furthermore, the changes in personnel are frequent. Some scholars argue that numerous, frequently changing decision-makers do not respond to the tort signal accurately. See id at 15–16. I am not about to enter the age-old debate about the effectiveness of large-scale operations in general, or corporations in particular, except to make a relatively simple point. The signal sent by the tort system does not differ in kind from other market signals to which we all assume corporations respond. It registers a cost for an activity and, therefore,

Although I have shown elsewhere that one can see even apparently aberrant punitive damage awards, like the $125 million award in the famous
Grimshaw case, as jury responses consistent with the socially beneficial use
of punitive damages,[70] it is hardly surprising that commentators would be
uncomfortable with my suggestion that the intuitions of a jury left largely
unfocused and uncontrolled by vague legal instructions should serve the
role of making adjustment in the overall deterrence signal. At first blush, a
case-by-case determination made by an inexpert and constantly changing
jury looks like a ridiculous way to adjust a system-wide signal compared to
a legislative or, more likely, an administrative determination that adjusted
the signal when necessary by a system of tort fines. The lay jury operating
in an ad hoc case-by-case manner would seem the worst system imaginable — that is, until one more carefully considers the alternatives.

The world of highly deterrable, calculating, potential injurers is distribution 3. That world is one in which all the technical advantages of expertise and scope associated with administrative agencies and tort fines can
be easily canceled by severe minoritarian bias. In such a setting, even
where significant increases in awards are needed to correct general shortfalls in the deterrent signal, such an agency might well do virtually nothing when the product manufacturers who would pay these increased awards
are the primary influence on the agency's decision-making. In such a situation, the inexpert, ad hoc jury seems to fit well Winston Churchill's comment about democracy — it is the worst system except for all the others.

The institutions available in most law and public policy settings are far
from ideal. In such a world, the gut feeling that there must be something
better is unreliable. I do not mean to suggest that valid reform is impossible. But valid reform does not substitute an unexamined and often undefined system for an existing one solely because of the inadequacies of
the latter. Such substitutions inevitably simply cycle through the same set
of alternatives. Yesterday's failure is offered up as today's panacea only to

---

ought to enter into the corporate calculus like any other cost. It is a complex cost, associated with a range of probable outcomes. But many, if not most, costs facing corporations have the same nature. Corporate financial managers face stochastically complex
cost pictures generated by financial markets. Costs of raw material and labor are subject
to fluctuation and significant aberrant movements. One does not have to be a student
of large-scale operations or corporate organization to understand that tort signals are no
more or less costs of production capable of integration into decision-making than any
other costs.

70. See Komesar, 65 NYU L Rev at 64–67 (cited in n. 35).

once again become tomorrow's failure. Careful, parallel examination of institutional choices is meant to break this cycle and the cynicism it fosters and, in that way, to promote valid reform.

The question of focusing civil liability on those best positioned to receive the civil liability signal surfaces beyond specific issues like punitive damages.[71] It raises more general concerns about the implications of civil liability on the likelihood of victim prevention of harm and, therefore, on the role of contributory negligence defenses. Several law and economics commentators have argued that modern product liability law has ignored the significant, even dominant, role of consumers as avoiders of injury.[72] These commentators argue for a much broader place for contributory negligence in the product liability context.[73]

However, the fact that consumers are often in a position to avoid injury does not by itself necessitate greater need to consider victim behavior in determining tort liability. The tort system must consider whether consumer prevention of harm would be increased by strengthening the contributory negligence defense. Where potential victims have low per capita stakes, there is a correspondingly low possibility that potential victims will receive the signals sent by this alteration in legal liability. Thus, even if consumers were always the lowest cost avoiders of product mishaps, there is good reason not to include a contributory negligence defense if it is unlikely that consumer behavior will be affected by the liability signal. In such a situation, society may be better off inducing somewhat more expensive avoidance from producers, who are more likely to receive the liability signal, than futilely attempting to induce a less expensive response from an inattentive population of potential victims. If avoidance from victims, however attractive, cannot be induced by existing systems, these victims' greater potential for prevention is irrelevant; in effect, it is an unreachable resource.

71. Joint and several liability raises issues parallel to punitive damages. See id at 68–70.

72. "There is growing empirical evidence that, for many products, the consumer's role in accident prevention swamps any effects of differential technological investments by providers." Priest, 22 Valp U L Rev at 13 (cited in n. 2).

73. See id at 10–14 ("[T]he presumption that product- and service-providers are vastly superior to consumers in the power to prevent injuries . . . has generated many of the problems of modern [tort] law."); Schwartz, 97 Yale LJ at 382–404 (cited in n. 18) (arguing for strict liability with contributory negligence defense rather than assumption of risk and comparative negligence).

WHO DECIDES WHO DECIDES: THE NEED FOR JUDICIAL
PROTECTION OF PRIVATE DAMAGE ACTIONS

Tort liability is a highly imperfect and expensive system of achieving improved safety and prevention. Yet it may in some contexts be the best possible system. In the product and service setting of distribution 3, the shifted distribution gives tort liability some distinct comparative advantages over either political or market process alternatives. Even in this setting, however, it is by no means obvious that the existing system of tort liability is the best we can do. Tort reform may be called for. Serious law and public policy choices concerning how to pursue safety in general and how to shape tort reform in particular remain to be made. In that vein, the analysis presented in this chapter should improve the quality of that decision.

The analysis in this chapter, however, raises important questions about which institution should make the tort reform choices. In other words, it raises question about who decides who decides — which institution decides which institutions should make the safety balance. Although decisions about tort liability and, therefore, tort reform have traditionally been made by the common law (by the courts or the adjudicative process), recently these decisions have shifted to the political process.

The analysis of distribution 3 showed why that shift may have occurred and why that shift is disquieting. Potential injurers and their insurers have become increasingly busy in the political process. Such greater activity, standing alone, would not be disturbing. Quite the opposite, costs and distortions caused by the tort system need to be considered, and the political process registers these problems through interest group effort. The disturbing feature is the relative representation of both sides of the issue. The skewed distribution can lead and, in this context, appears to have led to overrepresentation of the position of the potential injurer group. This overrepresentation has all the elements of minoritarian bias and can be seen as augmented by misled majority activity.

To the extent that this tale fairly characterizes the political process in the context of tort reform, the diminution in tort liability associated with the increasing tide of reform is disquieting. The tort reform process is biased. Even if some tort reform is necessary, the biased political process of tort reform is likely to go much farther than it should.

Courts can substitute for the political process in two different ways.

They can affect the scope of legislation by statutory interpretation or they can directly invalidate the legislation through their powers of constitutional judicial review. The courts have, in fact, responded to legislative alterations in tort liability in both manners. They have offered strained readings of statutory language in order to limit the force of tort reform legislation they consider dubious.[74] They have also invalidated various tort reforms as unconstitutional.[75] It does not take much effort to find a judicial perception of political malfunction and, in particular, of minoritarian bias lying behind these judicial decisions.[76]

However, even if I am correct that there is severe political malfunction, the existence of severe political malfunction is never a sufficient condition

74. See, for example, *Gates v Jensen*, 92 Wash 2d 249, 595 P2d 919 (1979) and the many examples in Guido Calabresi, *A Common Law for the Age of Statutes* (1982).

75. Damage caps have been a particular target of judicial review, and many have been struck down. See, for example, *Boyd v Bulala*, 672 F Supp 915, 918–22 (WD Va 1987) ($1,000,000 medical malpractice cap unconstitutional); *Boswell v Phoenix Newspapers, Inc.*, 152 Ariz 9, 12–19, 730 P2d 186, 189–96 (1986) (en banc) (statute precluding libel damages unconstitutional), cert denied, 481 US 1029 (1987); *Smith v Department of Ins.*, 507 So 2d 1080, 1087–89 (Fla 1987) (per curiam) ($450,000 cap on general "noneconomic" losses unconstitutional); *Wright v Central Du Page Hosp. Ass'n*, 63 Ill 2d 313, 325–31, 347 NE2d 736, 741–43 (1976) ($500,000 medical malpractice cap unconstitutional); *Kansas Malpractice Victims Coalition v Bell*, 757 P2d 251, 258–64 (Kan 1988) ($1,000,000 medical malpractice cap unconstitutional); *McGuire v C & L Restaurant Inc.*, 346 NW2d 605, 610–14 (Minn 1984) ($250,000 medical malpractice cap unconstitutional); *Pfost v State*, 219 Mont 206, 214–23, 713 P2d 495, 501–06 (1985) ($300,000 cap on government liability unconstitutional), overruled in *Meech v Hillhaven West, Inc.*, 776 P2d 488, 491 (Mont 1989) (4–3 decision); *White v State*, 203 Mont 363, 367–70, 661 P2d 1272, 1274–75 (1983) ($300,000 cap on government liability unconstitutional), overruled in *Meech v Hillhaven West, Inc.*, 776 P2d 488, 491 (Mont 1989) (4–3 decision); *Park v Rockwell Int'l Corp.*, 121 NH 894, 899–900, 436 A2d 1136, 1138–40 (1981) ($1,200 cap for job-related wrongful deaths of persons with no dependents unconstitutional); *Carson v Maurer*, 120 NH 925, 939–43, 424 A2d 825, 835–38 (1980) (per curiam) ($250,000 medical malpractice cap unconstitutional); *Arneson v Olson*, 270 NW2d 125, 135–36 (ND 1978) ($300,000 medical malpractice cap unconstitutional); *Lucas v United States*, 757 SW2d 687, 690–92 (Tex 1988) ($500,000 medical malpractice cap unconstitutional).

This suspicion of special interest legislation in the tort context is not limited to the recent round of tort reform. See, for example, *Brown v Merlo*, 8 Cal 3d 855, 882, 106 Cal Rptr 388, 407 (1973) (declaring unconstitutional California guest passenger statute); *Gates v Jensen*, 92 Wash 2d 246, 252–54, 595 P2d 919, 923–24 (1979) (en banc) (interpreting statute intended to overturn Washington State Supreme Court's famous decision in *Helling v Carey*, 83 Wash 2d 514, 519, 519 P2d 981, 983 (1974) (en banc), which had allowed finding of medical malpractice in face of medical custom, so narrowly as to preserve *Helling*).

76. For a particularly obvious example of this judicial perception, see *Brown v Merlo*, cited in the previous footnote.

for substituting the courts for the political process through constitutional judicial review or by the indirect route of strained statutory interpretation.[77] Comparing institutions requires precisely what it says — an examination of the *relative* abilities of the reviewed and the reviewer. Thus, given severe political malfunction, we need to seriously ask about the parallel abilities of the judicial process.

Here we are skirting the edge of a much larger universe. Tort reform decisions are only a microcosm of a much larger world of safety and health decisions. Much government action involves attempts to regulate safety and health. Minoritarian bias often infects these settings. This political malfunction may be even worse in many of these settings than in the tort reform setting because the dispersed interests that might favor regulation often do not even have the advantage of concentrated subgroups like the plaintiffs' bar. Severe political malfunction in the area of safety and health can lead to too much safety and health regulation as well as too little. Safety and health rationales are often employed to cover protectionist legislation meant to exclude competition, create monopolies, and redistribute income from dispersed consumers who must now pay higher prices to protected producers. This is the story told by the interest group theory of politics discussed in chapter 3.

In the terms of American constitutional history, the extension of judicial review in the face of severe minoritarian bias in the safety and health area, taken to its logical, single institutional conclusion, returns us to the era of economic due process — a period of judicial activism generally held in low repute. Worse, it would return us to economic due process in a world in which the size and coverage of the regulatory bureaucracy has grown immensely and in which the issues of safety and health are more technical and complicated than they were when the era ended in the 1930s.

My own opinion is that the relative abilities of the political process and the courts justify enhanced judicial scrutiny of tort reform. In this connection, I am heartened that many state courts have assumed such a role.[78]

77. For the purposes of this book, I will assume that all such substitutions occur through constitutional judicial review. A comparative institutional analysis of statutory interpretation would have primarily the same features. Given the vast literature on statutory interpretation, however, any attempt to explicitly consider this subject would make an already long book even longer. I will leave to another day or, hopefully, another author, the task of thoroughly developing a comparative institutional analysis of statutory interpretation.

78. See, for example, the cases cited in note 75.

But the issue of whether and to what extent tort reform decisions should be reviewed by the courts is one I will save for another day. It is too complex and too volatile to be handled as an aside here. The concerns with constitutional law and constitutional judicial review do, however, bring us to the subjects of the next two chapters.

}7{

Constitutional Law and Constitution Making

In the next two chapters I consider the role of comparative institutional analysis in understanding constitutional law and constitution making. By constitutional law, I mean the decisions of the Supreme Court of the United States. By constitution making, I mean the process of creating or drafting a constitution. The emergence of new nations and the radical political changes in older ones have made constitution making more than an arcane academic interest. The study of constitutional law, either its description or prescription, is complex, and constitutional law scholarship is immense. Yet the complexity and difficulty of constitutional law pales when compared to the task facing those who wish to understand constitution making and, more importantly, those who wish to make constitutions. In the process of writing this book, I have come to understand how difficult it is to address the issue of constitution making and yet also how important it is. In this chapter I address constitution making in only a preliminary fashion, limiting my observations to lessons that can be drawn from the making of the American constitution and from American constitutional law. Anything more would require a comparative study of constitutions, a task that I have not undertaken here.

It seems self-evident that constitutional law and constitution making are about institutional choice. Even the most cursory examination of the American Constitution reveals its dominant concern with the design of the American political process. The first three Articles of the Constitution detail the characteristics of the Congress, the Presidency, and the Supreme Court. The greatest controversies in the framing of the Constitution surrounded the makeup of the Congress and the methods of choosing the Congress and the President. Although handled in more vague terms, a great deal of attention was also given the issue of the responsibility of each of the branches of the federal government and of the roles of the federal and state governments.

No doubt, the Constitution reflects important and controversial goal or value choices. These include those vague notions appearing in the

196

Preamble plus the protection of a wide variety of other interests, including unfortunately a limited protection of slavery. But enunciation of these values and interests tells us very little about the Constitution we see. The tough choices are institutional choices.

Surprisingly, the two major paradigms of constitutional scholarship ignore the difficulty and importance of institutional choice. One paradigm, the fundamental rights approach, examines constitutional law solely from the vantage point of constitutional values and goals. The second, the original intent approach, trivializes the issue of institutional choice by truncating institutional choice to one institution — the original drafters or framers of the Constitution. As has been shown throughout this book, law and public policy cannot be understood by simply understanding or studying goals and values. Equally, the originalists' attempt to find the content of the Constitution (and therefore the nature of a wide variety of institutional choices) through the intent of the framers is a futile one. Originalist judges are in fact making institutional choices without acknowledging or even sometimes recognizing them. Inevitably, both fundamental rights analysts and original intent analysts make difficult and controversial institutional choices. But they do so without carefully examining the bases for these choices. I will return to these non-institutional theories in the next chapter.

Fortunately, in the last two decades, constitutional scholars have attempted more directly to address basic institutional questions. John Ely's widely known theory of judicial review reflects serious concern for the central role of institutional analysis in understanding American constitutional law. In addition to Ely, a number of other scholars have produced a variety of theories of the judicial role, both constitutional and statutory, based upon political malfunctions defined by the interest group theories of politics.

Unfortunately, there are two problems with these theories. First, they are single institutional. They define the role of the judiciary in terms of the performance of the political process without parallel comparison with the judiciary itself. Second, the conceptions of political malfunction employed by Ely and by the other constitutional analysts are incomplete. On the one hand, the interest group theory of politics, as we have already seen, focuses attention only on minoritarian bias. On the other hand, Ely's theory of political malfunction focuses only on majoritarian bias, thereby ignoring minoritarian bias.

In this chapter I examine and expand on these attempts to use institutional analysis to understand constitutional law in order to show how a fuller comparative institutional approach can help us understand constitutions. First, I examine the problems in John Ely's theory of constitutional judicial review, including its single institutionalism and its constrained theory of political malfunction. I next consider the attempts to employ the IGTP in constitutional analysis. Here I contrast the ability of the one-force model that characterizes this theory with that of the two-force model by examining two important constitutional moments — the framing of the Constitution and the famous *Carolene Products* footnote.

JOHN HART ELY'S APPROACH TO JUDICIAL REVIEW

In *Democracy and Distrust*,[1] John Hart Ely offers an institutionally based conception of constitutional judicial review that focuses particularly on the attributes of the political process. Ely's approach constitutes a serious and significant attempt at an institutional analysis of constitutional law. He sees the Constitution as concerned primarily with the mode of decision-making rather than with dictating specific decisions. His concern about the attributes of the political process is more than an afterthought. It is the central feature of his analysis.

Ely's theory has descriptive as well as normative aspects. He sees in the text of the Constitution, and in its interpretation by the Supreme Court, a basic concern with departures from the democratic political process.[2] To Ely, this concern is epitomized in the famous *Carolene Products* footnote, in which, as it signalled the end of the interventionist era of economic due process, the Supreme Court set out those circumstances in which judicial intervention might still be expected.[3] The strength of Ely's analysis lies in his insightful examination of the major features of constitutional law in terms of variation in the ability of the political process. The Equal Protection Clause, the First Amendment, and the dormant Commerce Clause, among others, receive a new interpretation.

That Ely has been able to affect constitutional analysis so powerfully is

1. John Hart Ely, *Democracy and Distrust* (1980). Not surprisingly, Ely's book has been widely cited and often discussed. Among the more cited critiques are Mark Tushnet, *Darkness on the Edge of Town: The Contributions of John Hart Ely to Constitutional Theory*, 89 Harv L Rev 1037 (1980); Laurence Tribe, *The Puzzling Persistence of Process-Based Constitutional Theories*, 89 Yale LJ 1063 (1980); and Paul Brest, *The Substance of Process*, 42 Ohio St LJ 131 (1981).

2. Ely, *Democracy and Distrust* at 73–77 (cited in n. 1).

3. *United States v Carolene Prods. Co.*, 304 US 144, 152 n 4 (1938). The text of the footnote appears in note 53.

both a tribute to his intellectual and expositional ability and a strong indication of the desperate need for institutional analysis in constitutional
scholarship. Ely has been able to significantly advance thinking on constitutional law with an approach to institutional choice that is at once both
insightful and seriously flawed. Like Posner's analysis of the common law,
Ely's analysis of constitutional law is single institutional, relying largely
on variation in political malfunction. In addition, Ely's conception of political malfunction ignores minoritarian bias — an important category of
political malfunction — and it also fails to systematically recognize the interaction between officials and constituents. That a theory with such defects should add so much to constitutional scholarship underlines the
inadequacies of non-institutional constitutional analyses. Understanding
the defects in Ely's approach facilitates the move to a better, more complete institutional approach to constitutional law.

Understanding the U.S. Constitution:
The Limits of Single Institutionalism

Ely understands that the reliability of the political process varies across
the range of social issues. For example, he sees the political process as more
suspect when it deals with race or speech issues. However, he does not
observe that the competence of the alternative institution — the judiciary —
may be similarly variable. Thus, while Ely explores the imperfections of
the judiciary with great gusto in his criticism of the fundamental rights
theorists,[4] he virtually ignores these imperfections in developing his own
theory. Accordingly, he does not compare the imperfections of the respective institutional alternatives.

In place of a careful comparison of institutional attributes, Ely substitutes a distinction between process and substance: the judiciary's role is to
police the political process and to correct political malfunction, while it is
the role of the political process to make substantive value determinations
and value judgments.[5] Like other shortcuts, this simple allocation of responsibility is not an adequate substitute for careful institutional comparison. The task of policing the political process in fact *requires* the judiciary
to make difficult and important value judgments and to substitute these
judgments for those made by the legislative process. In making these judgments, the judiciary is necessarily involved in precisely the tasks for which

---

4. Ely, *Democracy and Distrust* at 44–45, 56–60 (cited in n. 1).
5. Id at 181.

Ely supposes them ill suited.[6] Yet, these judgments are made under circumstances in which Ely suggests that the political process is also ill suited to make these judgments. To avoid this impasse, Ely's institutional analysis needs something more than his process/substance distinction can provide.

The essence of Ely's theory and his institutional argument is captured in two paragraphs worth full quotation here:

> The approach to constitutional adjudication recommended here is akin to what might be called an "antitrust" as opposed to a "regulatory" orientation to economic affairs — rather than dictate substantive results it intervenes only when the "market," in our case the political market, is systemically malfunctioning. (A referee analogy is also not far off: the referee is to intervene only when one team is gaining unfair advantage, not because the "wrong" team has scored.) Our government cannot fairly be said to be "malfunctioning" simply because it sometimes generates outcomes with which we disagree, however strongly (and claims that it is reaching results with which "the people" really disagree — or would "if they understood" — are likely to be little more than self-deluding projections). In a representative democracy value determinations are to be made by our elected representatives, and if in fact most of us disapprove we can vote them out of office. Malfunction occurs when the *process* is undeserving of trust, when (1) the ins are choking off the channels of political change to ensure that they will stay in and the outs will stay out, or (2) though no one is actually denied a voice or a vote, representatives beholden to an effective majority are systematically disadvantaging some minority out of simple hostility or a prejudiced refusal to recognize commonalities of interest, and thereby denying that minority the protection afforded other groups by a representative system.
>
> Obviously our elected representatives are the last persons we should trust with identification of either of these situations. Appointed judges, however, are comparative outsiders in our governmental system, and need worry about continuance in office only very obliquely. This does not give them some special pipeline to the genuine values of the American people: In fact, it goes far to ensure that they won't have one. It does, however, put them in position objectively to assess claims — though no one could suppose the valuation won't be full of judgment calls — that either by clogging the channels of change or by acting as accessories to majority tyranny, our elected representatives in fact are not representing the interests of those whom the system presupposes they are.[7]

6. Id at 43–69.
7. Id at 102–3.

There are several questionable propositions in this seemingly compelling argument. I have discussed many of them elsewhere.[8] For my purposes here, I want to focus in particular on two of these mistaken propositions — that an institution cannot correct or police itself and that determining the existence of a political malfunction is sufficient for constitutional judicial review. These propositions, central to Ely's analysis, are repeated in one form or another by other analysts. Buried within them are important analytical faults that can be understood once one takes a more careful look at the functioning of institutions and institutional choice.

Ely explains why "correction" or process should be the business of the judiciary only in the passage we have been examining and then only in one sentence: "Obviously our elected representatives are the last persons we should trust with identification of [legislative malfunctions]."[9] To Ely, this assertion points to judges as guardians of the political process because they are "comparative outsiders to the governmental system."[10]

Ely's assertion that the political process and its central actors should not be entrusted with the task of identifying and correcting legislative malfunctions manifests a simple principle — that one cannot reliably judge or correct oneself. The fox cannot guard the chicken coop. Although this principle, correctly qualified and employed, certainly has relevance to the allocation of institutional responsibility, it is far from a sufficient basis for a major institutional choice like the disqualification of the political process. It identifies only a potential imperfection in one of the alternative institutions — the political process. An institution attempting self-correction may be open to some degree of distrust, but, given the inevitable existence of imperfections in alternative institutions like the judiciary, recognition of a problem in the political branches is an insufficient basis for institutional choice. Simple maxims that grant institutional superiority to one institution simply do not work in the complex world of institutional choice.

It is particularly surprising that Ely should take so simplistic a view given his sophisticated appreciation of the complex institutional character of the U.S. Constitution. In *Democracy and Distrust,* Ely shows the Constitution's central focus on institutional design. A wide variety of checks and balances are built into the divisions of responsibility between the three

8. See Neil Komesar, *Taking Institutions Seriously: Introduction to a Strategy for Constitutional Analysis,* 51 U Chi L Rev 366, 398–414 (1984).
9. Ely, *Democracy and Distrust* at 103 (cited in n. 1).
10. Id.

parts of the federal political process — the House of Representatives, the Senate, and the President — and into the division of responsibility between the federal and state political processes. Underlying all these divisions of responsibility are significant variations in the rules of election, assuring that the various parts of the political process are elected by different constituencies, by different methods, and for different terms.[11] This complex structure of government can only be understood as an attempt to have the political process police itself. Various parts, variously elected and beholden to different constituencies, form the avenues of self-policing — the checks and balances. No constitution can depend solely on so fragile an institution as the judiciary to successfully insure that the rules of the game are followed. The great threats to violation of the rules come from forces that judges cannot control.

For example, the single greatest threat to the rules and indeed to the game comes from the monopoly of force that characterizes government. The military and the police are central functionaries in any constitutional government. But they are also its major threats. Rule by the military and the secret police often turns constitutions into empty documents. In the U.S. Constitution, the primary source of the control against usurpation comes from the division of responsibility among the political branches and from the dynamics of citizen participation. The U.S. Constitution divides responsibility for the federal standing army between the Congress and the President, and it at least initially allocated the responsibility for the military in general between the federal and state government through division of control over the state militias. These militias were the source of most of the armed forces for the early history of our country. The right to bear arms in the Second Amendment provided additional protection for the existence of a nonfederal military. As always, institutional choice involves difficult and sometimes perilous tradeoffs. State control over the militias and lack of a central standing army contributed to the risk of secession and civil war.

Although a variety of complex lessons for constitution making are

11. In the original Constitution, the Senate was elected by the state legislatures, the House by direct election, and the President by the electoral college. US Const, Art I, § II. Senators represent (and are now elected by) a state-wide constituency. US Const, Amend XVII, cl 1. Members of the House represent substate districts (whose boundaries are determined by state legislatures). US Const, Amend XIV, § 2. The President represents the entire nation. US Const, Art II, § 1, cl 2. Senators serve for six years. US Const, Amend XVII, cl 1. Members of the House serve for two years. US Const, Art I, § 2, cl 2. The President serves for four years. US Const, Art II, § 1, cl 1.

buried in the tradeoffs and choices of the American constitutional experience, one lesson is clear. Any protection against usurpation by the military has to come from the structuring of the political process — from internal checks and balances — not from the courts. The federal courts have been largely docile and ineffectual in the face of strong claims by the military. In times of war, the courts have allowed usurpation of traditional civil rights, including one of the sorriest moments of mistreatment of racial minorities — the Japanese relocation.[12] If we have survived usurpation by the military, it is because over time the political process policed itself, not because the courts policed it.

Even within the traditional arenas of judicial activism that Ely means to describe with his theory, the political process is not completely unable to police itself. Consider, for example, Ely's first form of political malfunction. Is it obvious that attempts to "choke off the channels of political change" in order to retain power for the "ins" would not or could not be deterred or controlled in the absence of judicial intervention? Our political process has many public officials and political actors with a great diversity of desires. This diversity of individuals and desires impedes the formation of a stable majority capable of choking off change. For most of American constitutional history, the courts were inactive about process, voting, and speech. During this period legislatures, not courts, produced reforms, the franchise was extended, and the press functioned.[13]

Nor have the political branches shown themselves completely unable to combat legislative prejudices and stereotypes — the second type of malfunction that Ely identifies. Remedies for gender discrimination have come as often from the political process as from the judiciary. The political process, for example, eventually provided suffrage for women through the Nineteenth Amendment.[14] Similarly, both after the Civil War and during

12. *Korematsu v United States,* 323 US 214 (1944).

13. One could, of course, contemplate a massive totalitarian suppression of speech, assembly, and the franchise. Under those conditions, the internal functions of the political process would have difficulty correcting the suppressions. Bayonets and tanks could silence effective political dissension. But faced with such an extreme failure of democratic institutions, the debate about the proper scope for judicial intervention would become moot, since the judiciary would be powerless; the power of the judiciary depends on a functional political process.

14. US Const, Amend XIX. For a list of other legislation enacted to correct gender discrimination, see, Education Amendments of 1972, Pub L No 92–318, 86 Stat 235, 373, codified at 20 USC § 1681 (1982); Act of Sept. 6, 1966, Pub L No 89–554, 80 Stat 378, 523, codified at 5 USC §§ 7201, 7204(b) (1982); Equal Pay Act of 1963, Pub L No 88–38, 77 Stat 56, codified at 29 USC § 206(d) (1982); see also note 15 and statutes cited therein.

the past two decades, Congress acted to curtail racial discrimination that afflicted state political processes.[15]

I do not mean to argue, nor do I believe, that political attempts to correct the problems in the political process have been sufficient, or overwhelmingly attractive, or that they have left no significant role for judicial intervention. I do contend that the political process is not inevitably the least desirable choice for correcting these problems — not when the choice is among imperfect alternatives. Since some correction can and does occur within the political process, one cannot declare a priori that the judiciary is better qualified to identify and correct political malfunctions. Whether the political process is the last we should trust is a complex comparative institutional issue, not a simple single institutional one.

In the complex world of institutional choice, foxes might be assigned to guard the chicken coop where the alternatives (bears, weasels, and so forth) are worse. Bad is often best because it is better than the available alternatives. Institutions can and do police themselves because they are complex and interactive. Forces within the institutional process can operate to reduce if not eliminate the worst mistakes or defects. Although constitutional judicial review has and can play a valuable role in the constitutional system, the U.S. judiciary plays only a small part in the policing, correcting, or general running of the system. In the main, the political process can and must police itself.

Thus, one of Ely's basic assignments of institutional responsibility is wrong. Correction or process-policing, the task Ely assigns the judiciary, is and must be done primarily by the political process. We come then to the second and more generally criticized assignment of institutional responsi-

---

15. See, for example, Civil Rights Act of 1968, Pub L No 90–284, 82 Stat 73, codified in scattered sections of 18 USC, 25 USC, 28 USC and 42 USC (1982); Voting Rights Act of 1965, Pub L No 89–110, 79 Stat 437, codified at 42 USC §§ 1971, 1973–1973bb–1 (1982); Civil Rights Act of 1964, Pub L No 88–352, 78 Stat 241, codified as amended at 28 USC § 1447, 42 USC §§ 1971, 1975a-d, 2000a & note 2000h–6 (1982); Civil Rights Act of 1960, Pub L No 86–449, 74 Stat 86, codified as amended at 18 USC § 831, 1071, 1074, 1501, 1504, 19 USC § 1971, 20 USC § 241, 260, 42 USC §§ 1974–1974e, 1975d (1982); Civil Rights Act of 1957, Pub L No 85–315, 71 Stat 634, codified as amended at 5 USC § 294–1, 28 USC §§ 1343, 1861, 42 USC §§ 1971, 1975; Civil Rights Act of 1875, ch 114, §§ 3–5, 18 Stat 336, 337, current version codified at 18 USC § 243, 42 USC § 1984 (1982); Civil Rights Act of 1871 (Ku Klux Klan Act), ch 22, 17 Stat 13, current version codified at 42 USC §§ 1983, 1986 (1982); Civil Rights Act of 1870, ch 114, 16 Stat 140, current version codified at 42 USC §§ 1971, 1981, 1987, 1989–1991 (1982); Civil Rights Act of 1866, ch 31, 14 Stat 27, current version codified at 42 USC §§ 1982, 1986–1987, 1989–1992 (1982).

bility. Substance, according to Ely, is the task of the political process not the courts. Ely's process/substance split, and especially his assignment of substance solely to the political process, is the Achilles heel (or perhaps, more accurately, the black hole) in his analysis. It has been roundly criticized.[16]

But Ely's perception of a separate sphere or job for the judiciary is, I believe, widely shared by constitutional scholars. It appears in the popular maxim that courts do not (or at least should not) legislate and in the idea that courts are in the ethereal business of identifying and propounding long-term principles of justice. Supposedly, constitutional judicial review can go on without courts remaking the basic public policy determinations previously made by the political process. This view is a fiction. It is most easily seen as a fiction in a theory like Ely's that explicitly recognizes the necessary role of institutional considerations. But the fiction is hidden in the folds of most constitutional theories.

This fiction that the courts have a separate universe of responsibility shows up in the concluding sentence of the passage previously quoted from Ely. According to Ely the judicial task is "to assess claims . . . that our elected representatives in fact are not representing the interests of those whom the system presupposes they are." The description of the task is incomplete. Determining that the political process insufficiently represents the interests of the public (or suffers from any malfunction) is insufficient to produce a constitutional decision. When the courts invalidate legislation, they must do more than decide that the political process is defective. They must also decide whether the resulting governmental decision is invalid.

Defective political processes may in fact produce good legislation whether goodness is measured by resource allocation efficiency, distributive justice, or any other criterion. Invalidating legislation simply on the basis of a malfunction can invalidate good government action. Therefore, even if the interest of a group is insufficiently represented, unrepresented at all, or even perversely represented in the overt hostility of prejudicial legislatures, a resulting legislative decision can sometimes be the same as that produced by a political process where all the defects are removed and the interests of the group are adequately represented. My point is not that the legislative decision *will* be the same. My point is that it *can* be the

16. See, e.g., Tribe, 89 Yale LJ (cited in n. 1) and Gerard Lynch, *Book Review,* 80 Colum L Rev 857 (1980).

same. As such, the reviewer must not only decide whether, to what extent, and in what form a malfunction exists but must also decide whether to remake the decision. In doing so, the reviewer cannot automatically conclude that a decision different from the one made by the defective process is preferable.

Consider the following hypothetical example based again on the nine box diagram from the *Boomer* setting; again imagine that we are dealing with a nine-voter jurisdiction. Suppose that there are two regulations each of which will prohibit the concentrated minority, depicted by E, from doing something that would harm the majority.[17] For the purposes of expositional simplicity, I will assume the social goal of resource allocation efficiency:

A	B	C
D	E	F
G	H	I

For regulation X, the impact of the regulation on E will be − $4,000 and the impact on each member of the majority will be + $1,000. For regulation Y, the impact of the regulation on E will be − $8,000 and the impact on each member of the majority will be + $500. We are now concerned with whether a given regulation will be passed by one of three political processes — an efficient process, a majoritarian bias process, or a minoritarian bias process.

The first process, the perfect process from the perspective of efficiency, weighs the *aggregate* costs and benefits and decides in favor of the largest net benefit. Such a process would decide in favor of regulation X ($8,000 benefit, $4,000 cost) and against regulation Y ($4,000 benefit, $8,000 cost). The majoritarian biased process would count only the *number* of voters benefited versus the *number* of voters harmed. Such a process would pass *both* regulations — eight voters are benefited and one is harmed by both. The minoritarian biased process is more difficult to describe in simple terms. But, as we know, it gives undue weight to the concentration of

17. The same regulations can also be seen as obtaining a benefit for the majority at a cost to E.

interests and, therefore, can be seen as rejecting both regulations because both are opposed by the concentrated minority, E. The results can be summarized in the following table (where R stands for "regulation"):

	X	Y
Efficiency	R	No R
Majoritarian biased	R	R
Minoritarian biased	no R	no R

The judicial reviewer's quandary is now apparent. A reviewer may know that a severe political malfunction is present in the process. He or she may even know the type of malfunction—majoritarian or minoritarian. But knowing of a malfunction does not tell the reviewer whether the legislative decision is inefficient. If the reviewer invalidates on the basis of the existence of a malfunction, one efficient and one inefficient action will fall. Indeed, given the facts of the hypothetical example, society will be no better off for such review. If the review requires resources, then such review would produce a net loss and itself be inefficient. It seems important to find a reviewer that cannot only spot malfunction but also spot inefficiency.

We often observe sweeping invalidation of legislation that suffers from a particularly severe political malfunction. But this strategy is only sensible as a categorical way of remaking the substantive decisions. It cannot avoid remaking them. The sweeping invalidation of legislation based on the existence of some forms of political malfunction is sometimes associated with traditional strict scrutiny under the Equal Protection Clause. Such sweeping invalidation is more sensible the lower the chances that the biased process would yield valid decisions and, conversely, less sensible the greater those chances. But the basic point remains—the attractiveness of review depends on the chances that the reviewing process will invalidate bad rather than good legislation. Good review requires more than recognizing political malfunction. Good review depends on the ability of the reviewer to do better than the reviewed. The tough challenge of comparative institutional analysis cannot be avoided by supposing that the reviewer is making a different type of decision than is the reviewed.

The need to remake tough public policy decisions and, therefore, the fragility of Ely's process/substance distinction can be seen at the very core of Ely's sense of "process." Reflecting his affection for the famous *Carolene Products* footnote 4, Ely places heavy emphasis on the courts' "process" role under the First Amendment and the Equal Protection Clause of the Fourteenth Amendment.[18] But an examination of the issues raised in each of these areas reveals a vast array of those difficult substantive value judgments that Ely claims belong to the political process.

Ely's view of the First Amendment is simply stated: the First Amendment deals with speech — political speech predominantly — and with the press. The free exchange of ideas is basic to the functioning of the political process. Ely's notion that the First Amendment concerns political information and is linked to the political process certainly follows a long tradition of constitutional interpretation.[19] Many speech cases involve political speech, and many involve concerns about the throttling of that speech by politicians adverse to the message.

Other commentators have broader conceptions of the meaning of the First Amendment,[20] but even if one accepts Ely's narrower view, there is still no escaping the fact that speech cases require the judiciary to make difficult substantive decisions. First Amendment cases, after all, are not just speech or press cases; they are also cases about national security, the raising of armies, violence in the streets, the orderly use of public thoroughfares, the functioning of the judicial system, the privacy and morals of the populace, and the education of the young.[21] In other words, they implicate subjects normally assigned to the political branches. If Ely were asked where these subjects belong in his constitutional order and were not told

18. Ely, *Democracy and Distrust* at 93–94, 98 (cited in n. 1).

19. See Thomas Emerson, *The System of Freedom of Expression* 7 (1970); Alexander Meiklejohn, *Free Speech and its Relation to Self-Government* 22–27 (1948); Alexander Meiklejohn, *Political Freedom, the Constitutional Powers of the People* 107–24 (1960); Robert Bork, *Neutral Principles and Some First Amendment Problems*, 47 Ind LJ 1, 20–35 (1971); Harry Kalven, *The New York Times Case: A Note on "The Central Meaning of the First Amendment,"* 1964 S Ct Rev 191, 204–10; Kenneth Karst, *Equality as a Central Principle in the First Amendment,* 43 U Chi L Rev 20, 23–25 (1975).

20. Some would argue that a further purpose of the First Amendment is the protection of "personhood," or the dignity of individual thought. See, for example, Emerson, *The System of Freedom* at 6 (cited in n. 19); Laurence Tribe, *American Constitutional Law,* 905–10 (1978); Karst, 43 U Chi L Rev at 25–26 (cited in n. 19).

21. See, for example, *Terminiello v Chicago,* 337 US 1 (1949); *West Va. State Bd. of Educ. v Barnette,* 319 US 624 (1943); and *New York Times Co. v United States,* 403 US 713 (1971) (per curiam).

that speech issues were also present, he would surely respond that these are substantive matters involving determinations of basic value judgments and should therefore be assigned to the political branches.

We only need to recall the earlier discussion of the *Pentagon Papers* case, an important First Amendment case, to see both the insufficiency of the finding that the political process is malfunctioning and the resulting necessity that the judiciary make difficult substantive judgments. It would be difficult to believe that any of the members of the *Pentagon Papers* Court were unaware of the distinct possibility that the Nixon administration might have wanted to suppress the Pentagon Papers in order to "choke the channels" of the political process by suppressing information for reasons other than national security. That national security concerns were not the sole or even the dominant reason for the government's attempt to suppress the Pentagon Papers did not mean, however, that the Papers would not have been suppressed by a perfectly functioning political process in which all valid concerns were well represented.

This possibility caused at least the dissenting and swing votes to worry about the possibility that the government's position was valid even if the governmental decision-making process that produced it was suspect. Even the "absolutists" had to make the judgment that the chance of a valid outcome was low enough to ignore that possibility on a general basis. Significant suspicion of the government was not sufficient. The Court had to consider its ability to remake the complex and important substantive issue at stake.

A look at Ely's other core subject — the representation of minorities and its grounding in the Equal Protection Clause — yields similar conclusions. According to Ely, the Equal Protection Clause is meant to correct a problem with the legislative process: classifications based on prejudice, whether deriving from open hostility or from self-serving stereotypes. Either because they are members of the majority or because they serve the wishes of the majority, political representatives often fail to represent those groups against whom this prejudice is directed.

However, despite this element of failure of process, Equal Protection cases, like First Amendment cases, require the judiciary to make important and difficult substantive determinations. Equal Protection cases can and do involve a broad range of social issues. Prejudice, after all, may lie behind any form of legislation. The identification of a serious prejudice that influences the political process only tells us that there is a *tendency* to underrepresent certain interests. But the same decision might have been produced by an unbiased process[22]—a process, in Ely's terms, untainted by hostility or self-serving stereotypes. If, as Ely believes, a showing of prejudice should shift the burden to the government to demonstrate that the same policy decision would have resulted even if no such motive had existed, the judiciary is obliged to evaluate the basic substantive decision.

The inadequacy of a finding of political malfunction and the requirement that courts remake difficult substantive decisions is dramatically illustrated in *Korematsu v United States,*[23] where the Supreme Court addressed the constitutionality of the exclusion of persons of Japanese ancestry from designated areas of the West Coast. Korematsu was a native-born American of Japanese ancestry convicted of refusing to obey a military order to leave his home.[24] The military order of exclusion had been issued by the regional military commander pursuant to powers granted by Congress and the President.

There can be little doubt that the governmental action involved in *Korematsu* was a product of the sort of severe political malfunction that underlies the equal protection component of Ely's theory of judicial review. In a few pages of his dissent, Justice Murphy laid bare the real possibility that the worst sort of racial stereotypes were at work. He described a racist attitude toward individuals of Japanese ancestry on the part of General DeWitt, the military commander who issued the relocation order.[25] He showed that pressure for the order had been applied by special interest groups concerned with eliminating commercial competition from Japanese-Americans who had had the temerity to undersell white producers.[26] In short, Justice Murphy presented strong grounds to distrust the process that had made the relocation decision.

Even the majority, which upheld the constitutionality of the government action and the associated conviction of the defendant, saw strong

22. This realization comes through in the Court's cryptic footnote 21 in *Village of Arlington Heights v Metropolitan Hous. Dev. Corp.,* 429 US 252, 270 n 21 (1977), where the Court noted that proof that the village was motivated by prejudice does not automatically require invalidation of its actions if the same action would have resulted absent prejudicial purpose.

23. 323 US 214 (1944).

24. Because Korematsu was convicted only of disobeying the exclusion order, the Court did not address the constitutionality of the further order that he report to an "assembly center to be relocated"—most likely to a relocation center, id at 222, or, in the phrase of the petitioner explicitly disavowed by the Court, id at 223, a concentration camp.

25. Id at 236 (Murphy dissenting).

26. Id at 239.

reason to distrust the political process. In an opinion authored by Justice Black, the Court for the first time enunciated the modern equal protection test associating the judicial role with the use of a suspect racial classification. The Court declared that "all legal restrictions which curtail the civil rights of a single racial group are immediately suspect" and would be subject to "the most rigid scrutiny."[27] To satisfy this test, the government must show "pressing public necessity."[28] The majority included Justices Black and Douglas, who were to be strongly associated with the protection of minority rights, and Chief Justice Stone, who had authored the *Carolene Products* footnote. They were aware of the defects of General DeWitt and the political process. Indeed, the "most rigid scrutiny" they proposed for "suspect classifications"[29] suggested that they were uncomfortable with the government's decision.

Yet despite the grounds for distrust of the political process and an announcement of the "most rigid scrutiny," the majority of the Justices simply accepted the government's assertions that some residents of Japanese ancestry were disloyal and that these disloyal residents could not be separated expeditiously from loyal citizens. As a prominent modern commentator has noted, "In retrospect, the Supreme Court's tolerance of the wartime excesses of Congress seems wrong, but in retrospect it is also clear that the Court saw no reasonable alternative to deference."[30]

Justice Jackson, in dissent, stated the Court's predicament clearly:

> I cannot say, from any evidence before me, that the orders of General DeWitt were not reasonably expedient military precautions, nor could I say that they were. . . .
>
> The limitation under which courts always will labor in examining the necessity for a military order are illustrated by this case. How does the Court know that these orders have a reasonable basis in necessity? No evidence whatever on that subject has been taken by this or any other court. There is sharp controversy as to the credibility of the DeWitt report. So the Court, having no real evidence before it, has no choice but to accept General DeWitt's own unsworn, self-serving statement, untested by any cross-examination, that what he did was reasonable.[31]

27. *Korematsu,* 323 US at 216.
28. Id.
29. Id at 216.
30. Tribe, *American Constitutional Law* at 355 (cited in n. 20).
31. *Korematsu,* 323 US at 245 (Jackson dissenting). Faced with this dilemma, Justice Jackson even argued that the Court should refuse to decide the constitutionality of the government's actions and refuse the military access to civil courts to enforce its

Yet, the Court did not have to accept the government's assertions blindly. It could have rejected the commander's report and the government's assertions and made its own determinations about the relevant issues. Justice Murphy was willing to do this. While conceding that a very real threat of invasion existed at the time the order was issued, Justice Murphy argued that a sweeping exclusion based on race was not necessary.[32] He pointed to the experience in England where tribunals had separately assessed the loyalty of over 70,000 German and Austrian aliens and interned only 2,000.[33]

Korematsu poignantly, even painfully, shows the insufficiency of a judicial determination that the political process is malfunctioning—even severely malfunctioning. Constitutional invalidation of a governmental action requires that courts substitute their decision for the decision of the malfunctioning political process. In *Korematsu*, this meant that the courts were faced with deciding whether to decide the sort of issue that they would normally completely shun as a political question.[34]

Thus *Korematsu*, like the *Pentagon Papers* case, shows that in constitutional adjudication courts must do more than find the presence of severe political malfunction. They must also choose between the malfunctioning political process and an adjudicative process that often suffers from ignorance, systemic bias, and limited resources. If they choose themselves, they must remake the public policy determination made by the political process. They must substitute their own imperfect determination of substance

---

orders. Id at 243–46. One should not overestimate the practical significance of such a refusal. Given the resources of the military in this war zone, the courts were not really necessary to it. Korematsu had been taken from his home and placed in a relocation camp without court order. Justice Jackson would, in effect, have declared the issue nonjusticiable on a basis closely aligned to the political question doctrine.

32. Id at 241–42 (Murphy dissenting).

33. Id at 242 n 16.

34. In retrospect, the majority choice was wrong. High-ranking government officials from both the War Department and the Justice Department apparently suppressed information indicating that mass internment was unnecessary and that individual loyalty hearings were a feasible alternative and specifically kept this information from the Supreme Court during the *Korematsu* hearings and those for *Hirabayashi v US*, 320 US 81 (1943) (an earlier War Powers case). See Peter Irons, *Justice at War: The Story of the Japanese American Internment Cases* 199, 201–2, 205, 207, 285, 292, 317 (1983). One cannot avoid the disquieting reality, however, that a similar case could again arise in time of war or national emergency and again present the courts with the same difficult choices ex ante that confronted the *Korematsu* court, whatever historic investigation showed ex post. The Supreme Court, like other decision-makers, must make decisions in significant ignorance.

for the imperfect determination of substance made by the political process. That is the character of constitutional review.

Despite the long tradition of denial by judges and commentators, judicial review requires remaking public policy made by the political process. The uncountable number of governmental decisions potentially subject to review and the minuscule judicial resources available for review mean that courts are forced to focus basic attention on institutional choice — on the allocation of decision-making authority. Courts are forced to refuse serious judicial review to vast categories of often important and highly imperfect government actions. The limited scale of judicial resources alone forces courts to abandon a serious review of the vast majority of government activity. The courts must make tough institutional choices. But, when the courts decide to decide and offer serious judicial review, the courts must do substance. If they decide that they are better decision-makers, they must then decide the underlying public policy question.

Ely is correct, in my view, when he asserts that the Constitution basically serves to allocate decision-making responsibility rather than to directly impose specific substantive results. He also is correct when he argues that problems with the political process are and should be important in determining that allocation. However, Ely's single institutional analysis with its process/substance dichotomy is insufficient to define the role of judicial review. In short, the issue is institutional choice and the analysis must be comparative, not single, institutional.

Ely's Concept of Political Malfunction: Ignoring Minoritarian Bias

There is one further problem with Ely's institutional argument. To Ely, "malfunctions" in the political branches are the basis for judicial intervention. While such malfunction alone is not a sufficient condition to determine when and how to intervene, it is an important feature of comparative institutional analysis. Malfunction in the political branches, however, is not necessarily limited to the two forms Ely identifies, namely, attempts by those in power to choke off the channels of political change and the systematic disadvantaging of some minority out of simple hostility or prejudice.

The most glaring absence from Ely's sense of political malfunction is minoritarian bias. In chapter 3, I argued that the one-force model of the interest group theory of politics was too limited because it focused attention solely on the overrepresentation of concentrated minorities. Ely, on the other hand, has ignored minoritarian bias and focused on the underrepresentation of minorities and the overrepresentation of majorities—majoritarian bias, in my terms, or majority tyranny in his. Although majoritarian bias is a severe form of political malfunction, so is minoritarian bias. It is more pervasive and may in total be more damaging to society. Why does Ely ignore it?

If Ely allowed minoritarian bias as one of the forms of political malfunction that triggered judicial review, he would have a difficult time accommodating his theory to *Carolene Products,* a touchstone of his approach. *Carolene Products* involved legislation that had all the earmarks of rent-seeking. Yet in that case, the Court announced its retreat from concern about such legislation and from the doctrine of economic due process in general. In subsequent decades, the Court has made it increasingly clear that it will not examine most economic and social legislation despite strong evidence of severe minoritarian bias.

From a comparative institutional standpoint, it is relatively easy to understand the case for judicial rejection of economic due process or for rejection of judicial protection against minoritarian bias in general. Even in the presence of severe political malfunction, we would not expect or want to substitute judicial decision-making if it would be worse. The scale of the judiciary, its technical competence, the need for its resources elsewhere, and the biases inherent in the dynamics of the adjudicative process all help to explain why minoritarian bias might not be a central concern of American constitutional law.[35]

But what can be understood in a comparative institutional picture cannot be understood as long as the analysis is single institutional, as is Ely's. For Ely, the sole touchstone is serious political malfunction. Minoritarian bias is as serious a systemic political malfunction as is majoritarian bias. In both instances, important interests are unrepresented.

The common rhetoric of constitutional law explains the absence of judicial review of most economic legislation based on the benign nature of the political process in this context or at least on the basis of the ability of the political process to eventually correct bad outcomes. Ely simply repeats the common theme. But the common theme is wrong. There is good reason to believe that there is a significant, systemic political malfunction in the area of "social and economic legislation." Rent-seeking is not

35. I will explore economic due process and the judicial response to minoritarian bias more extensively in the subsequent discussion of Bruce Ackerman's analysis of the *Carolene Products* footnote and Richard Epstein's call for a return to economic due process.

simply the imagining of right-wing ideologues. It exists and it is serious. To make his single institutional theory fit *Carolene Products,* Ely must refuse to recognize an important form of political malfunction.

Another feature of Ely's conception of political malfunction makes it unattractive even if expanded to include both majoritarian and minoritarian bias and placed in a comparative framework. Ely conceives of political malfunction at least in the equal protection context in terms of the motives of governmental officials—their hostility to minorities or their self-serving stereotypes about minorities. Ely's focus on the motives of public officials largely ignores the interaction between those officials and the mass of non-official political actors—voters, interest groups, lobbyists, and so forth. But, as I indicated in chapter 3, illicit motivation is neither a necessary nor a sufficient condition for severe political malfunction—minoritarian or majoritarian. Influential constituents can get their way even in the face of public-interested officials by overrepresentation of their view through lobbying and propaganda or by replacing one public-interested official with another whose conception of the public interest adheres more closely to the position desired by the better represented group. Ely's focus on legislative motivation would seem to ignore a large range of serious political malfunction.[36]

In summary, Ely's analysis of constitutional law provides a powerful alternative to the non-institutional analyses that surround it. Yet, it is single institutional. That severe limitation produces the defective process/substance distinction and forecloses a broader and more robust conception of political malfunction that includes minoritarian as well as majoritarian bias. The lesson to be gathered from the defects in Ely's analysis is not, as some would insist, the irrelevance of institutional analysis.[37] Ely's failure is that he did not do enough institutional analysis. He failed to base his institutional analysis of the political process on a systemic enough base and to compare the political process with its alternative, the adjudicative process, in a consistent, parallel manner.

36. An emphasis on the motivation for legislation is reflected in equal protection law in the motive or purpose test for implicit suspect classifications. To the extent that that test reflects a judicial perception of political malfunction similar to Ely's, it is subject to the same criticisms I have just applied to Ely. Even to the extent that that test reflects a concern about judicial as well as political malfunction, it is still an awkward and inferior way of dealing with an important issue. I discuss this issue in Neil Komesar, *A Job for the Judges: The Judiciary and the Constitution in a Massive and Complex Society,* 86 Mich L Rev 657, 708–11 (1988).
37. See Tribe, 89 Yale LJ (cited in n. 1).

THE USE OF THE INTEREST GROUP THEORY OF POLITICS IN
CONSTITUTIONAL LAW AND ANALYSIS

The interest group theory of politics has been frequently applied both
to constitutional law and to the allied field of statutory interpretation.[38]
Most of these applications use the political malfunction identified by the
interest group theory of politics as the justification for an increased judicial
role. Like Ely's approach, these efforts are single institutional.[39] They make
their case by focusing on the degree or existence of political malfunction
without careful, parallel consideration of the abilities of the judiciary. To
the extent that they consider the characteristics of the judiciary at all, they
tend, like Ely, to suggest that the judiciary would not be faced with serious
substantive determinations under their suggested expanded programs.

I have discussed the problems of such single institutional analysis at
length in connection with Ely and will return to it in connection with
Richard Epstein's theory of the Takings Clause. At this juncture, I want to
explore the comparative advantages for constitutional analysis of the two-
force model of political malfunction over the one-force model associated
with the interest group theory of politics. In that connection, I will examine two constitutional law topics—the framing of the U.S. Constitution
and the meaning of the *Carolene Products* footnote—using the two-force
model as compared to several analyses that use the one-force model. The
discussion of the *Carolene Products* case and its famous footnote leads into
the discussion of modern constitutional law, economic due process, and
the Takings Clause (all considered in the next chapter) and returns us to
broader questions of institutional comparison. Discussion of the framing
of the Constitution and of the *Carolene Products* footnote also provides
insights valuable to an understanding of constitution making in general.

38. Examples of the constitutional law applications include Erwin Chemerinsky, *The
Supreme Court, 1988 Term—Foreword: The Vanishing Constitution,* 103 Harv L Rev 43
(1989); Richard Epstein, *Takings* (1985); Bernard Siegan, *Economic Liberties and the Constitution* (1980); Martin Shapiro, *Freedom of Speech: The Supreme Court and Judicial Review*
(1966); Cass Sunstein, *Interest Groups in American Public Law,* 38 Stan L Rev 29 (1985).
Examples of statutory interpretation applications include Frank Easterbrook, *The Supreme Court, 1983 Term—Foreword: The Court and the Economic System,* 98 Harv L Rev 4
(1984); Jonathan Macey, *Promoting Public-Regarding Legislation Through Statutory Interpretation,* 86 Colum L Rev 223 (1986); Cass Sunstein, *Interpreting Statutes in the Regulatory
State,* 103 Harv L Rev 405 (1989).

39. For a summary of the single-institutionalism of these works, see Einer Elhauge,
Does Interest Group Theory Justify More Intrusive Judicial Review?, 101 Yale LJ 31, 66–87
(1991).

The Framing of the Constitution

We can see the benefits of the two-force model with its attention to interaction between majoritarian and minoritarian bias by contrasting it to some recent attempts to analyze the Constitution in one-force (minoritarian bias) terms. In the view of two recent analyses of the Constitution, it was the intent, and the achievement, of the original Constitution to increase the costs of special interest activity, thereby decreasing such unattractive activities as factionalism and rent-seeking. Cass Sunstein concludes that the framers of the Constitution, and in particular James Madison, intended to create a government immune from the clamoring of interest groups.[40] In terms of our previous discussion, Sunstein asserts that the Constitution was designed to raise the costs of interest group activity and thereby to create as much slippage as possible so as to allow legislators greater opportunity for independent deliberation about the public interest. Subsequently, in two articles which rely in part on Sunstein but make more explicit use of the interest group theory of politics, Jonathan Macey argues that one can understand the gist of the Constitution as an attempt to reduce the amount of rent-seeking activity:[41]

The Constitution employs a bicameral legislature, with houses of widely different sizes. The American constitutional system also institutes a regime of checks and balances by creating both a federal judiciary that is insulated from political pressure because its judges have life tenure and salaries that cannot be reduced, and a federal executive with authority to veto acts of Congress. In addition, each of the three branches of government must appeal to different constituencies for political support, thereby further reducing the power of interest groups to affect political outcomes. Finally, the Constitution envisions a federal form of organization in which citizens are free to travel among the several states, thereby reducing the incentives of individual states to engage in transfer activities.

Each of these features of the Constitution provides independent support for the hypothesis that the Constitution was designed to impede rather than to facilitate rent-seeking.[42]

40. Sunstein, 38 Stan L Rev (cited in n. 38).
41. Jonathan Macey, *Transaction Costs and the Normative Elements of the Public Choice Model: An Application to Constitutional Theory*, 74 Va L Rev 471 (1988) and *Promoting Public-Regarding Legislation Through Statutory Interpretation: An Interest Group Model*, 86 Colum L Rev 223 (1986).
42. Macey, 74 Va L Rev at 509–10 (cited in n. 41).

Macey supports his view that limiting "the ability of interest groups to achieve anti-majoritarian outcomes in the legislature was a primary goal of the new Constitution" by pointing to the expressed wishes of the framers of the Constitution, and in particular James Madison, as well as to the views of prominent constitutional scholars, like Sunstein and Bruce Ackerman, who I will discuss subsequently.[43]

From the vantage point of the one-force model, Sunstein's and Macey's arguments seem appealing. Higher costs of political participation decrease the amount of special interest activity and thereby decrease the waste of rent-seeking and increase the independence of elected officials to deliberate the public interest. From the vantage point of the two-force model, however, both the intent of the framers and the character of the Constitution they produced look significantly different. The historical record indicates that those who drafted and debated our Constitution understood both aspects of the two-force model — the special interest or minoritarian bias that animates the analyses of commentators like Sunstein and Macey and the majoritarian bias that they neglect. Indeed, contrary to the assertions of Sunstein and Macey, Madison and the Federalists seemed most concerned with majoritarian not minoritarian bias. The Constitution they created may have increased the second while decreasing the first.

The framers, or at least those who authored the Federalist papers, recognized the existence of both forms of bias, expressed concern about both, but seemed to worry most about majorities. James Madison, in particular, placed great emphasis on the danger of majoritarian excesses:

> If a faction consists of less than a majority, relief is supplied by the republican principle, which enables the majority to defeat its sinister views by regular vote. It may clog the administration, it may convulse the society; but it will be unable to execute and mask its violence under the forms of the Constitution. When a majority is included in a faction, the form of popular Government, on the other hand, enables it to sacrifice to its ruling passion or interest both the public good and the rights of other citizens. . . .
>
> [T]he majority . . . must be rendered, by their number and local situation, unable to concert and carry into effect schemes of oppression. . . .
>
> [A] pure Democracy, by which I mean a Society consisting of a small number of citizens, who assemble and administer the Government in person, can admit of no cure for the mischiefs of faction.[44]

43. Macey, 86 Colum L Rev at 243 (cited in n. 41).
44. Federalist 42 (Madison) in Henry Dawson, ed, *The Federalist Papers* 59–60 (1863).

And also:

> Wherever the real power in a Government lies, there is the danger of oppression. In our Governments the real power lies in the majority of the community, and the invasion of private rights is *chiefly* to be apprehended, not from acts of Government contrary to the sense of its constituents, but from acts in which the Government is the mere instrument of the major number of the Constituents. This is a truth of great importance, but not yet sufficiently attended to. . . . [45]

Madison's comments also reveal the major Federalist response to the perceived danger of majoritarian excesses: the insulation of federal government decision-makers from local majorities.[46] They sought this insulation in several ways. First, these decision-makers were physically distanced. The national capitol was generally much further from most citizens than the seats of state or local government; physical distance was no small factor at a time when travel was so difficult. Second, each of these decision-makers was to represent a large number of constituents, thereby making organization of a majority more difficult. Third, they served for relatively long terms ranging from two to six years. As such, their constituents had far less frequent access through the ballot box and a more complex record to decipher and judge. Fourth, the Senate and President were indirectly elected — the Senate by state legislatures and the President by the electoral college.[47]

By contrast, their opponents, the Anti-Federalists, appeared far more concerned about minoritarian bias than the Federalists. The Anti-Federalists feared that indirectly elected Senators serving long terms would devolve into an aristocracy and combine with the indirectly elected President to allow an easy conduit for "the advantage of the few . . . over the many."[48]

45. Letter from James Madison to Thomas Jefferson (Oct. 17, 1788), reprinted in *The Mind of the Founder: Sources of the Political Thought of James Madison* 206 (1973) (emphasis in original).

46. These comments also show the systemic or institutional nature of Madison's conception of political malfunction. Madison's view of politics is not based on the motives or mind-set of public officials. Majorities are most to be feared because they are least likely to have their influence checked within the larger political system. Whether or not Madison's view that majorities were most to be feared is correct, his argument reflects a sophisticated perception of the systemic nature of political malfunction.

47. See David Epstein, *The Political Theory of the Federalist* 59, 95–97, 99–100, 105 (1984).

48. *Comments of George Mason*, in Jonathan Elliot, ed., *The Debates in the Several State Conventions, on the Adoption of the Federal Constitution: As Recommended by the General Convention at Philadelphia, in 1787*, 493–94 (1983). See also, *Comments of Patrick Henry*, in id at 503–4; *Comments of James Monroe*, in id at 220.

In response, they unsuccessfully sought rotation in office, shorter terms, the possibility of recall, and easier impeachment.[49] They also feared that the House was insufficiently numerous to enable it to be "a representation of the people" and, therefore, that it would be subject to influence and corruption.[50] They feared "the superior opportunities for organized voting which they felt to be inherent in the more thickly populated areas."[51] They feared that a Supreme Court not subject to popular control would favor the rich.[52] These are all signs of concern about minoritarian bias.

This analysis of the Anti-Federalist position indicates that minoritarian bias might have been curbed in many ways not adopted in the Constitution. Such curbs were not adopted, at least in part, because the design of the Constitution and any attempts to curb rent-seeking were more complex and interesting than Macey, Sunstein, and others who employ the one-force model recognize. In particular, they were not adopted because the dominant Federalists feared majoritarian bias more than they feared minoritarian bias.

Without a recognition that majoritarian as well as a minoritarian bias is possible, it is easy to assume that, when Madison speaks of "factions," he must be speaking about minoritarian or special interest groups. But that is not the case. Madison's own words, the reaction of the Anti-Federalists, and the character of the Constitution all indicate that if a decrease in rent-seeking was the object of the framers, it was a decrease primarily in majoritarian rent-seeking, and if legislators were to be protected against the pressure of factions, it was primarily majoritarian factions against which they were to be protected. Because the two biases trade off against one another, any attempts to reduce one may in fact increase the other. It is entirely possible, therefore, that our Constitution was designed to reduce majoritarian rent-seeking or protect against majoritarian factions, but may have done so at the expense of increasing minoritarian rent-seeking and the influence of minoritarian factions.

49. See *Comments of Patrick Henry,* in id at 50. See also note 48 and materials cited therein.

50. *Essays of Brutus, Essay of Nov. 15, 1787,* in Herbert Storing, ed, 2 *The Complete Anti-Federalist* 380 (1981); *Letters of Centinel, Letter I* in id at 142; *Letters from the Federal Farmer, Letter of Oct. 10, 1787,* in id at 235; *Comments of Melancton Smith* in *Debates* at 248–49 (cited in n. 48); *Comments of William Grayson* in id at 281–82.

51. Kenyon, *Men of Little Faith: The Anti-Federalists on the Nature of Representative Government,* 12 Wm & Mary LQ 3, 13 (1955).

52. *Essays of Brutus, Essay of Mar. 20, 1788* in *The Complete Anti-Federalist* at 438–39 (cited in n. 50); *Comments of George Mason,* in *Debates* at 495 (cited in n. 48).

Because of the relative versus absolute cost effects discussed in chapter 3, increasing the costs of political action can lead to more rent-seeking or more factional activity. The entire logic of minoritarian influence and bias is the greater ability of concentrated minorities to deal with the cost of understanding and affecting political outcomes. Concentrated interests flourish when high costs of participation, most often the high costs of information, make the dispersed majority dormant. Here the relative cost effects on the majoritarian opposition may exceed any absolute effects on concentrated minorities, and these concentrated interests may find political activity more, not less attractive, causing an increase, not a decrease, in rent-seeking activity.

This tradeoff between minoritarian and majoritarian bias with its interaction between absolute and relative cost makes characterizing the Constitution more difficult. The supposed isolation of public officials, which Sunstein praises, may purchase protection from majoritarian bias but only by increasing the potential for minoritarian bias. Greater distance, more complex modes of selection, and larger and more diverse constituencies may provide protection of public officials from the masses — but not complete isolation. Other paths of influence, and therefore sources of bias, remain and in fact flourish. Access may be more expensive, but it is more efficacious when the competition of more diffuse groups is eliminated. For those, like Sunstein and Macey, who see politics solely from the one-force perspective, increased costs of access unabashedly reduce rent-seeking and increase legislator independence. But these results are by no means inevitable. A concentrated minority may find it more costly to reach the ear of government officials, but they often find it much more profitable to do so.

The two-force model provides insights into the quandary facing the framers and into the character of the document they gave us. Its insights into institutional design may be particularly important today when constitutional design is of more than historical interest. As new nations or reborn old nations attempt to structure their political processes, understanding the tradeoffs inherent in the choices about the form and character of the political process is increasingly important. In such endeavors, the two forces of majoritarian and minoritarian influence, and their tensions, tradeoffs, and interactions, require attention.

The *Carolene Products* Footnote

We can see the importance of the two-force perspective in a more contemporary constitutional setting by examining the famous *Carolene*

Products footnote 4, the often-discussed, provocative precursor to much twentieth-century constitutional law concerning individual rights.[53] This footnote appears in one of several cases that marked the end of the era of economic due process — the period approximately between 1905 and 1935 in which the Court invalidated a wide range of legislation regulating economic transactions. The *Carolene Products* case involved a federal statute prohibiting the interstate sale of "filled milk" — a whole milk substitute.[54] In upholding the constitutionality of the legislation, the Court articulated a strong presumption of constitutionality and, therefore, a limited judicial role in connection with "regulatory legislation affecting ordinary commercial transactions."[55] To this pronouncement, the Court attached footnote 4.

In this footnote, the Court suggested that the same strong presumption of constitutionality might not apply to three categories of legislation: legislation that appears on its face to violate a specific prohibition of the Constitution; legislation that restricts the political process; and legislation

53. *Carolene Products* footnote 4 reads:

> There may be narrower scope for operation of the presumption of constitutionality when legislation appears on its face to be within a specific prohibition of the Constitution, such as those of the first ten amendments, which are deemed equally specific when held to be embraced within the Fourteenth.
>
> It is unnecessary to consider now whether legislation which restricts those political processes which can ordinarily be expected to bring about repeal of undesirable legislation, is to be subjected to more exacting judicial scrutiny under the general prohibitions of the Fourteenth Amendment than are most other types of legislation. On restrictions upon the right to vote, see Nixon v. Herndon, 273 U.S. 536; Nixon v. Condon, 297 U.S. 233; on restraints upon the dissemination of information, see Near v. Minnesota ex rel. Olson, 283 U.S. 697, 713–714, 718–722; Grosjean v. American Press Co., 297 U.S. 233; Lovell v. Griffin, supra; on interferences with political organizations, see Stromberg v. California, supra, 369; Fiske v. Kansas, 274 U.S. 380; Whitney v. California, 274 U.S. 357, 373–378; Herndon v. Lowry, 301 U.S. 242; and see Holmes, J., in Gitlow v. New York, 268 U.S. 652, 673; as to prohibition of peaceable assembly, see De Jonge v. Oregon, 299 U.S. 353, 365.
>
> Nor need we enquire whether similar considerations enter into the review of statutes directed at particular religious, or national, or racial minorities; or whether prejudice against discrete and insular minorities may be a special condition, which tends seriously to curtail the operation of those political processes ordinarily to be relied upon to protect minorities, and which may call for a correspondingly more searching judicial inquiry.

304 US at 152 n 4 (some citations omitted).

54. For a more complete discussion of the legislation in the case and its connection to minoritarian bias, see chapter 3, note 31 and the sources cited there.

55. 304 US at 152.

directed at religious, national, or racial minorities. Of these three categories of legislation, the second two have received virtually all the attention.
Of these two, the third is the most discussed. Attention has focused particularly on the phrase the Court used to describe the minorities: "discrete
and insular minorities."[56]

This deep concern for protection of "discrete and insular minorities" is
reflected in John Ely's theory of constitutional judicial review and in the
pattern of modern equal protection law. Yet not everyone is comfortable
that this time-honored concern for "discrete and insular minorities" is
well founded. In a provocative and insightful article, Bruce Ackerman argues that the Court's emphasis in *Carolene Products* on the protection of
insular and discrete minorities is, at least, wrong in our time and was perhaps wrong even at the time the footnote was written.[57]

A careful examination of Ackerman's argument provides a way to understand both footnote 4 and the role of theories of political malfunction
in constitutional law generally. It once again shows the value of the two-
force model. Ackerman argues that insularity and discreteness are political
assets rather than disadvantages. Employing an analysis that reflects the
same considerations that underlie the IGTP, Ackerman argues that small
size, compactness, and discreteness make organization and monitoring
easier for the groups involved and therefore make it easier to overcome
free rider problems and to produce the kind of group representation in the
political process not so easily attained by larger, more dispersed, less well-
defined groups. Similarly, the costs of informing or educating a smaller,
more compact, more easily identified group are lower; it is therefore easier
to organize them and to bring them into the political process in an active way.

It is not Ackerman's position that racial, religious, and ethnic minorities, who were the prototypical insular and discrete minorities of the *Carolene Products* footnote, are overrepresented or treated extraordinarily well
by the political process. He acknowledges the existence of severe prejudice
both in the process and in society in general towards these groups. But, he
argues, they are relatively better off having reached the pluralistic bargain-

---

56. The attention given this footnote is remarkable. A former Supreme Court Justice
has called it "the most celebrated footnote in constitutional law." Lewis F. Powell, Jr.,
Carolene Products *Revisited,* 82 Colum L Rev 1807 (1982). In turn, others have termed it
the "great and modern charter for ordering the relations between judges and other agencies of government." Owen Fiss, *The Supreme Court, 1978 Term—Foreword: The Forms of
Justice,* 93 Harv L Rev 1, 6 (1979).

57. Bruce A. Ackerman, *Beyond* Carolene Products, 98 Harv L Rev 713 (1985).

ing table, through better political organization, than are more dispersed, less identifiable, more anonymous, and, generally, less organizable groups. He points particularly to women, the poor, and homosexuals. To the extent that these groups are less protected than traditional insular and discrete minorities, Ackerman believes that the "insular and discrete minority" language of paragraph three of the *Carolene Products* footnote disserves the general purpose of that footnote — to assert a role for the judiciary in those instances in which the political process severely malfunctions.

Ackerman's article serves an important role because it examines anew and with critical energy a bromide of constitutional law and does so with a sophisticated perception of the dynamics of political activity. His emphasis on the strength of concentrated minorities provides a valuable contrast with the position of John Ely, for whom concern about majoritarian bias is the core of modern American constitutional judicial review. As we saw in chapter 3, Ackerman is correct when he emphasizes small size, easy identification, and even geographical compactness as important ingredients in the representation and indeed the overrepresentation of certain concentrated minorities. In this book, such overrepresentation is termed minoritarian bias. In this sense, Ackerman's view is consistent with the views and positions of the IGTP.[58] But whatever the other merits of the Ackerman article, its analysis is incomplete for the same reasons that the IGTP is incomplete — the failure to understand the implications of the two-force model.[59]

Thus, while insularity and discreteness may be advantages in the context of minoritarian bias, they are disadvantages in the context of majoritarian bias. Indeed, the existence of an insular and discrete minority increases the chance both of majoritarian activity against that minority and of targeting that minority for majoritarian bias. The simple symbols associated with racial, religious, and ethnic categories increase the possibility that the usual dormant majority can be activated, will recognize its interests, and will target that minority. These same attributes make these minorities safe targets. Members of the majority feel comfortable that they

---

58. It is not at all clear that Ackerman would feel comfortable being associated with this company. See id at 719.

59. For critical examination of Ackerman's analysis of politics from a different perspective, see Daniel A. Farber and Philip P. Frickey, *Is* Carolene Products *Dead? Reflections on Affirmative Action and the Dynamics of Civil Rights Legislation*, 79 Cal L Rev 685, 699–716 (1991).

will not become members of the minority and themselves suffer the disproportionate burdens of majoritarian bias. A geographically confined, easily identifiable group increases the possibility that the target group will be distinct, easily targeted, and unlikely, at some future time, to include members of the majority.[60]

The extent to which insularity and discreteness are advantages in the political process depends on whose political participation we focus on— the minority in question or its majoritarian opposition. Ackerman is correct that insularity and discreteness of the minority are advantages in terms of the political participation of that minority. But the insularity and discreteness of the minority are also advantages to the political participation of the opposing majority. Insularity and discreteness make the minority a safe target and often increase the possibility of majority activity by making the presence of simple symbols more likely.[61]

One can see this story played out in the plight of the German Jews in the 1930s, an important backdrop to the framing of the *Carolene Products* footnote. The German Jewish community most likely had all the advantages in organization and communication that Ackerman ascribes to discrete and insular groups. As a general matter, European Jews, sometimes forced by law into insular ghettos, formed the kind of communities where the lack of exit, the closeness of connections, and even the presence of

60. The implications of the broader scope of the two-force model also show up in the treatment of "immutability." Ackerman, like Supreme Courts subsequent to *Carolene Products,* finds the notion of immutability inherent in the concepts of insular and discrete. Also like the Court, Ackerman treats immutability solely in terms of exit—a category is immutable if a member cannot leave. Using the concepts of Albert Hirshmann, Ackerman argues that immutability is a political advantage because a mutable classification whose members cannot be well identified will suffer from organizational problems as these members, because of their anonymity, exit rather than stay and employ the voice of political participation. Although some individuals can escape the dire effects of the legislation, such exit weakens the political efficacy of the group. As his example, he points to homosexuals.

Ackerman's use of the term immutability, like its use by the Supreme Court, however, misses an aspect of immutability closely related to insularity and discreteness. The category can be immutable because people cannot leave it, but it also can be immutable because people cannot enter it. It is this entrance meaning of immutability which promotes majoritarian bias by assuring members of the majority that they need not fear being subject to the onerous position assigned minority members. In this sense, immutability is a clear political disadvantage. From this vantage, homosexuality may be more immutable and more subject to majoritarian bias than Ackerman's definition of immutability would allow for.

61. For a more extensive discussion of the meaning of discrete, insular, and immutable, see Komesar, 86 Mich L Rev at 675-77 (cited in n. 36).

quasi-governmental infrastructures made for the significant possibility of collective action. Even the more assimilated German Jews would have had some of these advantages, certainly more than the diffuse German population. But, armed with the simple symbols of religious distinction strengthened by a long history of anti-semitism and the promise of little negative impact on the gentile population, the Jews of Germany and in turn the Jews of Europe were the targets of an activated majority precisely for the reasons that would, and likely did, activate them as a minority. As a general matter, an active majority can overwhelm an active minority.

Ackerman might respond to this analysis by asserting that in the 1990s, unlike the 1930s, episodes of majoritarian bias are unlikely. Such an argument seems at least implicit in his view that discrete and insular minorities have, by political participation, improved their protection against such bias over the ensuing sixty-year period. I hope that his observation is correct, although the recent experience in the Balkans and in other areas in constitutional transition suggests that the seeds of majoritarian bias are, unfortunately, very durable.

The greater frequency of minoritarian bias does not, however, necessitate a retreat from the position held in the third paragraph of the *Carolene Products* footnote. Such a retreat, like any reform of law or public policy, would only be justified by a comparative institutional analysis in which the relative frequency of majoritarian and minoritarian bias is but one factor. That analysis would depend upon the severity as well as the frequency of these political malfunctions, the degree to which they are corrected or correctable by other elements in the constitutional setup besides direct judicial review, and the character and capacity of judicial review itself. The importance of the allocation of judicial protection justifies a closer examination of these factors.

As noted in chapter 3, those episodes in our political history usually pointed to as the most shameful and severe — Jim Crow laws, and the general treatment of African-Americans, the treatment of Native Americans, and the forced relocation of Japanese Americans — are instances in which harm has befallen compact and easily identifiable minorities at the hands of active or activated majorities. But even if, after factoring in lower frequency, the overall severity of majoritarian bias were not greater than that of minoritarian bias, we would still not know whether the concern for insular and discrete minorities expressed in the third paragraph of the *Carolene Products* footnote was wrongheaded. We would need to assess the efficacy of alternative strategies for protection against minoritarian or majoritarian bias.

In fact, we need look no further than the *Carolene Products* footnote itself to see the existence of strategies alternative to direct judicial review. In paragraph two of the footnote, the Court indicates greater judicial concern about "legislation which restricts those political processes which can ordinarily be expected to bring about repeal of undesirable legislation." As examples, the Court points to "restrictions upon the right to vote . . . restraints upon dissemination of information . . . interferences with political organizations . . . and . . . prohibition of peaceable assembly." These political protections can provide powerful antidotes to minoritarian bias. They all aim at making information, organization, and the vote more generally accessible. As such, they decrease the relative advantage of concentrated interests who trade upon their superiority in gathering information, organizing, and gaining access to power through nonvoting channels. What perfects the process vis-à-vis minoritarian bias, however, may not decrease and in fact may even aggravate majoritarian bias. Governmental officials whose manipulations of programs reflect the will of the majority have little to fear from public exposure or increased voting by the general public. Nazi officials in the 1930s, U.S. officials in charge of the Japanese relocation in the 1940s, and southern politicians in the recent past did not feel any need to hide their racial or religious discrimination from the general public.

In the simplest sense of majoritarian bias set out in chapter 3, majoritarian bias is generated when simple democracy works too well. The majority knows its interest and votes it. In this informed manifestation of voting power, however, a minority suffers disproportionately. From this vantage, even judicial responses like the basic rule of American voting rights — one person-one vote[62] — that are well suited to dissipate minoritarian bias can reinforce majoritarian bias. In the extreme, if it were possible to fully perfect the process by making every citizen totally aware of his or her own interest and able to immediately translate that interest into an effective vote, minoritarian bias would disappear, but majoritarian bias could be worse.

We again have an example of the absolute and relative cost effects discussed in chapter 3. Factors that raise the cost of political participation but

---

62. See *Baker v Carr*, 369 US 186 (1962) and its progeny.

raise these costs more for one side of an issue than for the other may in fact increase both the efficacy of and the amount of activity by the side less affected by the rise in costs. In turn, when these costs are lowered, making political participation for both minority and majority less costly, the end effect may be to increase the relative cost to minorities, decrease the probability of minoritarian bias, and increase the probability of majoritarian bias. From this viewpoint, the protections promised in paragraph two of the *Carolene Products* footnote may decrease the need for further protections against minoritarian bias but leave unaffected or even increase the need for further protections against majoritarian bias. As such, the protections of direct judicial review promised to discrete and insular minorities in paragraph three may be all the more necessary.

But even if, after all the indirect protections of political participation promised in paragraph two, minoritarian bias remains the more severe form of political malfunction, it still would not follow that direct judicial review and protection of diffuse, anonymous, and mutable majorities is the correct response. That depends on the capacities and character of the judicial review strategy. The need for careful examination of the propensities and abilities of the judiciary can be seen by again returning to *Carolene Products*—this time to the case, not the footnote.

The case to which the famous footnote is attached is one of several in which the Supreme Court announced its retreat from economic due process. Most modern constitutional scholars, including Ackerman, applaud this decision. But the abandonment of economic due process severely reduced judicial protection of one of the most diffuse and anonymous majorities — consumers.[63]

Taxpayers and consumers are the most diffuse and anonymous of large groups. Here the protections of political participation manifested in paragraph two of the footnote will likely have the least effect because the per capita impacts are so small and health and safety issues are often so complex that it is unlikely that these political losers will even recognize their loss, let alone operate to overcome the free rider problems enumerated by Ackerman, so as to find a place at the pluralist bargaining table. The harm done to society by the resources extracted from these groups and the resources expended on the legislation to produce that extraction may very well be the greatest cost of political malfunction. Furthermore, the implicit

---

63. As indicated in chapter 3, n. 31, the "filled milk" legislation in *Carolene Products* had all the earmarks of rent-seeking legislation.

"tax" on goods and services inherent in this legislation is likely to be highly regressive, hitting most severely the poor whose fate justifiably concerns Ackerman.

Yet, with all of this, few would embrace a return to economic due process. Any serious attempt to root out minoritarian bias by judicial review would confront courts with the overwhelming task of examining virtually all forms of legislation and remaking all the public policy decisions inherent in that legislation. The scale of activity inherent in such an endeavor would completely overwhelm the judicial system as presently constituted or even as feasibly augmentable. Because health, safety, and other issues associated with consumer protection are so important, yet so complex, and especially because they so greatly involve the assessment and weighing of consumer and citizen preference, there must be considerable doubt as to the general competence of the judicial process to substitute its determinations on these issues even for an admittedly severely flawed political process. In addition, as I showed in chapter 5, the character of litigation gives the judiciary a form of minoritarian bias that makes it a good match for the review of majoritarian bias legislation but a bad match for the review of minoritarian bias legislation.

The existence of serious minoritarian bias in a wide range of legislation creates a crisis for the theories of both Ackerman and Ely. Ely bases his theory of constitutional judicial review on the existence of serious political malfunction and yet ignores minoritarian bias. His theory explicates the institutional choices made in the *Carolene Products* footnote, but it ignores the other institutional choice made in *Carolene Products* — the choice to reduce the judicial role in connection with legislation subject to severe minoritarian bias. Ackerman, like Ely, focuses his attention on the institutional choices made in the footnote. He argues that the choices were wrong and that it is the diffuse and dispersed who are most severely underrepresented in the political process. But he also must deal with the other institutional choice made in the case. He must explain why the most severe manifestation of the underrepresentation of the diffuse and dispersed should be ignored by the courts.

There are good reasons to support the institutional choice of the *Carolene Products* Court to retreat from economic due process. I just indicated some of these and will examine them more fully in the discussion of Epstein's recent attempt to return the courts to economic due process. But the theories of Ely and Ackerman are not equipped to deal with economic due process in good part because they take a one-force rather than a two-force approach to understanding political malfunction. Even though they emphasize a different force, they run up against similar analytical difficulties.

In his confrontation with the *Carolene Products* footnote, Ackerman un-wittingly demonstrates the importance of the two-force model. When he turns the tables on the Court and argues that insularity and discreteness are political advantages, he makes a major contribution by compelling constitutional scholars like John Ely to consider the other side — the other force — left out of paragraph three and its focus on insularity and discrete-ness. But two forces exist. Insularity and discreteness are advantages in some contexts, but they are disadvantages in others. The two-force model identifies these different contexts and the characteristics of those issues and interest groups that are most likely to be associated with each of these contexts. Ackerman, Ely, and other constitutional analysts must deal with these implications of the two-force model, and they must do so in a full-blown comparative institutional analysis.

SUMMARY

In this chapter I have discussed those existing approaches to constitu-tional law that have taken institutions seriously.[64] In that context I have explored both important moments in the shaping of American constitu-tional law and the role of the two-force model of politics in understanding them. In particular, I have examined the complex but essential trade-off between majoritarian and minoritarian bias and its role in understanding

---

64. I have omitted a prominent example of institutional analysis. In his work, *Judi-cial Review and the National Political Process* (1980), Jesse Choper argues that the dynamics of the political process themselves provide an adequate, albeit imperfect, means for re-solving most issues associated with federalism and separation of powers and that the Supreme Court would be wise to turn its attention and resources away from these issues and toward individual rights (169–70).

Choper's admirable concern for the workings of the political process, his rich descrip-tions of that process, and his recognition of the central importance of allocating scarce judicial resources reveal a basic emphasis on institutional attributes. But he leaves the knottiest institutional issues in constitutional law untouched. Although he calls for a greater allocation of judicial resources to the issues of individual rights, he gives little conceptual guidance on how to determine which social questions are to be addressed by the judiciary as issues of individual rights and to what extent. All legislation or public sector action affects individuals, and virtually all such activity affects some individuals detrimentally. A court advised to turn from federalism and separation of powers to in-dividual rights will still be left to face the most basic and difficult institutional questions. It must still determine which of the vast range of social issues will receive its attention and, more importantly, the degree of that attention.

the framing of the U.S. Constitution and the *Carolene Products* footnote, the precursor of contemporary constitutional judicial review. In these examples and others such as the structuring of the political process to minimize the dangers of the military, there are some nascent lessons for constitution making in general. The challenge of developing these lessons will have to await future work. There are also lessons here about the role of institutional choice in understanding American constitutional law and, in particular, constitutional judicial review. These lessons I explore more fully in the next chapter.

}8{

American Constitutional Law: The Contours of
Judicial Review

In this chapter I address what is considered the central feature of American constitutional law — constitutional judicial review. As the last chapter indicated, constitutions must be about a great deal more than the role of the courts. Even in the American context, where constitutional judicial review has found its greatest flowering, the courts play a relatively minor role in the functioning of the government and even in the preservation of constitutional balance. Yet constitutional judicial review is an important subject that deserves attention.

The role of one institution (the judiciary) as reviewer of another (the political process) seems an obvious issue of institutional choice. But, aside from the creative but single institutional and one-force analyses discussed in the last chapter, there has been little serious institutional analysis, let alone comparative institutional analysis, of constitutional judicial review.

I have addressed the comparative institutional analysis of constitutional judicial review from several vantages elsewhere.[1] Here I would like to examine the subject from the perspective of the jurisprudence of the Takings Clause. This perspective has a contemporary flavor provided by recent calls for radical expansion of judicial review under the auspices of the Takings Clause and by recent judicial forays in that direction. The jurisprudence of the Takings Clause provides a useful analytical microcosm for the exploration of the contours of constitutional judicial review in general.

In a much cited book, Richard Epstein has called for massive expansion of the takings doctrine in the name of the goal of Lockean libertarianism and its articulation of a fundamental right — the protection of private property.[2] The failings of Epstein's ambitious proposal for judicial review raise familiar themes such as the insufficiency of goal choice, the value of a two-force model of politics, the need for a realistic understanding of the limits

1. See Komesar, *A Job for the Judges: The Judiciary and the Constitution in a Massive and Complex Society,* 86 Mich L Rev 657 (1988) and Komesar, *Taking Institutions Seriously: Introduction to a Strategy for Institutional Analysis,* 51 U Chi L Rev 366 (1984).
2. Richard Epstein, *Takings* (1985).

of the judiciary, and, in general, the problems created by failing to take institutional choice seriously.

I employ the lessons from the comparative institutional analysis of takings law to explore the concept of the minimal state so popular with many commentators as well as to construct a general overview of constitutional judicial review. I then take up the two non-institutional paradigms of American constitutional judicial review — fundamental values and original intent. Having examined constitutional law from a number of vantages, it becomes easier to understand the inability of these paradigms to address the difficult task of institutional choice and analysis. I close with an institutional perspective on the issue of legitimacy over which generations of constitutional scholars have labored.

THE TAKINGS CLAUSE AND ECONOMIC DUE PROCESS

The rejection of the era of economic due process has been a cornerstone of constitutional law scholarship and constitutional law opinions for nearly sixty years. For most of that period, government actions broadly lumped into the category of "economic and social" have been subjected to very little judicial attention. This inattention is sometimes explained by the generally meritorious nature of this legislation or at least the belief that there are no serious problems with the political process in these areas. The IGTP casts significant doubt on these explanations. Many examples of rent-seeking and minoritarian bias can be found in this category of governmental action. The very legislations involved in the cases that established the strategy of judicial inactivity are classic examples of rent-seeking. From the prohibition on the sale of milk substitutes in *Carolene Products* to the obvious attempt to curb competition from opticians in *Lee Optical*,[3] it is

3. *Williamson v Lee Optical of Oklahoma*, 348 US 483 (1955). The state regulations in *Lee Optical* made it unlawful for opticians to fit or duplicate lenses without a prescription from an ophthalmologist or optometrist. Further, the regulations made it unlawful to advertise or otherwise solicit the sale of frames, mountings, or other optical appliances. They also made it unlawful to rent or provide space for eye examinations or for the provision of visual care.

Despite the district court's findings that these regulations lacked even minimal connection to health and safety (and despite the obvious connection between the regulations and the suppression of competition), the Supreme Court had the imagination to construct the necessary minimal connections. The Court recognized that this might not be good legislation but suggested that any problems would have to be corrected by the political process.

Lee Optical is one of a series of cases in which the judicial scrutiny was so minimal and the Court's unwillingness to seriously consider any attacks on the legislation so manifest that they are sometimes referred to as the "hands off" cases.

extremely difficult to ignore the overrepresentation of special interests, often at the expense of dispersed consumer or taxpayer majorities. If this vast and important set of government actions is to be left without careful judicial scrutiny, it cannot be realistically justified because of the uniformly high quality of the public policy choices or the absence of good reason to distrust the political process.

In fact, recent Court decisions hint at a return to serious judicial examination of the "social and economic" legislation that was the target of economic due process, primarily in the context of the Takings Clause.[4] The judges who authored the cases have been coy on the subject of the dimensions of the new takings doctrine. Academic commentators, however, have not been so reticent in their prescription for a new takings doctrine and its approximation of economic due process. The most ambitious of these calls for an expanded interpretation of the clause is embodied in Richard Epstein's book, *Takings*. In that book, Epstein argues for a vastly expanded interpretation of the Takings Clause and with it an expanded role for judicial review. He anchors this proposal in an analysis largely informed by goal choice. In his view, the U.S. Constitution in general and the Takings Clause in particular are grounded on the views of John Locke.[5] Lockean libertarianism, with its emphasis on the protection of private property, forms the intellectual core of Epstein's call for an increased judicial role in the examination of legislation left largely unexamined since the 1930s.

In this section, I examine Epstein's proposal and the libertarian goal of protection of property he espouses because such an examination allows me to pull together several themes important to this chapter and book. First, it provides another example of the importance of a two-force model of politics by showing the analytical problems created for Epstein by his failure to understand the quite different effects of Takings Clause compensation on minoritarian bias and majoritarian bias. Second, examination of Epstein's proposal dramatically underscores the analytical gulf between

4. See, for example, *Nollan v California Coastal Commission,* 483 US 825 (1987) and *Lucas v South Carolina Coastal Commission,* 112 S Ct 2886 (1992).

5. The Takings Clause can also be linked to basic concerns about distributive fairness. Even if we assume that all government programs are beneficial to the public as a whole, it still remains very likely that not everyone will be benefited equally and, more importantly, that some may in fact be net losers. A concern for these net losers, and indeed the definition of net loser, can be derived from a number of seemingly quite different philosophical sources. Thus, for example, Rawls's concern for the worse off in his famous difference principle associated with his theory of distributive justice is consistent with the notion of basic concern for the losers in social programs. Similarly, the Pareto version of resource allocation efficiency can be fulfilled only if there are no net losers.

goal choice and law and public policy choice. Without a far more complete and sophisticated comparative institutional analysis, Epstein's strong commitment to the protection of private property is as consistent with a contracted Takings Clause and a diminished judicial role as it is with an expanded Takings Clause and an expanded judicial role. The failings of Epstein's proposal again show the problems created by the failure to compare institutions.

Richard Epstein's Proposal

Tucked neatly into the end of the Fifth Amendment is the Takings Clause: "nor shall private property be taken for public use, without just compensation." At present, the courts constrain their role in review of governmental action under the Takings Clause by defining the taking of private property in very narrow terms. The resulting jurisprudence of takings is characterized by strained distinctions and arbitrary cutoffs. Complete takings — those where the state takes title — are distinguished from partial takings — where title remains in the hands of the original owner. Among partial takings, physical invasions are distinguished from nonphysical invasions, and instances in which all market-recognized uses of the property are restricted ("zero value" restrictions) are distinguished from restrictions that are less encompassing. Acquisitions of title, physical invasions, and zero value restrictions are far more likely to be defined as takings even though the actual loss caused a property owner by these governmental actions may be less than the loss caused by governmental actions that do not fall into these categories. Arbitrary differences, such as accidents of location, seem to determine whether a claim of takings will be seriously considered.[6]

Epstein offers an intellectual approach to defining takings and private property that wipes away much of this intellectual hodgepodge. At base, Epstein argues that any government action that interferes with any aspect of the use of private property protected at common law constitutes a takings whether or not the government acquires title, reduces the value to zero, directly invades the premises, or fulfills any of the seemingly arbitrary criteria that characterize the existing takings jurisprudence. Epstein's definition of private property straightforwardly reflects economic reality. In terms of economic impact, it makes little difference whether the gov-

6. Compare *U.S. v Willow River Power Co.*, 324 US 499 (1945) to *U.S. v Cress*, 24 US 316 (1917) (on the river and up the creek); compare *U.S. v Causby*, 328 US 256 (1947) to *Batten v U.S.*, 306 F2d 580 (10th Cir 1962) (fly over and fly by).

ernment acquires title to ten of fifty acres or restricts use of all fifty acres in such a way as to reduce their value by one-fifth. Nor would it make any difference whether the government reduced the value of a business on the fifty acres by directly invading the space, such as by flying over it, as opposed to equally reducing the value of the business by creating a similar amount of noise and dirt from a neighboring property. A loss is a loss is a loss.[7]

In Epstein's expanded vision of the Takings Clause, once any interference with common law property rights has occurred, the government can resist invalidation of its offending actions on only three grounds. First, it can pay just compensation. Second, it can argue that it is protecting the rights of other private property holders against the restricted party. This so-called "nuisance" exception allows the government to sweepingly enforce the common law rights of injured or potentially injured private property holders. No compensation is due because the claimant had no common law property right to take the action that the government restricted. Third, the government can resist the payment of compensation in individual cases by arguing that compensation has, in effect, been delivered by the program itself. Thus, for example, a claimant might lose because of a zoning restriction placed on his or her land, but gain from a similar restriction imposed on the land of neighbors. In Epstein's terms, he or she has already received "implicit in-kind compensation."

At least until recently, government assertions of these defenses were treated with great deference by the courts. The courts accepted the government's claim of nuisance prevention or implicit compensation with little careful judicial examination, thereby largely eviscerating the takings doctrine for regulatory takings. Epstein allows for no such fatal gaps in his proposal. The government would have to prove that the program in no way interfered with a legitimate property interest or that any implicit compensation was full and complete. It would not suffice to have the government show that the allegedly offending program, to some extent, removed a nuisance or, to some extent, offered compensation.

The scope and scale of Epstein's takings doctrine is immense. Since Epstein's definition of property includes all possible economic resources including land, materials, labor, and even good will and trade name, virtually all forms of regulation and taxation would presumptively become

---

7. In fact, even Epstein's definition of property has some elements that arbitrarily limit compensation. I consider this point below.

takings. Each such program would then be subject to examination by the courts to see whether the program prevented the violation of some other property right and to further check whether, even if such prevention was the purpose, there were less intrusive means of achieving the purpose. In turn, each government claim that the program offered implicit compensating benefit would have to be checked by the judiciary to see whether the benefit existed and, more importantly, whether the benefit sufficiently compensated. Much of the activity of national, state, and local government would be called into question. Does Epstein mean to call for serious judicial scrutiny of all of this governmental action? Does he recognize that he may be calling for judicial invalidation of the modern welfare state?

The answer to both these questions is unabashedly yes. Epstein is calling for serious judicial scrutiny for this vast range of governmental action. And he is hardly cowed by the prospect of invalidating the welfare state:

> The New Deal *is* inconsistent with the principles of limited government and with constitutional provisions designed to secure that end. Any attack on this social legislation does not mean that the state cannot continue to govern, or that certain ruinous practices will continue to the detriment of the public at large. The police can function; the courts are open; the army is at the ready; common pools can be contained; holdout problems can be overcome; uncertainty can be handled. But the takings clause is designed to control rent-seeking and political faction. It is those practices, and only those practices that it reaches.[8]

It hardly seems a surprise that a libertarian like Epstein should be delighted with the prospect of government constrained to its minimum. Whether motivated by a desire for the protection of private property or by a desire to increase resource allocation efficiency by the removal of rent-seeking or by any number of other goals, constraining government to its minimum is popular. It seems natural then to turn to the courts in general and to the Takings Clause or even economic due process in particular to get the job done. But neither life nor law is that simple.

Even accepting a passionate commitment to libertarianism and the protection of private property and even recognizing all the evils of rent-seeking in the political process, Epstein's proposal still does not naturally follow. Very serious problems of institutional choice undermine Epstein's libertarian program. First, and most obviously, the amount and scope of judicial activity Epstein proposes violates the simplest senses of scale.

8. Epstein, *Takings* at 281 (cited in n. 1).

Without regard to the competence of the courts or the chance that they would make worse decisions than even a rent-seeking, liberty-usurping political process, the range and complexity of the issues that the courts must now consider would break the judicial bank several times over. Whatever the evils of government regulation or the goodness of judicial decision-making, reallocating such a mass of social decisions from the political to the adjudicative process is impossible without a change in the size of the judiciary so massive that it would alter the basic character of the judiciary.[9]

When one factors in judicial competence and the shortfalls and gaps in litigation patterns, there is significant reason to doubt that Epstein's program would advance any social goal, including libertarianism and the protection of private property. Contrary to Epstein's assertions, it is not at all obvious that, under his proposal, the police can function, the courts will be open, the army will be at the ready, let alone that such basic property right enforcement problems as common pools and holdouts will be solved. Depending on the hard realities of institutional choice, libertarianism can be as consistent with increased as with decreased government.

Takings and the Two-Force Model

Before I come to this general discussion of goal choice and institutional choice, however, I need to consider Epstein's argument that the requirement to pay compensation will correct political malfunction and make judicial review easier. In his discussion of the New Deal quoted earlier, Epstein asserts that "the takings clause is designed to control rent-seeking and political faction."[10] Epstein, like others who have employed the interest group theory of politics, sees government malfunction largely in terms

9. Epstein's only consideration of this issue is a one paragraph assertion that the problem will go away because government, confronted with new signals from the courts, will become minimal and will therefore stop creating faulty legislation to be reviewed. Id at 29. Epstein is proposing a complex set of tests to apply to a vast and varied range of government action. To expect that the dynamics of litigation on such a massive scale and faced with such uncertain outcomes would produce such a smooth convergence requires heroic assumptions. To expect that all the various levels and forms of government would so easily receive, decipher, and act from these complex signals requires assumptions about the operation of the political process and the incentives of its officials that are radically inconsistent with those assumptions that motivate Epstein's call for intervention in the first place. Given these possibilities, a one paragraph assertion, made without explanation or serious institutional analysis, that everything will converge must be considered at best a throw-away argument.

10. Id at 281.

of minoritarian bias.[11] As we have seen throughout this book, minoritarian bias is a major form of political malfunction wanting for correction. But, as we have also seen, judicial intervention in the form of economic due process presents the judiciary with tasks that outstrip its resources and abilities.

Epstein, however, argues that the Takings Clause and in particular the mechanism of compensation correct rent-seeking and other forms of minoritarian bias in a way that bypasses these difficulties. Such a result would greatly ameliorate any concerns about judicial resources and abilities. Moreover, Epstein uses this corrective feature to plug a serious gap that would otherwise scuttle his program. Unfortunately, compensation will not correct the political malfunction he envisions and, in fact, the existence of that malfunction poses special problems for compensation.

As Epstein notes, a great deal of the strength of his expanded Takings Clause depends on the level of generalization at which the issue of implicit in-kind compensation is examined. Epstein wants courts to test for the presence of disproportionate impact and therefore the absence of implicit in-kind compensation on a program-by-program, legislation-by-legislation basis. An alternative to Epstein's approach would be to test for disproportionate impact on a more aggregate or general level, such as the output of the government for a significant period (a year or five years or ten years). If such a general level of examination were employed, much of the maldistribution associated with individual legislation might well disappear. Losers under one statute or piece of legislation might be winners under another. Viewed in large aggregates, the benefits and burdens of legislation, though disproportionate in individual cases, often even out and would, therefore, require no explicit takings and no careful examination by courts. As Epstein puts it: "In the limit, a court could place all legislative initiatives past and future into a single hopper and proclaim that the benefits and burdens are always proportionate, thereby gutting the takings clause for general regulation."[12]

Yet, whatever its effect on Epstein's program, this single-hopper approach has major advantages. Rather than awarding compensation after

11. Epstein's references to political malfunction in most parts of his book seem to support this interpretation, and it is one reflected in his other works. This interpretation is also consistent with that given his works by such readers as Einer Elhauge, *Does Interest Group Theory Justify More Intrusive Judicial Review?* 101 Yale LJ 31 (1991).

12. Epstein, *Takings* at 210 (cited in n. 1).

each piece of legislation or regulation, the courts could wait for a reasonable period and check to see the extent to which any individual was in the aggregate a net loser. Whatever shortfalls still existed in implicit compensation could be made up by explicit compensation at that point. Such a system would avoid the significant expenses of operating and administrating a more particularized compensation program. Why take funds from Peter and Paul to pay Mary and then from Peter and Mary to pay Paul and then from Paul and Mary to pay Peter when, as might be true in many instances, in the end all are similarly impacted by government programs in general? In a nation of tens or even hundreds of millions of Peters, Pauls, and Marys, the administrative savings could be immense.[13]

Epstein rejects this aggregated compensation scheme that so threatens his program by arguing that aggregating the consideration of compensation would make everyone worse off because it fosters or at least allows a great deal of negative-sum legislation. Without a more disaggregated or individualized requirement of compensation, the political process is more likely to pass legislation in which there is, in the aggregate, more loss than benefit. In such a circumstance, Peter, Paul, and Mary may in the end share equally in the aggregate effects of regulation, but each would end up equally worse off: "Where each separate statute bears the sign of a negative-sum game, then their totality yields only a larger negative sum. If the losses from each statute are ten, then the losses of the two taken together are twenty, not zero."[14]

Epstein's argument is a straightforward application of the IGTP. Each citizen may be a member of a special interest and, as such, extract benefits from the rest. Each citizen as a member of a concentrated interest is the recipient of benefits of some legislation and, as the member of the dispersed majority, the bearer of the burdens of others. If, as is the view of Epstein and the IGTP, the legislation is inefficient, what each citizen receives as a member of the special interest is less than what each, in the aggregate, pays out as the member of the dispersed majority.

But the presence of negative-sum situations does not show us how the payment of compensation on a case-by-case basis would correct the situation. Epstein's answer returns us to the familiar notion of disproportionate impact—the skewed distribution. Where the impact of a piece

13. As an aside, such a global accounting of winners and losers would also seem more consistent with the concerns of fair distribution derived from a Rawlsian theory of justice than would more particularized compensation.
14. Epstein, *Takings* at 210.

of legislation or governmental program is more uniformly distributed, there are incentives within the political process that tend to avoid negative-sum legislation. Those corrective incentives are not present, however, where the distribution of benefits and burdens is disproportionate or skewed. Compensation, Epstein argues, turns skewed distributions to uniform distributions.[15]

Epstein is correct when he asserts that the compensation mechanism, at least as a rough approximation, can serve to correct political malfunction by removing disproportionate impacts and, therefore, insure that the political process will not enact negative-sum legislation. But the compensation mechanism corrects only one form of political malfunction, and, more importantly, it is not the form of political malfunction that Epstein identifies when he speaks of rent-seeking. Compensation corrects majoritarian bias, not minoritarian bias.

The analysis is in fact quite straightforward. Compensation is paid out of the general tax funds that the majority provides. If the majority controls the political process, as majoritarian bias supposes, then the requirement that the majority pay the minority for any losses inflicted by the majority would, standing alone, insure the removal of majoritarian bias (at least in terms of resource allocation efficiency). One can see this point by referring back to the nine box hypothetical setting I employed in chapter 7.

In that discussion, I examined examples of both minoritarian and majoritarian bias employing the same general set of numbers. There the concentrated minority ("E" in the diagram) would lose $8,000 from the government action while each of the eight members of the majority gains $500 for a total gain of $4,000. Here we have negative-sum legislation: a net social loss of $4,000. Under a simple majority model, the legislation would pass—eight votes to one. But, if compensation of E is required, the vote changes. All nine of the citizens of the jurisdiction will now be forced to bear the cost of compensation, presumably through taxa-

15. Epstein writes: "The great peril of political life arises where some group receives a large enough increase in its share of the total pie to offset the shrinkage in the size of the pie as a whole. Because the total pie has shrunk, the gains to the successful faction must be offset by an even greater loss to the rest of the population. It is just that loss that the disproportionate impact test seeks to avoid by preventing any coalition from subverting the public good. . . . The requirement of explicit compensation to the losers now helps insure that the political game will have a positive sum. In both pro rata and non-pro rata cases, therefore, the system is endowed with a set of structural incentives that minimizes these allocative effects, even when there is no direct knowledge of where certain takings produce net social gains or net losses." Id at 208–9.

tion. That means an average tax bill to each of the nine citizens of approximately $889 ($8,000 divided by 9). Each member of the majority will now be faced with a net loss from the government action. Each member of the majority would have to pay $889 to receive a benefit of $500, leaving a net loss of $389. Even E would be a net loser, since E would receive a net payment of $7,111 in compensation for a loss of $8,000, leaving a net loss of $889. Now the vote would be 9 to 0 against the program.

But if, as is more common for the rent-seeking regulation Epstein abhors, concentrated minorities control the political process, the requirement of compensation will not correct the political malfunction and insure the absence of negative-sum legislation. One can see this outcome in the earlier nine box hypothetical setting where I showed minoritarian bias. There the concentrated minority, E, received a benefit of $4,000 from the government action and each of the members of the majority lost $1,000. Because of the overrepresentation of concentrated interests associated with minoritarian bias and the IGTP, the concentrated minority prevails and again we get negative-sum legislation ($4,000 benefit minus $8,000 loss).

Compensation, however, will not correct this bias. Each of the nine members of the community would be taxed $889 to cover the $8,000 needed to compensate the losers. Because minoritarian bias means that the minority controls, if this taxation is to correct minoritarian bias, it must change the incentives of the concentrated minority — E in our example. In our hypothetical, E would now have his or her tax bill raised by $889, but that will not negate the high per capita stakes associated with the concentrated interest, in this case $4,000. E would still push for the negative-sum legislation.

Faced with my argument, Epstein might point out that at the least the requirement of compensation would cause the concentrated minority to be less interested in the unattractive legislation. E's benefit is reduced by $889 (the tax bill) from $4,000 to $3,111. Such an argument itself concedes the significant differences in degree between the impact of compensation on minoritarian bias relative to its impact on majoritarian bias. That difference in degree quickly approaches a difference in kind, however, once one recognizes that the dispersed majority is virtually always much larger than the eight members in the hypothetical. If the number were 80,000 (as would be the case for many towns or cities) or 800,000 (as would be the case for many counties) or 8,000,000 (as would be the case for many states), the impact of the compensation tax on a member of the concentrated minority becomes negligible. (The per capita impact is 8 cents in even the least populated of those jurisdictions.) I leave the reader to play with the numbers, but the end effect is that compensation would have virtually no corrective effects on minoritarian bias.[16]

Epstein's notion that compensation will correct rent-seeking and negative-sum legislation simply does not work. Because compensation comes from the general tax fund, the members of any concentrated minority pay only a small fraction of the increased taxes for compensation associated with the government action they propose. The costs of compensation — both the transfer costs and the administrative costs — come from general tax revenues and, therefore, primarily from the majority not the minority.[17]

In fact, in the presence of serious minoritarian bias, the availability of compensation may itself create negative-sum, rent-seeking government action. Like other government functions, the massive compensation program associated with Epstein's program would have a complex administrative apparatus and generate the distinct possibility of minoritarian bias. In a setting where, as Epstein's analysis shows, essential concepts like the presence or absence of nuisance and the extent of in-kind compensation

16. A more interesting possibility is that the payment of compensation would more dramatically bring home the costs of the project to the majority and, therefore, increase the possibility of majority reaction, thereby removing the possibility of minoritarian bias. In the simple hypothetical, a special tax of $889 might bring the eight-person majority to their senses and cause them to realize what E is up to. This possibility is simply beyond the purview of the one-force model employed by Epstein. Alas, however, the realities of taxation negate even this possibility. Compensation is only a small part of the total tax burden for most taxpayers in most jurisdictions and would likely remain so even given Epstein's program. More importantly, figuring out what part of total taxes are associated with compensation for a given program is likely to be as difficult and, therefore, as defeating of majoritarian activity as understanding the impacts of the program itself.

17. There is yet another reason why compensation would not cure minoritarian bias. With minoritarian bias, we have dispersed losers — many losers each with low per capita losses. As we saw in chapters 5 and 6, these very small losses are very unlikely to be litigated.

It may be that Epstein is imagining a public compensation system different from anything now in existence in which the government would provide compensation to the dispersed majority from taxes levied on the concentrated winners. Such an imagined system of compensation would require that courts not only identify the losers and the extent of their loss but also the winners and, to some degree, the extent of their gain. These are precisely the tasks that Epstein claimed the payment of compensation would spare the courts. But, even if such an unusual and difficult compensation system were feasible, the dispersed losers would litigate few, if any, claims; consequently, the system would create little disincentive for rent-seeking.

are difficult to define and measure, mistakes and manipulations in the compensation program can be expected. Given the existence of minoritarian bias, these mistakes and manipulations will not be random. Overcompensation will be paid to concentrated interests who will employ the various avenues of influence (bribery, replacement of officials, lobbying, or propaganda) to gain these favorable determinations.[18] Rather than decrease the attractiveness of rent-seeking, the prospect of compensation might increase its attractiveness because compensation would promise additional rent-seeking opportunities.

From the perspective of the one-force model of politics, a judicial requirement of compensation at best offers no possibility of correction of the political process and at worst threatens to increase malfunction. From the perspective of the two-force model, the requirement of compensation can have corrective effects. These corrective effects, however, are limited to legislation where majoritarian bias is present. As I have argued elsewhere, some forms of local land use are characterized by majoritarian bias.[19] But, even if the correction were worth the costs in resources and errors associated with an increased judicial role, it would be sensible in a much smaller ambit than Epstein seeks. He could not use the Takings Clause to disassemble the welfare state.

Epstein's assertion that "the takings clause is designed to control rent-seeking and political faction" is much like the similar assertion made by Macey and Sunstein about the framing of the Constitution. If the Takings Clause was "designed" to control rent-seeking and political faction, it was either designed to deal with *majoritarian* rent-seeking and political faction or it was misconceived. Like many of the other Federalist choices, the Takings Clause reveals a deep concern with majoritarian bias. The Takings Clause is not, by either its background or its operation, geared to deal with the rent-seeking associated with minoritarian bias — the conception of political malfunction employed by Macey, Sunstein, and Epstein.

The Protection of Property and Institutional Choice

In the discussion quoted earlier, Epstein assured us that his program to weed out the evils of the New Deal would not interfere with the essential

18. For a study of eminent domain showing that higher value (higher stakes) parcelholders receive more than fair market value and lower value (lower stakes) parcelholders receive less than fair market value, see Patricia Munch Danzon, *An Economic Analysis of Eminent Domain,* 84 J Pol Econ 473 (1976).

19. See, e.g., Neil Komesar, *Housing, Zoning, and the Public Interest,* in Burton Weisbrod, Joel Handler, and Neil Komesar, eds, *Public Interest Law* 218 (1978).

functions of limited government: "the police can function; the courts are open; the army is at the ready; common pools can be contained; holdout problems can be overcome; uncertainty can be handled."[20] These are the standard set of legitimate functions of the libertarian limited or minimal state. The protection of private property so important to libertarians like Epstein is dependent on these governmental functions. Anything that seriously impaired these functions would decrease rather than increase the protection of private property. The issue is whether and to what extent Epstein's program for an expanded Takings Clause would impair these functions.

There is a familiar problem here. The protection of property, like the protection of privacy or liberty or any other goal, needs both protection *from* and the protection *of* the government or political process. This tension makes simplistic associations of goal and institution, such as libertarianism and less government or libertarianism and more property "rights" via judicial protection, treacherous.

One can see the two-edged nature of protection of property in the famous zoning case, *Euclid v Ambler Realty,*[21] employed by Epstein to exemplify the working of his expanded Takings Clause. The Supreme Court's approval of residential zoning in that case began a judicial retreat from significant review of land-use regulation and allowed the creation of a vast empire of land-use regulation. To Epstein, this is an evil empire, and it is precisely this sort of judicial abdication that bothers him. In areas like land-use regulation, Epstein wants the courts protecting private property *from* the government.

But, to readers of this book, there should by now be something faintly disturbing about all this unambivalent affection for judicial protection, especially with its undying allegiance to the parameters of nuisance law. Under Epstein's program, courts will have the final word on the balancing of harms and benefits that underlie regulation. They will do so in two forms. First, courts define nuisance law and, as we saw in the discussion of *Boomer* in chapter 2, that usually requires them to weigh the relative merits of the competing uses. Second, even if the government is regulating a nuisance, the courts, under Epstein's program, are to decide whether and to what extent another less drastic means would achieve the same ends. As

20. Epstein, *Takings* at 281.
21. 272 US 365 (1926). In this case, the owner of a sizeable parcel of land in Euclid, Ohio, challenged the validity of a comprehensive zoning ordinance. The district court found the ordinance unconstitutional. But the Supreme Court upheld its validity, a result somewhat remarkable since it occurred during the era of economic due process.

noted earlier, when all of this judicial activity is projected over the range produced by Epstein's pervasive definition of property and joined with the additional judicial obligation to seek out net losers case-by-case, the task overwhelms the resources of the adjudicative process.

Aside from the question of judicial resources, however, there are problems concerning the competence of the judges and the dynamics of litigation. As the analysis of litigation in the *Boomer* case in chapter 5 and the discussion of distribution 2 in chapter 6 indicated, where there are highly dispersed impacts, common law nuisance litigation will be dormant despite societally serious breaches in the protection of private property. As such, the adjudicative process provides severely inadequate protection for private property. As population and technology increase, the number and variety of these dispersed-impact, property rights violations increase, as does the complexity of resolving the associated issues of property right definition. It is difficult for any court to integrate all the possible conflicting uses operating through complex effects such as change in traffic density, air and water pollution, recreation, and aesthetics, especially when these effects impact a large number of properties.

Anyone who is concerned with the protection of private property and who, like Epstein, begins with the treatment of private property at common law, must worry about the limitations of the adjudicative process and see the beginnings of the case for large-scale governmental protection of property, such as zoning.[22] Even for the most ardent libertarian, at some

22. Problems with the adjudicative process can even produce problems with the evolution of nuisance law and, therefore, with the list of events that constitute nuisances. This "nuisance list" is essential to Epstein's program. If the governmental regulation in question regulates activity not found on the list, it is invalid unless compensation is paid. In other words, the government cannot regulate the activity. It can only buy it or contract to have it removed. This "nuisance list" has come to play a role in actual takings law analogous to (but not as pervasive as) the one suggested by Epstein. See *Lucas v South Carolina Coastal Commission,* 112 S Ct 2886 (1992).

But problems in the dynamics of adjudication of nuisance add a highly arbitrary element to the determination of the content of the nuisance list. If the type of injury is one that falls primarily on a dispersed group, it is unlikely to be litigated and, therefore, unlikely to make it to the nuisance list even though the type of injury is more serious in the aggregate than injuries on the list. The same would be true if the sources of the injury were dispersed or difficult to trace, making the costs of adjudication too high. Such complex forms of pollution as the controversial greenhouse effect might fit here. Similarly, if a type of injury is recent or only recently discovered, it will have less chance of making it to the nuisance list than older forms of injury, even though the newer injury is even more serious. The protection against erosion of the beaches in *Lucas* might be such an example.

As a general matter, it seems odd for Epstein to so vehemently attack the arbitrary

margin, the protection of private property requires the substitution of the political process for the adjudicative and market processes.

It is easy to understand Epstein's desire to minimize government. The prospects of minoritarian or majoritarian bias create the possibility of overregulation and, in terms of the protection of private property, government usurpation of property rights. These same conditions can even produce underregulation — a failure to adequately use the engines of government to protect human and physical property. As the discussion in chapter 6 indicated, this tendency toward underregulation can culminate in government action that deregulates by, for example, reducing or eliminating tort liability.

But, from an institutional choice perspective, Epstein's sort of single institutionalism creates a vicious cycle. As the discussion of *Boomer* in chapter 2 indicated, the protection of property rights via the adjudicative process or by market transaction is severely imperfect. Therefore, there would seem to be a case for government action. Nonetheless, the political process is also a severely imperfect means of protecting property. To Epstein, these governmental imperfections establish a case for a significant

---

nature of the definition of property in the present takings law and then define property for his purposes with a "nuisance list" that has strongly arbitrary aspects. Epstein and others could use the old ploy of expectation to justify the list. But that argument has long been bankrupt. As a matter of description, no property owners know what is on the nuisance list. All of us depend on a general and amorphous sense of what is protected or protectable. As a matter of prescription, why would we want to limit protection either *by* or *from* the government to the nuisance list?

I can think of many reasons to limit the definition of property for the Takings Clause. Not surprisingly, the reasons all involve issues of institutional choice. But I can see no strong reason in terms of the goal of property protection to limit government regulation to the nuisance list or conversely to limit compensation by definitions of property emanating only from ancient common law processes. In this connection, Epstein generally seems to have an arbitrarily narrow definition of property for takings purposes.

If I read Epstein correctly, the owners of the Bates Motel (remember them, moviegoers?) could receive compensation if the government prohibited or even limited their motel use. But they could not receive compensation if the government built a new superhighway, thereby diverting traffic and business from their business. (That is what happened to the Bates Motel in the movie, *Psycho*, causing them financial harm and no doubt aggravating pre-existing psychological trauma.)

There are many good reasons why we might not want to extend governmental compensation to those injured by the movement of the road — including a desire to avoid a rash of cases in which it would be difficult to discern net losers from net winners from the building of the superhighway. But these are issues of institutional choice. Epstein's suggestion that those injured in this manner would not have common law rights simply evades the issue by depending on a "nuisance list" that is itself generated by arbitrary institutional features.

increase in the judicial role. In reality, however, they again only create a case for careful institutional comparison and choice.

All the institutional means of protecting property—of making the determinations Epstein calls for—are severely strained. The protection of property is no more associated a priori with more judiciary and less political process or more market and less political process than it is with the reverse. Without more serious comparative institutional analysis than that done by Epstein, libertarianism and the protection of private property is as easily associated with more government as it is with less government. The existence of rent-seeking (or any other severe political malfunction) is not sufficient to establish the need for a greater judicial role, just as the existence of severe impediments in the adjudicative process (or the market) is not sufficient to establish a greater governmental role. This statement holds no matter what the social goal—libertarian, egalitarian, or any other.

Epstein has assured us that, under his proposal, although the excesses of the New Deal would be in jeopardy, the basic functions of the minimal state would be unimpaired. But consideration of institutional implications he ignores casts significant doubt on his assurances. The courts may be "open," but they will be so busy reviewing takings claims and reviewing regulation that they will have little time left for their common law role as protectors of property and enforcers of contracts. Whether common pools will be contained and holdout problems will be overcome depends on the questionable ability of an adjudicative process that is poorly constituted to deal with these situations, especially with the more complex and more dispersed of these situations that would previously have been handled by governmental regulation.

Even whether "the police can function" or "the army is at the ready" is called into serious doubt by Epstein's program. Epstein's expanded version of takings will bring important military issues into the adjudicative process. The most obvious of these is the military draft. Under Epstein's broad definitions of takings and private property, the draft constitutes an uncompensated taking. Limiting the draft pool by age and sex as well as any number of other factors means that there is insufficient implicit in-kind compensation. Consistent with Epstein's analysis, each draftee would have to be paid for his or her lost opportunities. Since it is likely to be too complex to carry out a draft that required compensation, military service would have to be voluntary. Courts could, of course, waive or condition the right of compensation by the existence of a threat to national security. But that would raise all the issues we saw in *Korematsu* or the *Pentagon Papers* case.

A politically malfunctioning political process cannot be totally trusted to determine national security. But neither can the adjudicative process. At the least, this example of a tough institutional choice buried in Epstein's program makes it less than certain that an expanded Takings Clause will not affect whether "the army is at the ready."

Indeed, if Epstein is truly concerned with weeding out severe instances of rent-seeking, then the judiciary must review a wide range of government choices concerning the size, staffing, and funding of the military. Reflecting Epstein's emphasis on rent-seeking, concentrated interests such as defense contractors are likely to profit disproportionately at the expense of the taxpayer by contracts that call for more military equipment than is needed or that set a price far above the relevant market price. Under Epstein's definitions of private property, taxation constitutes the taking of private property. This taking constitutes grounds for the courts to carefully examine the character of a wide range of governmental decisions not explicitly included by Epstein on his list.

Under these circumstances, whether the army is at the ready, or for that matter whether the police can function and the courts are open, will largely be decided by the adjudicative process. The courts would be assigned the task of determining whether taxes are being extracted without justification for excessive defense and other public expenditure — examples of severe rent-seeking. But such an assignment of responsibilities would overwhelm both the physical capacity and the competence of the courts. The functions of the libertarian, minimal state would not be likely to survive such a substitution of the courts for the political process, although no one would doubt that the political process is severely, systemically imperfect in carrying out these assignments. Without a careful consideration of the relative abilities of the severely imperfect adjudicative process and the severely imperfect political process in each of these settings, it is not possible to decide whether any of these functions and, with them, the protection of property will be increased or decreased by an expanded judicial role.

Epstein is but one of many commentators who are frustrated by the rent-seeking evils they see in a wide range of governmental regulation. Increasingly, frustration with the political process and its evils leads social commentators to look to the adjudicative process as a central force in this constitutional design. As with Epstein, the panacea is constitutional judicial review — review of legislation by the courts. Although often sophisticated about individual institutions, these authors are distinctly unsophisticated about the relevant comparative institutional issues that must underlie their proposals.[23] Judicial review is far trickier than its proponents seem to believe. Issues of scale, competence, and systemic bias in the adjudicative process and of the degree and kind of bias in the political process under review must inform an adequate construction of the judicial role and, therefore, of constitutional rights. Constitutional judicial review cannot be everything. In the larger constitutional scheme, it cannot be much. It is a very scarce resource that must be used carefully.

The courts may play a central role in deciding who decides, but they cannot call their own number too often. The story of constitutional law is that they generally do not. Although perhaps for different reasons, like Epstein I believe that many zoning decisions are suspect because they involve serious political malfunction—both minoritarian and majoritarian—and, through the impact of zoning on social integration, can significantly harm society. Like Epstein and many others, I can see the heavy imprint of interest group politics on governmental action in general. But none of these misgivings provides sufficient grounds to call for judicial response. To justify intervention, courts must be able to do a better job than the malfunctioning political process, and, at least on a wholesale basis, they cannot. Should the present Court seriously be toying with Epstein's proposal—and I suspect that their hints in that direction are bluffs—they will quite likely beat a rapid retreat when faced with the strain on their capacity and ability.

THE CONTOURS OF JUDICIAL REVIEW

The discussion of the Takings Clause contains important lessons about constitutional law in general. Epstein is correct when he claims that existing takings jurisprudence is filled with seemingly arbitrary definitions and that key concepts such as private property and takings could support a much broader role for the courts. In this sense, however, the Takings Clause is like many other clauses in the U.S. Constitution that provide the wherewithal for open-ended judicial review. Examples here include the Privileges and Immunities and Equal Protection Clauses of the Fourteenth Amendment, the Due Process Clauses of the Fifth and Fourteenth Amendments, the various clauses of the First Amendment, and the Commerce Clause of Article I.

23. See, for example, William Riker and Barry Weingast, *Constitutional Regulation of Legislative Choice: The Political Consequences of Judicial Deference to Legislatures,* 74 Va L Rev 373 (1988), and Robert Cooter and Daniel Rubinfeld, *Economic Analysis of Legal Disputes and Their Resolution,* 27 J Econ Lit 1067, 1093–94 (1989).

In the era since the end of economic due process, the federal courts have often employed the language of the Equal Protection Clause to provide the basis for significant judicial intervention: "No state shall . . . deny to any person within its jurisdiction the equal protection of the laws." This seemingly broad language could support a judicial role of indeterminate scope. The requirement of equality inherent in the language is a notion broad enough to relate to all government action. The very essence of public policy is differentiating and distinguishing. Since every governmental decision involves choices about how different people will be treated, all government decisions involve issues of equal treatment. From this vantage, equal protection and substantive due process are simply alternative labels for judicial review of substance. As such, judicial review in connection with equal protection can in theory bring any government action to the courts for review.

But if clauses like the Equal Protection Clause or the Takings Clause can be all encompassing in theory, they must be and are significantly less than that in practice. The character of the American institutional makeup necessitates judicial review far less encompassing than review of all legislation. Even without regard to the relative ability of the judicial versus the legislative process, the difference in scale between those processes, discussed earlier, dictates a confined judicial role. We can expect that all potentially broad-based conduits to judicial review, such as Equal Protection, substantive Due Process, the Takings Clause, the First Amendment, or the Commerce Clause, will be defined in such a way that only a small percentage of governmental action receives serious judicial review.

This limited judicial role can be ascribed to judicial self-control stemming from the judges' view that it would be illegitimate for the great part of social decision-making to be made by unelected and largely unremovable judges rather than by legislatures or from the judges' view that they are not competent to make determinations in many of the substantive areas that would be brought to them. But even if judges felt no such qualms, judicial dominance of social decision-making is simply physically impossible. It boggles the mind to even imagine the judiciary seriously examining all governmental action. Government (aside from the judiciary) has grown much faster than the judiciary.[24] Massive long-term govern-

---

24. In 1980 the total expenditure of the federal judiciary was about $564 million. See Fiscal Service, Bureau of Government Financial Operations, U.S. Dept. of the Treasury, Doc. No. 3281, *Combined Statement of Receipts, Expenditures and Balances of the United States Government* 13 (1980) *(1980 U.S. Accounts).* While the statements of accounts in

mental programs like national defense, transportation, commerce, welfare, criminal justice, and education are administered by enormous agencies that employ millions of people. These programs produce reviewable action at a virtually uncountable rate.[25] The physical capacity of the courts to review governmental action is simply dwarfed by the capacity of governments to produce such action.

These severe limits on judicial resources do not preclude an important judicial role. The judiciary has the resources with which to review a significant, if relatively small, subset of governmental decisions and has done so for nearly a century.[26] But the big picture of social decision-making is

---

1980 U.S. Accounts make it difficult to calculate administrative costs for Congress, the executive, and the federal administrative agencies, a conservative estimate yields a figure in excess of $94 billion—over 160 times the budget for the judiciary. See id at 110–24, 132–508. In 1925, the analogous figures were approximately $19 million for the judiciary, see Division of Bookkeeping and Warrants, U.S. Dept. of Treasury, Doc. No. 2966, *Combined Statement of the Receipts and Disbursements Balances, etc. of the United States* (1925) *(1925 U.S. Accounts)*, and $424 million for the political branches, see id at 40–253, the latter less than 23 times the size of the former. In other words, the administrative budget of the political branches had grown more than seven times as fast as the budget of the judiciary.

Although the most dramatic source of the difference is the growth in administrative agency budgets (compare *1980 U.S. Accounts* at 140–502 with *1925 U.S. Accounts* at 49–253), even the figures for Congress and the executive proper dwarf those for the courts. In 1980, that figure was over $1.25 billion, or more than twice the judicial budget. See *1980 U.S. Accounts* at 110–24, 132–38. In 1925, the budget for the federal judiciary (excluding expenditures for penal institutions) was only about thirty percent less than the administrative budget for Congress and the executive; see *1925 U.S. Accounts* at 47–48, 131.

25. For example, the number of laws passed in a session provides some measure of legislative activity by federal and state governments. During the 98th Congress, 623 Public Laws were passed. Clerk of the House of Representatives, *Calendar of the United States House of Representatives and History of Legislation* (1983, 1984). Approximately 70,000 bills were enacted by the fifty states during the 1983–85 legislative sessions. Council of State Governments, *The Book of the States* (1986–87). No similar compilation of data exists for local governments.

No complete measure of federal administrative activity is available, although the number of documents published annually in the Federal Register for incorporation into the Code of Federal Regulations provides some indication of federal rule-making capacity. In 1986, 4,589 documents were published (5,154 in 1984 and 4,853 in 1985). Conversation with Internal Records Office, Federal Register, National Archives (June 1987). The quantity of state and local administrative regulations has not been reported. Kenneth C. Davis, *Administrative Law and Government* 8 (1975). Davis also states that the number of informal, reviewable decisions by federal, state, and local agencies is unknown but probably "runs in the hundreds of millions or billions annually."

26. There are several strategies of judicial decision-making that are produced by the pressures of limits on judicial capacity and competence. Faced with serious doubts about

simple and straightforward: the political process is the dominant decision-maker; the judiciary occasionally dominates, but is usually dormant. Thus, if one imagines a large space such as a classroom blackboard (a common image to academics) representing all governmental decision-making, all serious judicial review would be represented by a small corner of it.

Constitutional courts have constrained their role by the use of thresholds, cutoffs, and arbitrary distinctions. In the jurisprudence of equal protection and substantive due process, the courts have declared a division of judicial activity into two (or perhaps three) categories (strict and minimal, or strict, heightened, and minimal). The threshold to serious judicial scrutiny is guarded by concepts like suspect classifications and fundamental rights. I discussed suspect classifications earlier in connection with the *Korematsu* case in chapter 7. The notion of fundamental rights has little intrinsic meaning and most certainly does *not* mean that the courts will decide

---

the political process, along with strains on its resources, the Court might well respond with a sweeping declaration that all laws of a particular type are invalid. Both sweeping validations and sweeping invalidations husband the Court's resources. As we saw in chapter 5, however, such sweeping determinations run serious risks of producing poor public policy, especially where there is a significant potential for relevant variations among the covered cases and for limited judicial ability to distinguish them. In response to strains on its resources, the judiciary may also attempt innovative remedies such as looking for help from within the political process or seeking to replicate parts of the political process through panels roughly representing the range of community interests. I have come to call the former the "trusty buddy" approach. One can see it at work, for example, in Justice Brennan's concurring opinion in *United Jewish Organizations v Carey*, 430 US 144, 175 (1977) (Brennan concurring), where "considerable deference" is accorded the judgment of the Attorney General in his capacity as "champion of the interests of minority voters" under § 5 of the Voting Rights Act, 42 USC § 1973(c) (1982). One can also see it in the Court's willingness to define the scope of statutory violations more broadly than similar constitutional violations. In *Washington v Davis*, 426 US 229, 246–48 (1976), for example, the Court enunciated an "intent" test for racial classifications that violates the Equal Protection Clause of the Fourteenth Amendment (or the Equal Protection aspect of the Fifth Amendment Due Process Clause) while retaining the broader "impact" test for violations of civil rights statutes. See *Griggs v Duke Power Co.*, 401 US 424, 429–33 (1971). One sees the effort to replicate the political process through the use of a representative panel in the approach of the district court in *Chance v Board of Examiners*, 330 F Supp 303 (SDNY 1971), discussed in Michael Rebell and Arthur Block, *Educational Policy Making and the Courts: An Empirical Study of Judicial Activism* 75–122 (1982). The role of the panel as a replication of the political process is a theme advanced in William Clune's book review of Rebell and Block. See William Clune, *Book Review*, 93 Yale LJ 763, 774–75 (1984). The point of recognizing the constraints imposed on the judiciary by the limits of its physical resources is simply that the judiciary must consider those constraints in determining how it will respond to a given social issue. The existence of this constraint is part, but not all, of an adequate analysis of institutional choice.

the most fundamental issues of public policy.[27] On the whole, these constructs help the courts limit and focus the judicial role. To be clear, nothing about these constructs or the language of the applicable constitutional provisions inherently limits that role. The courts define these constructs, and it is these definitions that define and confine the judicial role.

Most constitutional scholarship focuses on the small corner of American public policy in which the courts play an active role and, in particular, the edges or borders of that small corner. Many scholars have suggested that the simple classifications of judicial scrutiny are misleading. Strict is not always strict. Minimal is not always minimal. There is a continuum of judicial scrutiny or of the judicial role rather than simple discrete cutoffs. The question then, of course, is what defines the continuum — what causes variation in the judicial role. As I have suggested throughout this book and, in particular, in the discussions of the *Pentagon Papers* and *Korematsu* cases, this variation in scrutiny is driven by the factors that determine institutional choice — by the relative strengths and weaknesses of the reviewer (the adjudicative process) and of the reviewed (the political process). I have made this point in greater detail elsewhere.[28] But the important point here is that the continuum, whatever factors define it, is dominated by a significant range of zero judicial activity produced by the realities of institutional choice.[29]

The courts define constitutional terms like "takings," "property," "equality," and "liberty" not in the abstract but against the omnipresent background of institutional choice. The resulting definitions employed in constitutional jurisprudence are always arbitrary. They are the product of judges and more broadly an adjudicative process struggling with the tough issues of institutional choice. I believe that many judges understand that

27. I discuss fundamental rights more extensively in the next section and in Komesar, *A Job for the Judges: The Judiciary and the Constitution in a Massive and Complex Society*, 86 Mich L Rev 657, 718–21 (1988).

28. See id and Komesar, *Taking Institutions Seriously: Introduction to a Strategy for Constitutional Analysis*, 51 U Chi L Rev 366 (1984).

29. I suspect that the character of American institutions and the reality of modern American equal protection law also suggests a significant discontinuity at the point where this zero response sets in. That is, those issues that receive any non-zero level of judicial scrutiny are likely to receive some appreciable amount of such scrutiny. It is simply difficult for me to imagine the tiny degrees of judicial responses necessary to justify a continuum in the vicinity of zero. As such, the vast range of social issues would receive no judicial scrutiny and the rest would receive degrees that might vary but would not drop below some minimum amount. Thus, somewhere after the courts respond by saying "that is provocative and we might consider it," there is a significant and rapid drop to "don't bother us; go see your legislator."

they are making institutional choice. But even when they do not, the institutional realities are brought home to them by the workings of the various institutions. I will return to this subject in the subsequent discussion of legitimacy. The important point here is that constitutional law requires difficult institutional choice and cannot be defined by constitutional language taken in the abstract even when these terms are further defined by philosophical goals like Lockean libertarianism or Rawlsian justice. Ultimately, the difficult comparison between the political and adjudicative processes molds the patterns of constitutional law and the terms of constitutional jurisprudence. It behooves judges and commentators to explicate and better understand this comparison.

Non-Institutional Approaches: Fundamental Rights and Original Position

Thus far I have argued that institutional choice and comparative institutional analysis are essential to constructing a constitution and understanding constitutional law. But if I am correct, then constitution makers, interpreters, and scholars are set a difficult task. Outcomes are driven by factors that vary from one setting to another. Worse yet, the results are often equivocal and messy. Institutional superiority is not always obvious, and superiority is often a choice of bad over worse. When one factors in the possibility of variation in outcomes because of variation in the choice of social goals and values, constitutional analysis becomes a challenging task.

It would be nice to find a less difficult way — a non-institutional way — to understand constitutions and constitutional law. In this vein, much constitutional scholarship about the role of judicial review involves little consideration of institutional issues. Instead, most theories of judicial review rely on a variety of images — judges reasoning toward moral evolution[30] or deliberating civic virtue[31] or discovering higher principles[32] or seeking and following the plan laid out by the framers.[33]

Buried in these images are two perceptions of the role of the judiciary

30. See, for example, Michael Perry, *The Authority of Text, Tradition, and Reason: A Theory of Constitutional "Interpretation,"* 58 S Cal L Rev 551 (1985); Michael Perry, *Noninterpretive Review in Human Rights Cases: A Functional Justification,* 56 NYU L Rev 278 (1981).

31. See, for example, Cass Sunstein, *Interest Groups in American Public Law,* 38 Stan L Rev 29 (1985).

32. See, for example, Owen Fiss, *The Supreme Court, 1978 Term — Foreword: The Forum of Justice,* 93 Harv L Rev 1 (1979).

33. See, for example, Raoul Berger, *Government by Judiciary* (1977); Robert Bork, *The Impossibility of Finding Welfare Rights in the Constitution,* 1979 Wash U LQ 695.

quite different in articulation and perceived outcome. One image looks to broad senses of moral philosophy to establish the content of constitutional rights and, therefore, the role of the judiciary. This view, which takes many forms, I call the "fundamental rights" approach to constitutional law. The other perception looks to the beliefs of the original drafters of the U.S. Constitution to define constitutional rights and, therefore, the role of the judiciary. This view I refer to as the "original position" approach to constitutional law.

The fundamental rights approach is often associated with a more expansive role for the judiciary; the original position approach is often associated with a more restrictive role for the judiciary. In turn, these approaches are associated with different substantive targets. The fundamental rights approach is "liberal" in its loose twentieth-century sense. It concerns itself with racial, sexual, and income inequality. The original intent approach is "conservative." It concerns itself with protection of property rights.[34] Thus, the two approaches can be associated with different social goals and interests.

Each of these approaches seems to offer a way to short-circuit all the messiness and ambiguity of institutional choice. For reasons derived from what we have seen, however, these easy ways will not suffice. In fact, the constitutional positions these analysts propose do not follow from their articulated approaches. Their ignorance of institutional choice leaves in significant doubt even whether the positions they take on judicial review will serve the values or ideologies that motivate these analysts. In the first two parts of this section, I discuss these two non-institutional approaches. In the third, I address the issue of legitimacy that seems to animate these two approaches and much of American constitutional scholarship.

The Fundamental Rights Approach to Constitutional Law

In one manner or another, most constitutional scholars tell the story of constitutional law, constitutional rights, and judicial review in terms of a search for fundamental values. They may refer to natural law, moral philosophy, tradition, or consensus, but the prescription is largely the same: it is the job of constitutional judges to search for fundamental values and

---

34. Richard Epstein is a clear exception to these maxims. He seeks an expansive judicial role in protection of property rights. He is a "conservative" fundamental rights analyst. Not surprisingly, the attractiveness of original intent seems to diminish at those moments when judicial expansion seems attractive, turning original intent devotees into fundamental rights devotees.

resolve constitutional issues accordingly. Judges have adopted the notion of "fundamental rights" as part of the jurisprudence of equal protection and substantive due process. This support from the judiciary has only increased the interest in "fundamentalness" on the part of scholars.[35]

Whatever the judicial and academic support for the notion of fundamental rights and the associated notions of search for moral principles and public values, these constructs cannot provide a way to avoid the struggles of serious comparative institutional analysis. In their most straightforward meaning, these approaches are inquiries into the issue of goal choice. As I have argued from the outset, goal choice is never sufficient to define law and public policy choice. Discerning that some goal, principle, value, or interest is socially important by itself tells us nothing about what law or public policy should be. In the constitutional context, it does not tell us the extent to which the judiciary should play a role in achieving this goal through greater constitutional judicial review. In other words, it does not tell us when or why any particular goal or interest will be associated with a constitutional right or with its complete absence.[36]

---

35. See, for example, Kenneth Karst, *The Freedom of Intimate Association,* 89 Yale LJ 624 (1980).

36. The mysteries of the notion of fundamental rights and values are as usual well-captured by Ely: "[T]he list of values the Court and the commentators have tended to enshrine as fundamental is a list with which readers of this book will have little trouble identifying: expression, association, education, academic freedom, the privacy of the home, personal autonomy, even the right not to be locked in a stereotypically female sex role and supported by one's husband. But watch most fundamental-rights theorists start edging toward the door when someone mentions jobs, food, or housing: those are important, sure, but they aren't *fundamental.*" Ely, *Democracy and Distrust,* 59 (footnote omitted).

From an institutional perspective, the explanation for the peculiar pattern of fundamental rights embraced by judges and scholars seems to lie in the institutional role served by the concept of "fundamental rights." In the present constitutional jurisprudence, a finding that legislation affects a fundamental right tends to remove that issue from the legislative process and allocate responsibility for its determination to the judiciary. See for example, *Griswold v Connecticut,* 381 US 479 (1965). If housing, jobs, food, commerce, taxation, national defense, and foreign affairs were declared "fundamental values," the judiciary would have to take a serious hand in their effectuation.

These subjects are not excluded from the list of "fundamental values" because they are socially unimportant. If anything, they are excluded because they are too important. More exactly, they are excluded because the relative institutional abilities of the legislative process vis-à-vis those of the judicial process are thought to favor the former. Although these interests are by no means handled perfectly by the political process, their scale, difficulty, and the basic need to tap the desires and needs of the populace generally make even that highly imperfect political process appear superior to the adjudicative process in connection with these interests.

Sensing the need for institutional choice, some of the proponents of the fundamental rights position have offered an institutional component to their arguments. Judges are the preferred searchers for moral principles and fundamental values because, compared to the officials of the political process (let alone to the headless and, therefore, mindless market process), independent judges are much more capable of the contemplation and deliberation necessary to discover and enunciate long-term moral principles and fundamental values.[37]

This pervasive image is inadequate for reasons indicated throughout this book. First, it cannot address the most basic question of institutional choice for constitutional law — the allocation of responsibility between the political and adjudicative processes. It is difficult to pick out many important social issues that do not involve basic principles or weighty moral issues. Control of unemployment and inflation, expenditures on health and education, immigration policy, control of the environment, and the location and quantity of housing are but a few of the issues that engage questions of principle and basic values. Yet, as a general matter, responsibility for these issues lies with the legislative process. The judiciary has

37. The following comments are representative. Harry Wellington writes: "If a society were to design an institution which had the job of finding the society's set of moral principles and determining how they bear on concrete situations, that institution would be sharply different from one charged with proposing policies. The latter institution would be constructed with the understanding that it was to respond to the people's exercise of political power; in America, that means interest group politics. The former would be insulated from such pressure. It would provide an environment conducive to rumination, reflection, and analysis." Harry Wellington, *Common Law Rules and Constitutional Double Standards: Some Notes on Adjudication*, 83 Yale LJ 221, 246–47 (1973) (footnote omitted).

And Michael Perry writes: "I will begin explaining my justification for noninterpretive review in human rights cases with some fairly uncontroversial observations about comparative institutional competence. In recent generations, certain political issues have been widely perceived to be fundamental moral issues as well — issues that challenge and unsettle conventional ways of understanding the moral universe and that serve as occasions for forging alternative ways of understanding. . . . Our electorally accountable policymaking institutions are not well suited to deal with such issues in a way that is faithful to the notion of moral evolution and, therefore, to our religious understanding of ourselves. Executive and legislative officials tend to deal with fundamental political-moral problems, at least highly controversial ones, when they confront such issues at all, by reflexive reference to the established moral conventions of the greater part of their particular constituencies. They refuse to see in such issues occasions for moral re-evaluation and possible moral growth." Michael Perry, *Noninterpretive Review in Human Rights Cases: A Functional Justification*, 56 NYU L Rev 278, 293–94 (1981) (footnote omitted).

played no role in most of these decisions, a minor role in some, and a major role in very few.

Questions of war and peace, which classically raise fundamental moral and political problems, are conspicuously absent from the judicial list. The issue of nuclear war, its control, and its meaning for national and international morality, for example, has strained our national sense of right and wrong for decades. At least as a matter of description, as we have seen, the courts have been reluctant to address questions of war and peace even when racism has been involved.[38] One might argue, of course, that such unwillingness to intervene reflects the fact that the political process has generally handled questions of war and peace well, but I can think of few arguments so likely to meet with a skeptical response. One might ultimately conclude that the political branches may be best suited to decide these issues, but their history of war-related decisions is nevertheless far from ideal.

Whatever is meant, then, by issues of principle or morality, no obvious correlation exists between these issues and the traditional allocation of decision-making responsibility between the judiciary and the political branches. These commentators may wish to make major alterations in the allocation of decision-making authority, but, unless they wish to allocate virtually all decisions to the judiciary, they must better distinguish questions of morality or principle from the presumably much larger set of questions controlled by the legislature.

Second, institutional choice based predominantly on contemplation and deliberation is basically incomplete. Contemplation, reasoning, dispassionate consideration, and the desire to consider the long view are fine attributes. If voters and their elected representatives consistently functioned in this way, many defects in the legislative process might well be eliminated. We would be approaching an idealized Rawlsian world. But the proposal is not to make the legislature more contemplative; the proposal is to substitute a more contemplative judiciary for the legislature. Social decision-making thereby gains, to be sure, contemplation and reason, but it loses a basic measure of public will, desire, and reaction available in the legislative process.

The choice is analogous to the choice between central planning and a market allocation of resources. The actors in the market are self-interested.

38. See the discussion in chapter 7 of *Korematsu v United States*, 323 US 214 (1944).

They can be described as driven by passion, ignorance, and shortsightedness. Consequently, the results of market allocation can fail to take account of important factors, thereby injuring third parties or even the market actors themselves. These market imperfections provide the impetus for considering such alternative modes of allocating resources as central planning. In a system of central planning, the actors are assumed not to be shortsighted or self-interested; contemplation and reason in service of the general public are supposedly the system's features. But even if a central planning scheme fulfilled these ideals, it would still be missing an important element. In the hurly-burly of market activity, despite the shortsightedness and because of self-interest, wants and desires are revealed. The information gained is not just a shopping list of goods and services preferred. It puts weights on these desires and provides a simple index — relative prices — by which to assess relative demand.

Though the market and the political process are seriously defective, greater contemplation, reason, and disinterestedness through judicial decision-making are not cost-free. If one abandons the market or the political process, information about the wishes of the public as citizens, consumers, or moral individuals must be obtained in some other manner.[39] It generally may be correct that moral truth, moral evolution, and basic conventional morality are not faithfully embodied in the output of the political process. To say as much, however, is merely to recognize imperfections, which alone does not advance discussion in a world of imperfect alternatives. The political process may be highly imperfect and yet still superior to any other alternative as the instrument of society's moral evolution.

The contemplative and deliberative judges that fundamental value commentators so admire are part of a larger process. As we saw in chapter 5, the high cost threshold produced by the attempts to create independence, deliberation, and evenhandedness serves to screen out not only the important input of desires and needs but also to remove whole areas of inquiry where interests are too dispersed to litigate. The limited size or scale of the adjudicative process makes impossible judicial determination of more than a small fraction of the morally important social issues. As I have said, there are important instances in which this small, frail institution can

---

39. For an excellent treatment of the shortcomings that derived from the analogous substitution of bureaucratic expertise for the political process in the Progressive Era, see Terrance Sandalow, *The Distrust of Politics,* 56 NYU L Rev 446 (1981).

serve society well — where social decisions are better made by the courts. But this ambit of decision-making must be defined by an analysis of institutional choice more robust and sophisticated, albeit more complex and less ethereal, than reference to contemplation and deliberation in search of long-term moral principles.[40]

40. Some fundamental rights analysts have attempted to avoid the difficulty of real institutional analysis by simply assuming that one broad grouping of goals or interests belongs to one institution and another grouping to another institution. A classic example of a futile attempt to associate philosophical positions and institutional outcomes is found in the approach of David A. J. Richards and Ronald Dworkin. Their logic operates as follows. The legislature is clearly the utilitarian determiner (the proposition is considered so obvious that no argument is offered). On this basis, rights which operate to invalidate legislation show the existence of strong anti-utilitarian principles in our Constitution. Further, since the legislature is utilitarian, it cannot check its own process against anti-utilitarian constructs. This must be done by the judiciary. Thus, the authors prove both the existence of anti-utilitarian principles and the role of the judiciary in protecting them. See David Richards, *Human Rights as the Unwritten Constitution: The Problem of Change and Stability in Constitutional Interpretation*, 4 U Dayton L Rev 295 (1979); Ronald Dworkin, *Taking Rights Seriously*, 90–94, 188–92 (1977).

The argument that utilitarianism is associated with the political process while anti-utilitarianism is associated with the judiciary is fatally simplistic. The majoritarian political process is hardly a perfect determiner of utilitarian outcomes; the analogous consideration of representation of citizen desires in chapter 3 shows that. A utilitarian Constitution would not necessarily allocate decision-making to the legislature, or indeed form that legislature in the most directly democratic manner. It is easy to conceive of trumps on the legislature in a utilitarian system. Therefore, the existence of such trumps does not indicate the existence of anti-utilitarian elements. In some instances courts removed from the political process may be superior determiners of the utilitarian good.

Nor is it by any means clear that the superior determiner of the anti-utilitarian ideal (or ideals) is the judiciary rather than the legislature or the executive, let alone whether we would prefer the federal or state judiciaries, legislatures, or executives. Even if we were to assume Dworkin's and Richards's first argument, that the legislature is always the superior determiner of utilitarianism, it does not mean that the legislature is not also the superior determiner of anti-utilitarianism. To be superior in one vein does not make the entity inferior in another.

The arguments about the inability of the legislature to police itself are not helpful. As we saw with similar arguments by Ely, these are simply arguments for institutional allocation by default, which cannot hold up in a sophisticated institutional analysis. Allocation by default is a common institutional argument made by constitutional scholars. In one fashion or another, problems with the political process are revealed and the judiciary swept into place by the assertion that since they are the only entity outside this defective political process they must be the determiner. But such arguments are flawed.

The legislative process is not monolithic. It does not fit the image of the evil individual who would hardly be likely to police himself or herself. There are millions of individuals — and numerous interests, positions, and factions — operating within the process. These positions operate to balance and control each other. The degree and form of this internal control varies over time. As we have seen, this is the mechanism of

The Original Position Approach to Constitutional Law

Originalism offers a second "easy way" around the difficulties of institutional choice. According to originalism, no one in the present generation needs to choose among social decision-makers since those choices were already made by the framers. There is, of course, the institutional choice whether to be bound by the decisions of the framers or to remake that decision now. Much of the debate about originalism involves the question of whether original intent should be followed. But that debate is largely pointless.

On virtually all important issues of institutional choice or substantive results, the Constitution and the intent of the framers remain equivocal.[41] Part of this indeterminacy stems from problems of evidence or data. But part comes from a basic conceptual problem. To understand the difference, I need to distinguish between original position and original intent. The first would hold that a constitutional law controversy is to be resolved in the manner that such a controversy would have been resolved if it had been raised at the time of the framing. Thus, for example, whether state decisions concerning voting are covered by the Fourteenth Amendment or whether the death penalty constitutes cruel and unusual punishment under the Eighth Amendment are issues to be resolved by asking how that issue would have been resolved at the time of the framing of the Fourteenth or Eighth Amendments.

The second standard, original intent, asks how the framers would resolve the issue now. That is, it asks how the framers or drafters would resolve the issue as it actually arises. It is the view of intent that informs common law interpretation of contracts and wills. The question is how the original party or parties would resolve the issue given all the circumstances — including all the changes in circumstances that inevitably ac-

---

control on which we rely in most instances. I would hardly argue that this is the ideal, or more importantly, even the optimal means of policing in all instances. But it cannot be dismissed a priori. Institutional allocation cannot be determined simply by a bromide like "one can't police oneself." In a complex institutional setting in which all institutions are highly constrained and imperfect, the defects in one process do not validate allocation to an alternative. These defects may be necessary conditions, but they are far from sufficient ones.

41. I discussed this subject at length in Neil Komesar, *Back to the Future: An Institutional View of Making and Interpreting Constitutions,* 81 Nw U L Rev 191, 194–210 (1987). The treatment here is a brief recap of that analysis.

company the passage of time. Here the judge-interpreter is the faithful agent of the drafters, attempting to resolve issues according to the desires of those drafters. Original intent is the ideal. Original position is at best a rough approximation of original intent. It reduces the need for extrapolation, but it does so by reducing the normative attraction of faithfulness to the original parties.

Even the narrower original position standard runs into serious, usually overwhelming, evidentiary problems. The brief text of the Constitution offers little detail on specific substantive outcomes or even on institutional allocation; most of the detailed provisions in the Constitution concern institutional design. Nor will an examination of the surrounding records yield unequivocal results.

Answers from the past are difficult to find for many reasons. The logistics of record keeping and the identification of relevant views among conflicting statements provide problems. Problems in the use of language, no doubt tempered by the framers' desire not to bind future generations unnecessarily, also led to equivocal results.[42] Perhaps most important, constitution framing in the American experience is a collective enterprise. The original Constitution was the product of group decision-making—the Philadelphia Convention and the state ratifying conventions. In turn, the Civil War amendments were the product of Congress and the state legislatures. Collective intent is extremely difficult if not impossible to define, let alone unequivocally establish in a particular instance. Like the analysis of other large processes, the analysis of constitution framing, an example of aggregate decision-making, forecloses simple extrapolation from individual decision-making and even harbors the possibility for counterintuitive results.[43] Despite the continuous assertion that inquiry into the original position dictates results, careful analysis indicates otherwise. I have dealt with these questions in detail elsewhere, as have many others.[44]

But even if the original position could be unequivocally determined, there does not seem to be any way to determine original intent in a manner that does not force the remaking of the original decisions. Throughout

42. Such problems of language are discussed in id at 198–203.
43. Prominent among these is the possibility of cycling which throws substantial doubt even on some of the most substantially documented assertions of original intent. See id at 203–10 (examining Raoul Berger's assertions about the Fourteenth Amendment).
44. See id and the sources cited there.

the law in general, there are many instances in which the touchstone of judicial interpretation is the intent of the drafter or drafters. These include the law of contracts, where the issue is the intent of the original bargainers; the law of deeds and conveyances, where the intent is either of the drafter or of bargaining parties; and the law of wills and trusts, where the issue is the intent of the now deceased drafter or testator. There are usually very few parties, often just one or two; the subject matter is always more confined than that of a constitution; the relevant elapsed time when the interpretation is made is usually quite a bit shorter than the time elapsed between the drafting and interpretation of the Constitution. Yet, in many instances, courts are unsuccessful in determining intent specific to the original parties. Instead, they are forced to ask not what this individual did or said, but rather what the *reasonable person* would have done or said.

This "reasonable person" standard is especially common in "changed circumstances" cases where it is argued that the original party or parties would have preferred a different outcome than specifically indicated in the document because underlying conditions have significantly changed. Thus, to take an example from private land-use restrictions, suppose the parties agree that the land in question can be used only for single family dwellings with no express exceptions. Many years go by and the surrounding neighborhood changes from residential to heavily industrialized. Should the restriction on the land be lifted? The original parties are now either deceased or, as adversaries in a lawsuit, unreliable sources of information on the implicit conditions for change.

Whatever the ostensible formulation, judges in these cases are inevitably forced to decide based on a reasonable person standard. Changed circumstances force an interpreter of a document to separate the original position taken from the purposes for taking the original position. To ignore the changed circumstances means ignoring the purpose of the provision — an important aspect of the intent of the original party or parties. The judge would no longer be the faithful agent of the original parties. But, once one extrapolates the purpose of the provision to present circumstances, the decision must be remade because the original party did not provide and could not leave specific instructions.

For constitutional interpretation, where the language is less specific, the time elapsed is generally longer, and the drafters are many, the likelihood of relevant changed circumstances is pervasive. Any serious inquiry into original intent, as opposed to original position, forces even the most scrupulous judge into remaking the decision in light of the underlying purpose.[45]

I cannot find in the concept of original intent any way around the difficult issues of institutional choice. Even the more normatively questionable but narrower original position standard will seldom yield a way around serious institutional choice. Much of what goes on under the aegis of originalism is unexplained, unanalyzed, and even unconscious institutional choice by the judges or commentators who espouse it. Since originalism does not make the relevant choices any easier in reality (as opposed to in rhetoric), the subterfuge (or self-delusion) of those who use it does not well serve constitutional analysis.[46]

There are no simple shortcuts around the difficult questions surrounding the allocation of social decision-making. By a gradual process of accretion, the federal judiciary has acquired a significant role in this allocation. Judges will have to play their part in deciding who decides, whether they want to or not.

45. There is a subtle qualification here on the issue of who decides who decides, and there are instances where more specific language in the Constitution can prove important. The prevalence of open-ended changed circumstances in constitutional interpretation does not mean that the job of reacting to the changed circumstances necessarily belongs to the courts. It only means that some future institution must decide. There are two alternatives to the courts — the conventional political process (Congress and the President) or the amendment process of Article V. It is common enough for the supporters of original intent to point to the amendment process as the prescribed mode for adjusting to changed circumstances. But that argument only restates the issue. If original intent is the touchstone, we must ask whether it was the original intent of the framers to adjust to all new facts by the cumbersome amendment process.

The question becomes which future institution should react to changed circumstances. It is reasonable to suppose that where the framers used highly specific language — as with the minimal age for the President — they intended to make a firm decision changeable only be amendment. Where the phrase used is more vague or open-ended, non-amendment sources of change appear more reasonable. Here the choice of who decides who decides once again forces the same recourse to balancing reasonableness as the choice of who decides. The issue is institutional choice and, unfortunately, that difficult issue cannot usually be resolved easily.

46. It is hardly surprising under these circumstances that original position or a general devotion to originalism seems to operate largely as a make-weight. A good example of this outcome comes in the controversial, recent takings case, *Lucas*, where Justice Scalia, an erstwhile proponent of originalism, dismisses a strong original intent argument by Justice Blackmun, who rarely shows such affection for originalism, by pointing out that adhering to the original position would cause bad results. *Lucas v South Carolina Coastal Commission*, 112 S Ct 2886 (1992).

The Issue of Legitimacy

The peculiar fascination with the analytically weak fundamental rights and original position approaches reflects the agonizing fixation of American constitutional law with the issue of legitimacy. Since American constitutional law (but not the American Constitution) is judge-centered, a central issue has been the legitimacy of the substitution of judge-made public policy for public policy made by the political process. Where do unelected judges come off making public policy? If they are the determiners of constitutional law and, therefore, institutional choice, what limits them? What limits their power to usurp power? Where are the principles that form the foundation for and define the extent of constitutional judicial review?

The original intent position has always offered the most comfort because it sees judges as simply servants of the "higher" democracy of the constitution makers. Judges do not make public policy; they simply apply the public policy determinations made elsewhere. Judges do not even make institutional choices; they simply apply the institutional choices made elsewhere. Originalism easily sidesteps the tough issues of legitimacy. But that position is not intellectually cogent.

Either because they do not like the outcomes of the original intent approach or because they too do not believe that there is a cogent original intent approach, the fundamental value scholars look elsewhere for the legitimacy of constitutional judicial review. They find this legitimacy in the special ability of judges to search for long-term moral principles. In turn, John Ely, a critic of the fundamental values position, finds and defines the special judicial role in his substance/process distinction. But again neither of these positions is intellectually cogent.

If I deny these answers to the legitimacy quandary, then what is my answer? I believe that institutional choice and comparative institutional analysis offer help in resolving the legitimacy issues. In the end, however, these issues are to some degree unresolvable. Even then, institutional insights can help us to understand why they are unresolvable and why the lack of resolution should not be so troubling.

The issue of unelected judges is largely a red herring. Many have commented that we do not have a pure democracy and that, therefore, decisions by unelected judges are acceptable. Such an insight only scratches the surface of the complex institutional picture of the U.S. Constitution. Judicial review is only one of many "undemocratic" institutional choices in the Constitution. To use the standard legitimacy formulation, why should senators, under the original Constitution elected by the state legislatures, make public policy? Why should a president, elected by an electoral college, make public policy? As it turns out, neither of these deviations from direct popular election now make any difference. The first was changed and the second has evolved into a conduit for the popular vote. But both these deviations from the popular election of representatives were parts of the original Constitution. In turn, why should representation ever be other than proportional to population? Why should public officials elected only every six or four or even two years make public policy? Why should public officials, that is representatives, make decisions at all? Why not a perpetual town meeting? Why have a remote national government rather than more immediately accessible local decision-making?

As we saw in the earlier discussion of the framing of the U.S. Constitution, some of these issues greatly disturbed the Anti-Federalist opponents of the Constitution. All of the issues involve choices of institutional design too complex to fit neatly into a dichotomy between democracy and non-democracy. Some, like the need for representatives, hardly seem undemocratic. It is only sensible to free up citizens from continuously participating in government. But, even for so simple a provision or so simple an explanation, tradeoffs occurred. As the earlier discussion of the framing showed, other choices involved important and controversial tradeoffs reflecting fears of the excesses of both majorities and minorities. The differences in the character of the various components of the government are part of a complex picture of checks and balances, and that picture involves various permutations of democracy.

The judiciary is part of a complex institutional picture produced by design, evolution, and accident. It is simple-minded to continuously single out that one component for discussion of legitimacy. That judges are unelected or serve for life is just a variant of the general theme of the complexity of institutional choice. Under some circumstances, for some issues, given some goals, it makes sense to have decisions made by unelected, life-serving judges. In other settings, it makes sense to have decisions made by senators elected every six years or by representatives elected every two years or by state legislatures elected in some manner specified by the states.

But what limits judges? Senators, congressmen, presidents, and state political officials can be removed at the voting booth after at most six years.

More importantly, there are many members of each legislature, and each house of the legislature must get the approval of the other house and of the executive. Federal legislation becomes law only by passing both houses of Congress. It usually requires the consent of the president. But nine unremovable judges can remake public policy without recourse to other institutions. What controls the power of the judges?

It would, of course, give the framers and the early members of the Supreme Court no end of amusement to hear such a question. The "least dangerous branch" largely disappeared from American decision-making for at least a century. In the earliest days of constitutional history, appointment to the supposedly highest court was considered less powerful than a place on the state courts. Chief Justice John Marshall, the crafter of constitutional judicial review, was faced with the quite real prospect of having judicial decisions simply ignored by the political process.

Even today, the Constitution provides the other branches with significant control over the judiciary. Federal judges can, in fact, be removed by impeachment. The size of the judiciary is determined by the Congress. The makeup of the courts is determined by the president and the Senate. More importantly, however, the adjudicative process is by its nature limited. It is small relative to the political and market processes and grows relatively smaller every year. It has a hierarchical structure that reduces its ability to grow. The dynamics of litigation keep major issues from it or at least limit its ability to affect them. Even the most aggressive constitutional courts cannot affect more than a small fraction of social decisions. The outer limits of judicial power, like the outer limits of the power of all the branches of government, lie in systemic or institutional attributes. For the judiciary, those systemic limits are relatively tight. The judiciary remains the least dangerous branch.

None of this analysis, however, provides the rules of judicial review that most people associate with legitimacy. No rules keep the unscrupulous judge strictly in line. More importantly, there are no rules to give precise guidance to the scrupulous judge. Institutional choice and institutional analysis are complex and difficult. This complexity is increased by the interaction between institutional choice and goal choice. We can expect differing opinions even from judges who share similar goal choices. Better institutional analysis can promise an improvement in the clarity and quality of constitutional decision-making. It may even cause some convergence in views among judges. But it hardly dictates a narrow range of solutions or eliminates legitimate controversy. If legitimacy requires the statement of principles that promise to allow the convergence of opinion among judges who follow them and apprehension of those who do not, then analysis of institutional choice cannot resolve the issue of legitimacy. Since institutional choice is an unavoidable aspect of all constitutional law, there is no real possibility of legitimacy in this strict sense.

SUMMARY

Institutional choice is the core of constitutional law and constitution making. Analysis of institutional choice must consider the relative merits of various alternatives for each relevant context. It cannot afford the single institutionalism of Ely and the IGTP analysts, let alone the non-institutionalism of fundamental rights and original intent analysts. Constitutional law and constitution making require a sense for the complex, systemic nature of large institutions and an appreciation of the quandaries presented by the tradeoff between minoritarian and majoritarian bias. For constitutional law, where the American Constitution already contains basic decisions about institutional design, the range of institutional choices is much less than with constitution making. American constitutional law scholarship focuses almost exclusively on constitutional judicial review where the relevant institutional choice is between the courts and the political process. As we saw in chapter 7, however, the combination and permutations in the subject matter of public policy and the resulting variations in the interaction between minoritarian and majoritarian bias create a challenging arena for the analysis of institutional choice even in the narrower constitutional law setting.

For constitution making, the choices are immense. There is the choice between present and future decision-makers — the choice between the framers and a wide variety of future decision-makers. There are then the many variations which future institutions may take. Based on dimensions like the level of government (federal versus state), the structure of the legislature (for example, two houses versus one house), the relationship of the executive and legislature, the structure and role of an independent judiciary, and the ability to delegate decisions to a large bureaucracy, the character of social decision-making and therefore the character of social decisions is determined. These choices also determine the balance between majoritarian and minoritarian influences and the extent to which any interest will be protected from or by the government. Even given the same goals and interests, different societies can and should make different institutional choices depending on social characteristics like diversity and ethnic makeup, history of ethnic or racial strife, land mass, and population density. Working out goal choice, institutional choice, and demographic characteristics is the challenge of constitution making.

The two inquiries, constitutional law and constitution making, are related. Constitution making precedes the evolution of the judicial role we call constitutional law. A written constitution or a long constitutional tradition may evolve a set of mores that become so embedded in the political dynamic that violation of these mores, even without constitutional judicial review, becomes politically costly to public officials. In the United States context with its judicial review (itself an evolved tradition), the role of the judiciary depends on the character of the political process reviewed and, therefore, reflects the choices made by constitution makers. As we have seen, at least in the American context, the political process is structured as a tradeoff of potential problems. Some of these problems are well suited for judicial reaction and others are less so. Some require or are amenable to one form of judicial reaction; other problems are amenable to other forms of judicial reaction. Thus the role that constitutional judicial review can play depends on how the political process is structured and how that structure interacts with the demographics of society.

American constitutional scholars and judges must accept the difficult task of institutional choice and analysis that lies at the core of constitutional judicial review. Any analysis that does not centrally focus on this task is largely useless. Any rhetorical device that pretends a way around the task is misleading. Constitutional judges have responsibility for a very scarce resource, and they must take that responsibility seriously. Constitutional scholars have the responsibility of aiding these judicial choices by clearly explicating and examining the institutional choices inherent in them. That task may seem unattractive to many constitutional scholars, but they should either accept their responsibility to deal productively with the real choices or retire from the fray.

}9{

Summary and Conclusion: Propositions, Audiences, and Reformations

I have argued that questions of institutional choice should be central to all analyses of law and public policy. I have also presented a method for meeting that obligation — the participation-centered approach to comparative institutional analysis. By way of more detailed summary, I present the following propositions along with an indication of where in the book they were developed. Neither the list of propositions nor the references are exhaustive, but they provide a useful overview.

Proposition 1: The choice of social goals or values is insufficient to tell us anything about law and public policy either descriptively or prescriptively. One must seriously consider institutional choice in order to understand or reform law and public policy. (Discussion of: resource allocation efficiency and the *Boomer* case in chapter 2; Rawlsian justice and the *Pentagon Papers* case in chapter 2; the economic approach to tort liability in chapter 6; Lockean libertarianism and Epstein's version of the Takings Clause in chapter 8.)

Proposition 2: Institutional analysis must be comparative. No matter how sophisticated, single institutional analysis is an insufficient substitute; it cannot evaluate the relative merits of imperfect institutional alternatives. (Discussion of: Posner's analyses of *Boomer* in chapter 2 and of custom in chapter 6; curing rent-seeking in the market and political processes in chapter 4; Ely's approach to judicial review in chapter 7.)

Corollary 1: Institutions often move together — when one is at its best, the others are often at their best; when one is at its worst, the others are often at their worst. (Discussion of: *Boomer* in chapter 2; comparison between the three institutions across various distributions in chapters 5 and 6.)

Corollary 2: There are, however, instances when an institution possesses significant comparative advantages. (Discussion of: the two shifted distributions in chapter 5; shifted distribution and product liability in chapter 6.)

Proposition 3: Institutional analysis should be participation-centered. As decision-making processes, institutions comprise the complex interactions of many participants; consequently, assessing the performance of the institution as a whole requires that one attend to the actions of all participants. The various participants' kind and degree of involvement in an institution are affected by the factors identified in the following corollaries:

Corollary 1: The motivation of individual participants, including public officials, is usually only weakly related to institutional behavior. (Discussion of: the limited relevance of motivation in chapter 3; Ely's conception of political malfunction in chapter 7; fundamental rights view of constitutional law in chapter 8.)

Corollary 2: The cost of information plays an essential role in determining institutional participation and, in turn, institutional performance. The cost and availability of information is an important consideration in the analysis of a wide range of subjects including the possibility of majoritarian activity (chapters 3 and 7), the dynamics of false advertising and misleading propaganda (chapter 4), and the determinants of deterrence, insurance, and litigation (chapter 6).

Corollary 3: In relation to the political process, the participation-centered approach provides more relevant, richer, and more robust insights when it employs the two-force model proposed in this book. With its interaction between minoritarian and majoritarian influences, the two-force model offers a more comprehensive model of political participation than does the one-force model of the interest group theory of politics. (Most of chapter 3; discussion of the framing of the Constitution and of the meaning of the *Carolene Products* footnote in chapter 7, and of the corrective role of compensation for takings in chapter 8.)

Corollary 4: In relation to the market, the transaction cost approach begun by Ronald Coase provides a participation-centered approach that can be augmented by more explicit consideration of the role of transaction benefits. The transaction costly, not the transaction costless, world is relevant to institutional choice. (Most of chapter 4.)

Corollary 5: In relation to the adjudicative process, the participation-centered approach provides far more insights than the singular focus on judicial independence that characterizes most legal analyses. The pattern of adjudication produced by the high costs of participation associated with judicial independence and the severe constraints on judicial resources and on judge and jury competence must be considered along with judicial independence to determine the performance and potential of the adjudicative process. (Chapter 5 and much of chapters 6, 7, and 8.)

Because of my special concern with law, I have given the adjudicative process — the courts — special attention. To many nonlawyers, this relatively tiny institution is lost in the folds of the larger governmental process. That these analysts have not given the courts careful attention is understandable. Far less understandable is the failure of many legal scholars to pay careful attention to the comparative institutional characteristics of the courts. The limits and abilities of courts relative to the far larger institutions to which they react are subjects that require attention in every episode of legal analysis.

Spurred by the failure of others to adequately consider institutional choice, I have been both a cheerleader for and a critic of the adjudicative process. Faced with the runaway bandwagon of tort reform, I call for greater respect for the relative abilities of the adjudicative process in the pursuit of safety. Faced with plans for open-ended expansion of constitutional judicial review by fundamental rights scholars like Richard Epstein, I call for greater awareness of the limits of the adjudicative process.

I am not an opponent of constitutional judicial review. Judicially protected constitutional rights are an invaluable component of the workings of the American Constitution. There are many ways in which these rights can be sensitively and creatively expanded. It is one of the purposes of this book to help judges determine how to use their limited resources in the most beneficial ways. In turn, I am not a proponent of judicial dominance of safety. Such dominance is an impossibility, and mindless adherence to tort liability is a mistake. The strategy for dealing with safety has always been and will always be a multi-institutional one dominated by the market and the political process.

My immediate concern in this book is to reform the way people think about law and public policy. It is time for those who use the tools of economics in analyzing law and public policy to free themselves from their fixation on resource allocation efficiency and from the constraints of narrow assumptions about personal motivations. They should recognize that their most robust insights come from institutional analysis and that more such insights will follow from more careful comparative institutional analysis.

Some of the most sustained efforts at institutional analysis are the single institutional analyses of those employing economics who focus, in the welfare economics tradition, on imperfections in the market or, in the newer public choice tradition, on imperfections in the political process. This single institutional work can play a role in more relevant comparative institutional work. But, thus far, single institutional analysis has largely served one-sided calls for political intervention (in the case of welfare economics) or against political intervention (in the case of public choice). Legal scholars who have picked up bits and pieces of both traditions and woven them into the rhetoric of their various proposals have not seriously confronted the tougher issues of institutional choice inherent in the severe malfunctions present in both of these major institutions.

Non-economic analysts of law and public policy must end their obsession with goal choice and embrace the enterprise of institutional choice. They may even have to borrow tools from economics — a task that may be less onerous as these tools are less associated with a single goal and a narrow vision of individual motivation.

My ultimate goal is to aid the reformation of society. Throughout this book, I have critically addressed analyses associated with a wide variety of goals ranging from resource allocation efficiency to protection of private property to distributive justice. To analysts focused exclusively on goal choice, these criticisms may be associated with attacks on the goals themselves, despite my protests to the contrary and despite the breadth of the range of goals I have considered. In reality, any and all of these goals are attractive to me. But, as I have repeated throughout this book, that means very little. Reform is not the embracing of goals. Reform is the designation of the means of achieving them.

The road to reform is a difficult one. The vision of institutions in this book is not heartening. Massive, interactive processes are difficult to reform. Yet there are moments when selective and focused action can be telling. Public-interested public officials may not dominate these processes, but they can matter. I have presented a way to determine when and where these moments exist and what configuration of institutions could provide the best way to better achieve social goals.

The message is clear. The toil and peril of institutional comparison is inescapable. Real reform is possible, though determining the right moments and the right forms for reform is always a challenge. The best choices we have or are likely to have will be imperfect and usually significantly so. Yet this clear message is often ignored. The aesthetics and simplicity of perfection continue to attract commentators who build theories and programs unsoiled by comparative institutional analysis.

I am reminded of the well-worn story about the chemist, the physicist, and the economist marooned on a desert island with nothing to eat but canned goods. They must find a way to open the cans or starve. The chemist and physicist conjure up and reject a large number of strategies while the economist sits comfortably by with a satisfied smile on his face. After the chemist and physicist have exhausted themselves with no solution, the economist clears his throat and begins: "Assuming a can opener . . ."

One cannot assume away the problem. One cannot ignore or assume away institutional choice in solving problems of law and public policy. But there are more subtle lessons. Abstraction is a necessary part of any approach to law and public policy, and, therefore, some aspects of reality must be ignored or assumed away. It is the art of analysis to abstract from the unimportant and focus on the important. While I have argued that institutional choice is too central to be treated lightly, I have proposed a participation-centered approach to institutional choice that focuses on a contained set of behavioral parameters.

More deeply buried in the story of the castaways are issues that may help to explain why institutional choice is ignored. Who wants to listen to chemists and physicists go on when no answer appears imminent? Yes, the economist's suggestion is a joke, but any six-year-old would grab the cans and bash them with a rock. Surely, that approach is better than sitting around talking. Unfortunately, law and public policy problems will not yield to rock bashing. To give up the metaphor totally, law and public policy problems will not yield to gut reactions and intuitions such as those that lie behind calls for reliance on politics and ideology. As this book has shown repeatedly, institutional choice is complex and often counterintuitive. Soul searching without sophistication may work for goal choice, but it will not work for institutional choice.

We are forced back to the difficult and frustrating world of comparative institutional analysis. I have offered a participation-centered approach to comparative institutional analysis. But I cannot claim that it is more than a rope bridge across the chasm of institutional choice. Much more must be done and the work promises to be frustratingly slow and difficult, although I am confident that serious and creative analyses of individual issues of law and public policy will add to and fill in the theory.

Unfortunately, escape from harsh realities is easier for real world scholars than for our three castaways. If the economist in the story does not shape up, we may assume he will starve. But no such straightforward fate and, therefore, straightforward incentives await analysts of law and public policy. They will eat just fine as long as they *appear* to be working on the problems of law and public policy. The issue then is how to move them to take on more difficult and less aesthetic, albeit more relevant, tasks. Fortunately, many are motivated to improve society. If I have done my job, these analysts will now carry forward the task.

Author Index

Abel, Richard, 188n
Ackerman, Bruce, 218, 223–26, 228–30
Alchian, Armen, 107n, 110

Bailey, Martin, 88n
Barry, Brian, 38–39
Becker, Gary, 88n
Berger, Raoul, 255n, 263n
Block, Arthur, 144n, 253n
Bork, Robert, 208, 255n
Bradley, Michael, 110n
Brennan, Geoffrey, 57n, 59n, 89n
Brest, Paul, 198n
Buchanan, Geoffrey, 67n
Buchanan, James, vii, 53n, 55n, 56n, 57n, 59, 89n, 116n

Calabresi, Guido, 22n, 137n, 154–55, 162nn, 171n, 193n
Carrington, Paul, 139n
Caswell, Julie, 116n
Chemerinsky, Erwin, 216n
Cheung, Steven, 115n
Choper, Jesse, 230n
Clune, William, 253n
Coase, Ronald, vii, 29, 31, 61, 99, 105–6, 107nn, 109–10, 113, 115, 272
Comanor, William, 116n
Cooter, Robert, 134n, 250n
Culbertson, John, 116
Currie, Daniel, 139n

Dahl, Robert, 12
Dahlman, Carl, 104n, 106n
Daniels, Steven, 139n
Danzon, Patricia, 179, 180n, 244n
Davis, Kenneth, 252n
Dawson, Henry, 218n
Demsetz, Harold, vii, 104n
Donohue, John, 110n

Downs, Anthony, 66–67, 71n, 165n
Dungworth, Terry, 168n
Dworkin, Ronald, 261n

Eads, George, 168n, 170n
Easterbrook, Frank, 216n
Elhauge, Einer, 216n, 239n
Ellickson, Robert, 110n
Elliot, Jonathan, 219n
Ely, John Hart, 6–7, 197–201, 203–5, 208–10, 213–16, 223–24, 229–30, 261n, 266, 269, 271–72
Emerson, Thomas, 208nn
Epstein, Richard, 11, 134n, 155n, 232, 234–50, 256n, 271, 273
Eskridge, William, 12n

Farber, Daniel, 57n, 58n, 59n, 84n, 86n, 224n
Fiorina, Morris, 56n, 68n, 85n, 92n, 95–96
Fiss, Owen, 255n
Fletcher, George, 155n
Frank, Jerome, 138n
Frickey, Phillip, 12n, 57n, 58n, 59n, 86n, 224n

Galanter, Marc, 163n, 173n
Gilligan, Thomas, 85n
Goodman, Frank, 139n

Hand, Learned, 155–56, 159–61
Handler, Joel, 73n, 224n
Hardin, Charles, 94n
Hart, Henry, 11–12
Higginbotham, Harlow, 108n
Hill, Charles, 57n
Hirschman, Albert, 143n
Hirschoff, Jon, 162n
Hoffman, Elizabeth, 110n

277

278

Horowitz, Donald, 139n
Huber, Peter, 139n, 153n

Irons, Peter, 212n

Johnson, Judith, 132n, 133n
Jordan, Ellen, 139n

Kalt, Joseph, 56n, 57n, 86n
Kalven, Harry, 208n
Karst, Kenneth, 208n, 257n
Kaufman, Irving, 146n
Keeton, Robert, 176n
Keller, Morton, 69n
Kelman, Mark, 53n, 58n, 59n
Kenyon, Cecilia, 220n
Klein, Benjamin, 118n
Klevorik, Alan, 162n
Komesar, Neil, 47n, 60n, 70n, 73n, 79n,
    133n, 156nn, 159n, 173n, 174n, 182n,
    184nn, 188n, 190n, 201n, 215n, 225n,
    232n, 244n, 254nn, 262n

Landes, William, 118n, 155n, 166n, 177n
Latin, Howard, 165n
Lee, Alton, 69n
Lee, Dwight, 86n
Leffler, Keith, 118n
Levmore, Saul, 177n
Linch, Gerald, 205n
Lindblom, Charles, 12
Locke, John, 232
Lowi, Theodore, 56n
Luneberg, William, 138n

Macauley, Stewart, 130n
Macey, Jonathan, 90n, 216n, 217–18,
    220–21
Marshall, William, 85n
Martin, Douglas, 133n
Marwell, Gerald, 70n
McCarron, John, 146n
McCormick, Robert, 71nn, 72n, 90n
Meador, Daniel, 139n
Meiklejohn, Alexander, 208n
Melamed, Douglas, 22n
Michelman, Frank, 40, 43n
Mikva, Abner, 53n, 58n
Miller, Gary, 92n
Miller, Geoffrey, 69n

Moe, Terry, 92n
Mueller, Dennis, 37n
Musgrave, Peggy, 12–13
Musgrave, Richard, 12–13

Niskanen, William, 92–93
Noll, Roger, 56n, 94
Nordenberg, Mark, 138n
North, Douglas, 56n

O'Connell, Jeffrey, 176n, 177n, 178n,
    183n
Oliver, Pamela, 70n
Olson, Mancur, 8
Ordesbrook, Peter, 74n
Owen, David, 186n, 187n, 189n

Palay, Thomas, 130n
Peltzman, Sam, 55n, 88n, 92n, 93n
Perry, Michael, 255n, 258n
Peterson, Mark, 187n
Pierce, Richard, 82n
Posner, Richard, 6–7, 13n, 17–21, 22n,
    23, 25, 28nn, 32n, 41n, 53n, 56n, 57n,
    70n, 71n, 85n, 104n, 105n, 111, 118n,
    113n, 139n, 141n, 145n, 147n, 155,
    157–59, 161, 165n, 176n, 199, 271
Priest, George, 153n, 170n, 185n, 191n
Prosser, William, 157n, 160n, 185n

Rawls, John, 11, 14, 30, 34–44, 46, 48–50,
    62n, 234n, 271
Rebell, Michael, 144n, 253n
Reuter, Peter, 168n
Revesz, Richard, 139n
Richards, David, 261n
Riker, William, 74n, 250n
Rose-Ackerman, Susan, 56n, 58n, 59n
Rosenzweig, Michael, 110n
Rubin, Paul, 56n
Rubinfield, Daniel, 134n, 250n

Sacks, Albert, 11–12
Sandalow, Terrance, 260n
Sarma, Syam, 187n
Scharpf, Fritz, 139n
Schlozman, Kay Lehman, 63n
Schwartz, Alan, 162n, 171n, 180, 181n,
    183n, 185n, 191n
Schwartz, William, 159n, 188n

Shanley, Michael, 187n
Shapiro, Martin, 216n
Shepsle, Kenneth, vii, 94n, 104n, 105n
Siegan, Bernard, 216n
Siegelman, Peter, 133n
Spitzer, Matthew, 110n
Stewart, Richard, vii, 162n
Stigler, George, 53n, 55n, 57n, 66–67, 70, 74n
Storing, Herbert, 220n
Sugarman, Stephen, 154n
Sunstein, Cass, 216n, 217–18, 220–21, 244, 255n

Teixeira, Ruy, 70n
Telser, Lester, 108n
Tiebout, Charles, 143n
Tierney, John, 63n
Tollison, Robert, 55n, 67n, 71nn, 72n, 90n
Tribe, Laurence, 198n, 205n, 208n, 211n, 215n

Tullock, Gordon, 55n, 56n, 67, 71n, 116n
Tushnet, Mark, 198n

van Stiujvenberg, Johannes, 69n
Viscusi, W. Kip, 181n
Vogel, Kenneth, 110n

Weingast, Barry, vii, 85n, 94n, 104n, 105n, 250n
Weisbrod, Burton, 73n, 244n
Wellington, Harry, 258n
Williamson, Oliver, 105, 106n, 107n, 108nn
Wills, Robert, 116n
Wilson, James, 86–88
Wilson, Thomas, 116n
Winston, Clifford, 88n
Woodward, Susan, 107n

Zacharias, Fred, 163n
Zeppos, Nicholas, 12n
Zupan, Mark, 57nn, 86n

Subject Index

abortion, 64
adjudicative process
  appellate courts, 124, 144–45
  class actions, 25n, 130–33, 137, 147, 167
  comparative advantage and the shifted distribution, 134–38, 148, 168–74, 192
  discovery, 126
  distribution of stakes: skewed, 128–29, 130–34, 136, 140–42, 148; uniform high, 129–30; uniform low, 128–29
  efficiency of the common law evaluated, 28–29, 133–34
  information, costs and stakes, 127, 131, 141, 142
  judges: agendas, ability to control, 130, 147–49; competence, 138–39, 141–42, 145, 210–12; general attributes, 123, 124–25; increasing numbers, 143–45; jury substitutes, 150–51; managerial and specialized, 144–45
  judicial independence: cause of high litigation costs, 126–28; fundamental rights approach, 258–61; participation, relationship to, 128–34; sources and attributes, 124–25
  juries: compared to administrative agencies, 138–41, 172, 179, 180, 181–82, 190–91; bias, 186–87; bribery and, 140; competence of, 138–42, 156–61, 172, 179–82, 190–91; general attributes of, 124–25; as subject to majoritarian bias, 141; minoritarian bias in, antidote for, 140–41, 172, 179–82, 190–91
  jurisdiction, 126
  justiciability, 126
  litigation: modes of controlling demand, tradeoffs, 146–49; relation-

  ship to stakes and costs, 128–33, 134–38, 165, 167, 168, 175, 260
  ripeness, 126
  scale: adjudicative versus other processes, 142–43, 237–38, 251–53, 260–61; constitutional judicial review, 213, 237–38, 250, 251–53, 260–61; constraints on expansion, 143–45
  specialized courts, 139, 145
  standing, 126, 147
  statutory interpretation, 137–38
administrative agencies: growth of the bureaucracy and the two-force model, 90–97; standards for judicial review, 147; versus juries, 138–41, 172, 179, 180, 181–82, 190–91
advertising and market rent–seeking, 115–21, 127
AIDS, 173n
Anti-Federalists, 219–20, 267
anti-trust law and policy, 99, 108–9
auto accidents, 164, 176–77, 178–79

Boomer v. Atlantic Cement Co.
  law and economics, single institutional, 14–28, 111, 157
  market, 98, 100–102
  minoritarian-majoritarian tradeoff, 77–79, 206–7
  compared to *Pentagon Papers* case, 48
  pollution, 26–28, 96, 129, 167, 175
  property law, 14–28, 246, 247
bureaucracy, growth of, 90–97, 194

Carolene Products footnote, 198, 221–30. See also *U.S. v. Carolene Products*
catalytic subgroups, 70n, 72–74, 82–84. *See also* political process: two-force model of politics, attributes

281